GEORGE WASHINGTON

Half-Hours in Southern History

JNO: LESSLIE HALL, Ph.D.
Professor of English and of
General History in the
College of William and Mary

HERITAGE BOOKS
2009

HERITAGE BOOKS
AN IMPRINT OF HERITAGE BOOKS, INC.

Books, CDs, and more—Worldwide

For our listing of thousands of titles see our website
at
www.HeritageBooks.com

A Facsimile Reprint
Published 2009 by
HERITAGE BOOKS, INC.
Publishing Division
100 Railroad Ave. #104
Westminster, Maryland 21157

Copyright © 1907 B. F. Johnson Publishing Co.

— Publisher's Notice —
In reprints such as this, it is often not possible to remove blemishes from the original. We feel the contents of this book warrant its reissue despite these blemishes and hope you will agree and read it with pleasure.

International Standard Book Numbers
Paperbound: 978-1-58549-988-5
Clothbound: 978-0-7884-8099-7

To
A Faithful Scribe
and
Loving Daughter of the Confederacy,
M. F. H.

PREFACE

This is a book of sketches and might be entitled, *A Sketch Book of Southern History*. It aims to give in brief outline the salient features of Southern heroism and achievement, and to state rapidly the South's side of the long controversy between the sections.

The author has tried to be fair, candid, and truthful. Extremists of either section will not like the volume. The fact that he is a Southerner, however, the author will attempt neither to palliate nor to deny; but he has aimed to write "with malice toward none, with charity for all."

The facts stated in this volume have been gathered from a thousand sources; none have been manufactured. Of Southern civilization, the author speaks from experience, as he remembers vividly two generations that represented the Old South so-called. The work is a labor of love; its object, justice to all.

WILLIAMSBURG, VA., *March 31, 1907.*

CONTENTS

	PAGE
ILLUSTRATIONS	13

CHAPTER I

	PAGE
THE SOUTH IN OLDEN DAYS	15
"BEFORE THE WAR"	15
NO "SOLID" SOUTH	17
"THERE IS GLORY ENOUGH FOR US ALL"	19
ROANOKE ISLAND, ST. AUGUSTINE, AND JAMESTOWN	21
"SIC SEMPER TYRANNIS"	27
Harvey and Berkeley	27
George III and His "Friends"	30
Taxation Without Representation	30
"Treason! Treason!"	33
VIRGINIA AND CAROLINA	36
Tea Parties	36
Mecklenburg and St. John's Church	41
INDEPENDENCE	44
1772 and 1775	44
The Year 1776	46
THE SOUTH IN THE WAR OF THE REVOLUTION	51
Heroes and Heroines	51
Maryland	51
Virginia	52
North Carolina	59
South Carolina	63
Georgia	68
Heroes of the Frontier	71

	PAGE
Troops and Battles	72
Miscellaneous	74
THE SOUTH AND THE CONSTITUTION	78
The Federal Convention of 1787	78
The States Create the Union	83
THE SOUTH'S PART IN MAINTAINING AND EXPANDING THE UNION	86
The War of 1812	86
The Mexican War	90
Miscellaneous	96

CHAPTER II

	PAGE
THE HOMES THAT MADE HEROES	98
"TRUTH IS MIGHTY AND WILL PREVAIL"	98
THE SOUTH'S HISTORY WRITTEN BY HER ENEMIES	99
TIRED OF HEARING HIM CALLED "THE JUST"	104
CULTURE AND REFINEMENT	105
MANLINESS AND SELF-RELIANCE	108
"OLE MARSTER"	111
"OLE MISTIS"	114
THE PLANTER CIVILIZATION	116
THE CAVALIER AND THE PURITAN	119
THE YEOMANRY OF THE SOUTH	123
TRUTH, PURITY, AND PIETY	126
SLAVERY IN THE SOUTH	131
THE FEUDAL BARON	134
THE "LAZY" PLANTER	138
UNCLE TOM'S CABIN AND OTHER SLURS	142
"OF THE OLD SCHOOL"	144

CHAPTER III

	PAGE
THE HUNDRED YEARS' WRANGLE	146
EARLY CAUSES OF ESTRANGEMENT	146
Lights and Shadows	146
Views of the Constitution	150
The League or Compact Theory	150
The Partnership View	153
Federalists and Anti-Federalists	156
LATER CAUSES OF ESTRANGEMENT	158
THE GREATEST CAUSE OF ESTRANGEMENT	162
Slavery in the North and the South	162
The North Sells Out	165
Who Did Sin?	167
"The Higher Law"	173
A New God Demanded	174
The Plot Thickens	175
The Last Straw	179
THE RIGHT OF SECESSION	181
New England Pioneers of Secession	181
Late New England Secessionists	185
Nullification in the North	189
"THE WAR"	192

CHAPTER IV

	PAGE
THE PRIVATE SOLDIER AND THE SAILOR	197
THE REAL HERO	197
WHO?	198
WHY?	199
"GIDEON'S BAND"	200
MR. ROOSEVELT EXPLAINS	201
"WEARIED OUT BY THEIR OWN VICTORIES"	203
THE SOLDIER'S JOYS	204
"WHAT IS LIFE WITHOUT HONOR?"	205

CHRIST IN THE CAMP 207
"PIRATES" 208

CHAPTER V

PAGE

THE WOMEN OF THE CONFEDERACY 215
    THE TRUEST PATRIOTS 213
    WIVES AND MOTHERS OF HEROES 214
    THE RECRUITING OFFICER 216
    "THE UNCROWNED QUEENS OF THE SOUTH" 217
    "STITCH, STITCH, STITCH" 219
    "GALLANT BLACK TOM" AND TREACHEROUS ISAAC 221
    WAR POETS OF THE SOUTH 222
    "STARVATION PARTIES" 223
    "A MINISTERING ANGEL THOU" 225
    CUPID AND "GENERAL LEE'S SOCKS" 226
    A STARVING NATION 227
    THE "TRIUMPHAL MARCH" THROUGH GEORGIA 230
    THE WOMEN DECLINE TO SURRENDER 232
    HEROINES IN HOMESPUN 234
    HER MONUMENTS AND HISTORIES 236

CHAPTER VI

PAGE

LEE AND HIS PALADINS 240
    LEE GOES WITH HIS STATE 240
    THE HALL OF FAME 241
    "MARYLAND, MY MARYLAND" 244
    MARYE'S HEIGHTS AND CHANCELLORSVILLE 245
    "ALL THE WORLD WONDERED" 247
    GRAPPLE OF THE GIANTS 250

CHAPTER VII

	PAGE
JACKSON AND HIS "FOOT-CAVALRY"	253
"POOR WHITE TRASH"	253
JACKSON'S POLITICAL VIEWS	254
"STONEWALL"	255
THE TRUE STONEWALL JACKSON	257
THE THUNDERBOLT OF WAR	260

CHAPTER VIII

	PAGE
SHILOH AND ITS HEROES	262
THE HERO OF TEXAS	262
"FREEDOM SHRIEKED WHEN KOSCIUSKO FELL"	263
"COMMON ERRORS"	264

CHAPTER IX

	PAGE
THE SOUTH SINCE THE WAR	266
A PROSTRATE NATION	266
THE WOLF AT THE DOOR	268
THE HOUNDS OF PEACE	270
THE REIGN OF TERROR	272
THE FREEDMAN'S BUREAU	274
THE SCHOOLMARM IN TRADITION	275
RECONSTRUCTION THROUGH DESTRUCTION	277
THE CARPETBAGGER AND THE SCALAWAG	280
THE THIRD TRIUMVIRATE	282
THE KU KLUX KLAN	285
RECONSTRUCTION BY THE SOUTHERN PEOPLE	287
THE RACE PROBLEM	291
MORALS AND RELIGION	297
ZACCHEUS IS COMING DOWN	301

CHAPTER X

	PAGE
CONCLUSION	305
Recapitulation	305
Patriotism	307
INDEX	311

ILLUSTRATIONS

	OPPOSITE PAGE
GEORGE WASHINGTON *(frontispiece)*	
JOHN MARSHALL	16
PATRICK HENRY	32
THOMAS JEFFERSON	48
JAMES MADISON	80
JAMES MONROE	96
ANDREW JACKSON	128
JEFFERSON DAVIS	160
HENRY CLAY	176
JOHN C. CALHOUN	192
J. E. B. STUART	208
JOSEPH E. JOHNSTON	224
R. E. LEE	240
T. J. JACKSON	256
ALBERT SIDNEY JOHNSTON	264
N. B. FORREST	288

Half-Hours In Southern History

CHAPTER I

THE SOUTH IN OLDEN DAYS

I

"Before the War"

ALL our lives, we have heard about the times "before the war," and this is a familiar phrase among our people. "The war" is an era with us of the Southern states. Our fathers and grandfathers have told us, around the old fireside, of the good days they saw before the terrible clash between the sections. "Before the war," "during the war," "since the war"—all are household expressions south of the Potomac. Not even the war with Spain has robbed us of these phrases; the war of the '60's is still "the war" among our people.

"Before the war"—that was a joyous era with our beloved people. Not altogether blissful, to be sure,—for life is never that—but bright, happy, and hopeful. Of course our fathers had their troubles and disappointments; life, even then, had its sunshine and its shadows; but their sunshine was brighter than ours, and the day was longer.

They had a beautiful old civilization, and their homes were refined and comfortable, many of them elegant; while friends true as steel thronged around them, ready to enjoy their boundless hospitality and to return it on a lavish and open-handed scale.

In political affairs, the South was vastly better off than it is to-day, far happier in the Union, not only recognized, but trusted with leadership for several decades. Her statesmen had a prominent part in the conduct of the government, more than three-fourths of the presidents before 1860 being men of Southern birth or of Southern antecedents.

Opportunities being given, the South gave the Union many of its greatest soldiers. Still others were sprung from families that had recently migrated from her borders to found new commonwealths beyond the Ohio. Immediately you think of George Washington, Francis Marion, Light Horse Harry Lee, Daniel Morgan, William Henry Harrison, Zachary Taylor, and Andrew Jackson, whose names will be ever famous in the military annals of our earlier periods.

"Before the war," no impassable gulf yawned between North and South. Of course there was some unpleasantness; indeed, at times, some bitterness. Various questions arose, and some of them made New England threaten at times to leave the Union, so as to get away from her Southern sisters. This, however, generally "blew over," as we say, and did not keep Southern men from being called to high and honorable places in the government. How is it now in this so-called "era of good feeling"? What high and honorable places does any president give your father or any of your relatives? What Southern gentlemen are sent to represent the United States at the courts of any great European

JOHN MARSHALL

nation? How many Southern vice-presidents have been elected in your day? What party in your state wishes to push some eminent man of your state for the presidency, and thus blight his political career forever?

Why is this? Why is the South thus isolated, cut off from the rest of the Union? Why this "Solid South" that you read about so often in the newspapers? It is on account of "the war" and of the problems that have resulted from it. The causes of this war and the nature of some of these problems we shall talk over in the following pages. We regret that such talks are necessary. We regret that, after forty years of peace, the South's side is so generally misunderstood, is so inadequately treated in many books and in the schoolroom. Whatever the reasons for this, it is high time for Southern teachers to be up and doing. The youth of the South must be told the true story of Southern heroism, of Southern genius, of Southern fortitude, and must be taught, clearly and fully, why the South left the Union that she did so much to create and to make illustrious.

II

No "Solid South"

"The Solid South" is a phrase born within recent years. It is the child of war and bitterness. We love to think of the days when there was no such phrase in our language and no such fact in our history. Local jealousies and sectional animosities have, of course, existed from the earliest periods of our history, but they were not bounded by the Potomac river. No surveyor's line, no river, separated two great unfriendly sections of our country; that is comparatively recent. The North voted enthusiastically for numerous Southern presidents. The North called Washington twice to the head of the American army and twice to the presidential office. She called Marshall to the Supreme Bench, and has put him among her idols. More recent alienation between the sections is unnatural and unnecessary. If Virginia and New England disliked each other during the early days of our history, so did New York and New England; Connecticut and Pennsylvania. To-day, however, the South is in many respects almost cut off from the Union, almost as little connected with the Federal government as Korea or Madagascar.

Not so was it in the revolutionary and *ante-bellum* eras. Did Adams and Ellery and Roger Sherman and Rush and Franklin go off in a corner and act without the advice of the Southern delegates? The answer rises to your lips: "No; they worked hand in hand with the great patriots of the South, and wrote their names alongside those of Carroll, Wythe, the Lees, Jefferson, Rutledge, Middleton, John Penn, George Walton, and other men whose fame can never perish."

Who was called to lead the armies of the young nation in its fight for independence? Did sectionalism place the sword in weak and impotent hands? No, those were better days than ours; for we have seen a Fitzhugh Lee, gallant chevalier and statesman, left to play soldier, clean camps, administer capsules, in the swamps of Florida, when he should have been leading the armies of his country to the walls of Havana. We have seen the same distinguished man assigned an insignificant part in the government of Cuba after that island came under the care of the United States. Our forefathers, however, saw a better sight. They saw John Adams, of Massachusetts, urge George Washington, of Virginia, as commander-in-chief of the American army, and saw a throng of New England people shout applause, as the great son of Virginia accepted his sword under the Cambridge elm, on the soil of Massachusetts. They saw such great Northern soldiers as Anthony Wayne and Nathaniel Greene follow the Virginian to victory under the same banner as Marion, Sumter, and Pickens of South Carolina; "Light Horse Harry" Lee, Hugh Mercer, Andrew Lewis, and Daniel Morgan, of Virginia; Francis Nash and William R. Davie, of North Carolina; Joseph Habersham, of Georgia; John Sevier and Isaac Shelby, heroes of the frontier.

> "Give us back the ties of Yorktown!
> Perish all the modern hates!
> Let us stand together, brothers,
> In defiance of the Fates;
> For the safety of the Union
> Is the safety of the States!" *

III

"There Is Glory Enough for Us All"

In drafting the constitution, also, men of the North and of the South stood shoulder to shoulder. Just as they

---

*James Barron Hope, Yorktown Centennial poem.

risked their "lives," their "fortunes," and their "sacred honor" together, so they sent their greatest men to consult together as to the kind of government they should form for themselves and their posterity.

Of the details of the constitution of 1787, we shall speak more fully in a later section of this chapter. Here we may pause for a few remarks by way of introduction. A Southern state, Virginia, led the way in calling for a convention to frame a constitution for the thirteen free and independent states. It was Madison and Washington, of Virginia, who saw more clearly than almost any other men north or south that the young nation just cut loose from England needed a strong government to keep it from falling to pieces at home and from being despised abroad. Along with these patriots, we should mention Alexander Hamilton, the brilliant statesman of New York, and both Madison and Hamilton are often spoken of as "the fathers of the constitution." Another great man of that era was John Jay, afterwards chief-justice. When we think of the constitution, we cannot fail to think of Washington, whose personal influence alone induced many men to vote for the great paper that was ready in September, 1787, to be submitted to Congress and to the several states for adoption. In all these details, we see clearly that the great men of all sections worked hand in hand for the general welfare. Neither section can claim all the glory; the "honors are even."

In the foregoing sentences, we have seen in generous emulation men from both sides of the Potomac. Again, in the convention that drafted the constitution, we find, besides several already mentioned, Rufus King, of Massachusetts; Benjamin Franklin, James Wilson, Robert Morris, and Gouverneur Morris, of Pennsylvania; John Dickinson, of Delaware; and Roger Sherman, of Connecticut, standing shoulder to shoulder with Daniel Carroll, of Maryland; Edmund Randolph and George Mason, of Virginia; Hugh Williamson and William R. Davie, of North Carolina; Abraham Baldwin and William Few, of Georgia; John Rutledge, Charles and Cotesworth Pinckney, of South Carolina.

IV

Roanoke Island, St. Augustine, and Jamestown

A great poet tells us, "The poetry of earth is never dead." This means that the poetical in life, in the universe, appeals incessantly to humanity, and that, as long as man has sorrows to bemoan and joys to cheer him, the poet will be needed to inspire and console him.

Not all poetry is written in words, and clothed in rhythmical language. If there are, as Shakespeare says, "sermons in stones," there are also poems in places, in great events, and in the great ideas that thrill mankind. There is something thrilling, something too deep for utterance, welling up within us as we look at the "old gateway" and the "ivy-mantled tower," coming down to us as relics of antiquity. He who has no such poetry in his soul, though he may not be quite "fit for treasons, stratagems, and spoils," lacks that imagination which gives to life and to travel "the glory and the freshness of a dream."

With romance and poetry, our Southern past is glorious.

Carolina has her Roanoke Island, associated with the name of Walter Raleigh, whose whole career is wrapped in romantic glamour. It is the glory of the South that this great chevalier and soldier stands in the forefront of her history.

Of Roanoke Island you have read in your histories. Here was made the first English settlement in the New World; and "the lost colony of Roanoke" is the most pathetic romance in our history. The word *Croatan* carved upon that tree will be the sad enigma of the centuries; and myriads of children yet unborn will wonder whether the settlers were murdered by the savages, died of starvation, or perchance were adopted into some tribe of Indians.

Another sacred shrine is St. Augustine, Florida. All Americans love to visit the old town and look at its ancient gateway. It was on this spot that the white man made his first permanent settlement in America, and, though the relations between the Spaniards, whose ancestors planted this town, and the race to which we belong have not always been pleasant, we feel a solemn thrill as we think of the time when the great white race to which we both belong first planted a home on this mighty continent.

Still dearer to us of English blood are the **ruins of Jamestown**. The feelings that stir our hearts as we stand under the shadow of the old tower are too deep for utterance, and we almost beg to be left alone with our awe and our solemn meditation.

Whence those deep feelings, those unutterable emotions? It is the reverence for antiquity, the lofty sentiment that raises us above the brute creation. Misers are not without it; hard-hearted lovers of the "almighty dollar" cannot resist it; and hundreds, if not thousands, of the richest in our land visit that spot every year, tread reverently its sacred sward, read the inscriptions upon its old tombstones, and hear in imagination the echoes of the old bell that used to call the fathers of America to the house of worship.

Dear to every American should be that now deserted island. Proud should Virginians be that they are custodians of that shrine with its sacred memories; for it was on that spot, on the 13th of May, 1607, that the first permanent English settlement in America was made. There the first English home in America was established; there Reverend Robert Hunt, the first English minister in America, read the new liturgy of the reformed Church of England, and under a spreading canvas, with the green sward of nature as his carpet, "sang the Lord's song in a strange land." Its tower no longer rings with the reverberating peals of holy bells, calling to meditation and to prayer. Only the dead are there. All is in ruins. Yet we feel, as we stand in those sacred precincts, that the poet* was right when he said,

"Yes, give me a land that has legends and lays."

What other section has a Pocahontas? Others here and there have a kind Indian woman shielding the whites from treachery and cruelty; but Pocahontas, "the Princess of the Forest," the daughter of kings, the mother of statesmen that have been and that are to be—she will ever stand alone, unique, on the canvas of history, inspiring the artist's brush, the historian's pen, and the poet's lyre.

---
*Father Ryan.

The saving of John Smith by Pocahontas may some day be proved a myth by historians. With the people, however, the great masses, who love everything romantic and poetic, Pocahontas will forever bend over Smith, between him and the club of the cruel Indian, and save him from the bloody death that hangs over him. Maidens, too, will ever sigh over the love affairs of Pocahontas, and drop a tear of sympathy. They will think how cruel it was that she should be told that Smith had died in England and that, believing this, she had listened to the wooings of Rolfe, while her own "dear Captain" was thinking of her in England far away.

Why is the year 1619 immortal in our annals and why is the date July 30, 1619, mentioned with rapture and with reverence by our historians? The same lofty sentiment explains it. It is the inborn respect for antiquity, the reverence for what is venerable in our history. Because in that year and on that day, there met, in the church at Jamestown, the first American Congress, the first body of lawmakers that ever came together on this continent, and there and then the twenty-two burgesses, or representatives, of Virginia, with an independence and an earnestness never surpassed and rarely equalled, discussed some of the most important questions that ever engaged the attention of a legislative assembly of any people.

Possibly, "state pride" might lead the present writer to exaggerate the importance of this great assembly: let us hear what John Fiske, of Massachusetts, says of the charter under which this assembly met: "The Magna Charta of Virginia . . . . hardly second to any other state paper of the 17th century." This is from a Northern historian, fair to the South generally, but not especially anxious to glorify any section other than New England. John Esten Cooke, the Virginian, says of this same assembly, "The event was a portentous one. The old world had passed away, and the new was born."

And these first American lawmakers were worthy of the day. They took up the greatest subjects that ever engaged the attention of a legislative body. They passed on the rights of certain men to seats in the assembly, that is, on the eligibility of some of their own members; discussed the dangers arising from cruel Indian neighbors; discussed agriculture, their main source of support; made laws in regard to the church, which was then an established or state church; and took steps to found a college for the education of their sons, thus making the South the pioneer in the higher education of America.*

This same assembly petitioned the London Company at home to grant them authority "to allow or disallow of their orders of court, as his Majesty hath given them power to allow or disallow our laws." This is the claim of local self-government. It sounds the first note of the great contention between local self-government and outside interference, the contention which fired the eloquence of Patrick Henry in 1765, flashed from the sword of Washington ten years later, and nerved the arm of Lee and his heroes in the great war for Southern independence.

Two years later, another great idea was planted in Virginia. Sir Francis Wyatt was sent from England as gover-

---

*In this connection we may state that the first female college in the world was established in Macon, Georgia.

nor, and brought with him a "formal grant of free government by written charter," "the first charter of free government in America" (1621).

The South, then, was the cradle of American civilization. If Thanet is dear to all Englishmen as the place where their fathers first set foot upon the soil of England, if Athens is proud of her Acropolis and loves every foot of its great rock, every American must feel a thrill of awe and of sacred rapture, as he treads the verdant sward of Jamestown and thinks of the day when the *Susan Constant,* the *Godspeed,* and the *Discovery* cast anchor off that green peninsula, and the great Anglo-Saxon race planted its first home on the new continent.

In concluding this chapter, let us go back for a moment to our text which is taken from the verses of a great poet who said that his name was "writ in water," but who, because he believed that the poetry of earth was never dead and has taught others to believe it, is now numbered among the immortals. Yes, in this practical, money-loving age, we need more than one Keats to help us "hitch our wagon to a star."

However, there are still many that feel the poetry of earth. Even wealthy stockbrokers and porkpackers sometimes find poems in places. Some would buy the shrines of the South and ship them to Chicago. Shall we sell the tower of Jamestown? Shall a syndicate have it and move it to Cincinnati? What rich young university shall buy the poetry and the glory of old William and Mary College? When shall we auction off the old gateway at St. Augustine? Would Carolina sell King's Mountain for its weight in gold and silver? Shall the tomb of Washington be moved from Mount Vernon to some Northern city where more may visit it?

"There is grandeur in graves, there is glory in gloom,"

sings one of our heartbroken poets;* and he knew it all by experience. He sang out of a full heart. He had stood by the ruins and had sat by the graves. He tells us, in his own language, what Keats had already sung, that "the poetry of earth is ceasing never;" but that, as with other forms of beauty, "its loveliness increases, it will never pass into nothingness."

V.

"Sic Semper Tyrannis"

(1) HARVEY AND BERKELEY

In resisting tyranny, also, the South may claim priority. Her sons have always loved freedom and hated tyrants.

In the histories of Virginia, you have read a good deal about "the thrusting out of Sir John Harvey." This was, we may say, a "bloodless revolution."

Harvey was the governor of Virginia, sent out (1629) by Charles I, king of England, and was a worthy disciple of his tyrannical master. Besides being a tyrant, Harvey was unprincipled in money matters, "robbing the treasury and trying to sell lands belonging to individuals." The Virginians called an Assembly "to hear complaints against the

*Father Ryan.

Governor;" and "On the 28th of April, 1635," as the old record quaintly puts it, "Sir John Harvey thrust out of his government, and Capt. John West acts as Governor till the King's pleasure known." After a short contest with the people of Virginia, Charles yielded, and Harvey vanished into nothingness.

About forty years later, the Virginians again rose up in rebellion. This time, they were armed, and ready to play *sic semper tyrannis* with an orchestra of gun and cannon. We refer of course to Bacon's Rebellion.

For many years, the Virginians and the New England colonists had had grievances against England. The Navigation Acts, first passed in 1651, were pressing hard upon all the colonies, compelling them to ship their tobacco and other produce to England in English ships, prohibiting them from purchasing manufactured goods from any country but England, and from trading with each other in any article of importance. This meant ruin and starvation to our colonial fathers.

In 1673 came something still more galling. In this year, "the merry monarch," Charles II, to reward two of his favorites for their valuable services—probably for telling smutty jokes well or for inventing new pleasures—granted them "that entire tract of land and water commonly called Virginia," to have and to hold for thirty-one years. This was practical confiscation.

In 1676, came the straw that broke the camel's back. The once-popular and beloved governor, Sir William Berkeley, had grown peevish and tyrannical in his old age, and was afraid to give arms to the Virginians, for fear they might use them against him and his royal master. When the Indians rose up in 1676, Berkeley refused to grant a commission to a brave and eloquent young planter who wished to lead his people against the Indians. After parleyings and wranglings between the followers of Berkeley and of the young planter, Nathaniel Bacon, civil war broke out, and hundreds of men fought on each side. Suddenly Bacon died of a fever, and the "rebellion" ended. His grave is unknown to this day. He was buried secretly, so that Berkeley might not "hang, draw, and quarter" the dead rebel, as he no doubt intended to do.

History settles accounts strictly with men like Berkeley. They go down to oblivion "unwept, unhonored, and unsung." So with the once-honored and courted vice-regal governor of Virginia. His name is rarely mentioned save in scorn or in contemptuous pity. At his home near Williamsburg, no traveler drops the tear of love or heaves the sigh of admiration. Bacon, on the contrary, is honored in America. Northern and Southern writers unite in singing his praises. Monuments are even now going up to perpetuate his memory; and, by a strange freak of fortune, his name has been given to the post-office recently established at Greenspring, the old home of Berkeley.

Bacon, then, is the first American rebel against armed tyranny. His faithful lieutenant, Thomas Hansford, is the first American martyr to liberty. Well may Virginia cherish the memory of such sons! Well has she earned the right to blazon *sic semper tyrannis* upon her scutcheon,—that motto under which her sons have fought under rebels whose fame grows brighter with the ages.

If Virginia had her Harvey and her Berkeley, New England had her Andros, and North Carolina her Tryon. Only in the matter of priority did Virginia have the advantage of her sister colonies; for it was not till 1691 that the people of Boston rose up against Andros, "the tyrant of New England," and shipped him back to old England; and, in 1771, some of the brave men of the "Old North State" rose up against the infamous Tryon and fought against him at the river Alamance.

Probably no one thing did more to bring on the Revolutionary movement than the conduct of several of these royal governors like Andros, Tryon, and Dunmore. In selecting such men, England showed herself perversely blind to her own interests and indifferent to those of her colonies. It would seem that America had to be free, and that "offenses must needs come;" but "woe to him by whom the offense cometh."

(2) GEORGE III AND HIS "FRIENDS"

(a) "TAXATION WITHOUT REPRESENTATION"

In judging England for her treatment of our colonial ancestors, we must remember that she was no worse than other nations. The relation between colonies and the mother country is far more pleasant now than in earlier periods of modern history. In the eighteenth century, colonies were supposed to exist entirely for the benefit of the mother country; the idea of mutual benefit was hardly dreamed of except by a few statesmen, who were regarded as political dreamers.

These facts will help us to understand why the English parliament frequently reënacted the Navigation Laws, and made them harsh and galling. This of course produced hard feeling against the mother country. Moreover, our ancestors resorted to all kinds of means to evade the Navigation Laws; and thus many of our people got into the bad habit of taking the law in their own hands—which, if not checked, will undermine the foundations of government, and ruin any race or nation.

English people often say that American children are taught to hate England. If so, it is the fault of the books and the teachers. Whatever indignation we may justly feel should be directed rather against George III and his advisers, his ministers, as we call them. Even then, however, we should remember that George had a constitutional tendency towards insanity, and that he was not always responsible. Moreover, he had bad advice, bad teachers, from his very boyhood. His mother, for instance, was a highstrung woman, and brought him up with the idea that he must "be king;" and in 1760, at the age of twenty-five, he tried to rule according to the methods of the Stuarts, one of whom had been beheaded (1649), and another driven into exile (1685).

In studying about the American Revolution, furthermore, we should know something about the parliaments of that period. In our day, parliament is a representative body. It is elected by the great mass of English male citizens. It knows the wishes of the people, and is governed by public opinion. In George's day, a handful of freeholders elected members of parliament. Prominent landholders gave away seats, and left them in their wills to their sons and others. You can see, then, that England was an oligarchy, and that the masses had little voice in the government.

The king, too, had far more power than at present. His personal sovereignty was vastly greater. He could intimidate parliament and browbeat his cabinet, both of which things George did habitually.

In spite of all that we have said, however, the English people must bear a part of the blame. They fired up angrily when they heard that America was defying England. They thought they ought to stand by the government, just as many of us Americans think in regard to matters of our day. "My country, may she ever be right, but right or wrong, my country"—this is the feeling of a great number of patriotic men in all ages.

"Taxation without representation" was a popular political phrase of the pre-revolutionary era. Used by the eloquent James Otis, of Massachusetts, it spread throughout the colonies. It was a popular but vague phrase. Its real meaning depends upon the meaning of "representation." Many Englishmen said that the Americans had as much representation as a large number of people in England. Some in both countries thought that America should have actual representatives in parliament; but many others thought that this was impracticable. What the colonists really wanted was taxation by their local assemblies; and this was what George III vehemently refused them. So the long quarrel continued. "The irrepressible conflict" between the mother and the daughter was drawing nearer. The bitterness engendered in those days and in a later pe-

PATRICK HENRY

riod is gradually passing away; and it is to be hoped that the present century will see the two great Anglo-Saxon nations bound by indissoluble ties of love and amity.

(b) "TREASON! TREASON!"

Two years after James Otis, another great orator of revolution stepped into the arena. This was Patrick Henry, the "tongue of the Revolution." In 1763, he made his famous speech in the "Parsons' Cause" at Hanover Courthouse, Virginia, voicing the pent-up feelings of his countrymen against George III and his advisers.

In 1758, the tobacco crop having failed, the Burgesses had enacted that all debts payable in tobacco, then a species of currency, might be paid in money at the rate of two pence a pound. In 1763, tobacco being very scarce and very high, some of the vestries, in settling with the parsons, fell back upon this "Two-Penny Act," though it was virtually repudiating two-thirds of the salary of the minister. The matter might have been settled peaceably between the clergy and their people if the king had not meddled, in order to use his "prerogative," as he called it. In the suit of the Rev. James Maury against his vestry, the latter engaged Patrick Henry, an awkward and ungainly-looking young lawyer, to protect their interests. He criticized the clergy so bitterly that those present left the courthouse in mingled fury and dismay. He launched such thunderbolts of wrath at George III, that the leading counsel for Mr. Maury said to the court that he wondered how the justices could tolerate such treasonable language. The jury gave the parson one cent damages instead of several hundred dollars. It was really a verdict against the king for interference.

This trial has become famous in history. It was really the case of the people of Virginia against George III, and "the first formal defiance" hurled by America at England, says Fiske, the Massachusetts historian.

Two years later still, came the Stamp Act (1765). Of Henry's speech in Williamsburg, we need not speak in detail in this volume; it is described in all your histories. To pay a stamp tax on all legal papers, contracts, wills, newspapers, lawyers' licenses, pamphlets, and various other written and printed matter, was annoying and burdensome; but the main thing, as already intimated, was the principle. Our fathers were willing to be taxed by their own assemblies, but not by a parliament across the ocean. When the blood is hot, reason becomes clouded. Soon the phrase "no taxation without representation" became "no legislation without representation"—which meant of course that the colonists would shake off allegiance to England, if the men using that phrase should take the leadership.

Henry's speech on the Five Resolutions made an epoch. "Virginia rang the alarm bell," says a Northern writer. "Virginia gave the signal to the continent," wrote General Gage, the British commander. Virginia, however, was divided; on one side were the "big wigs" and aristocracy; on the other, the yeomanry, led by Patrick Henry. The vote was very close; and the morning after the House of Burgesses voted and adjourned, one of the boldest resolutions was found to have been torn from the secretary's record.

All students of history have doubtless heard of Peyton Randolph. He was a member of the House of Burgesses, and rushed out crying, "I would gladly give five hundred guineas for another vote." What could he have meant? Not that he wished to buy a vote; for that, though common in England at that time, was not dreamed of in Virginia. He of course meant that, if he could honorably do so, he would gladly pay this large sum to vote twice; for, by so doing, he would produce a tie, and leave the decision to the Speaker, who would vote against the five resolutions. Nine years later, this same Peyton Randolph was one of the leaders against George III and his ministry.

Virginia was the most fearless of the colonies. No other had taken so bold a stand on the Stamp Act. Some had protested before the act was passed; but, after its passage, there were no signs of resistance until Henry threw down the gauntlet. Even James Otis declared the Five Resolutions treasonable, and said that America must submit. The action of Virginia gave new nerve and boldness to the other colonies. Massachusetts suggested a Congress of all the colonies. This body, representing nine colonies, met in New York, October 7, 1765. The most enthusiastic response to the call came from South Carolina; and one of the leading spirits of the Congress was her representative, Christopher Gadsden, "the learned scholar," the "broad-minded man of rare sagacity and most liberal spirit," a man too little noticed in American history, but destined to shine brightly when history is written fairly and accurately. Virginia was not represented. Her House of Burgesses was prevented from meeting, being dissolved by the royal governor, Francis Fauquier.

This Stamp Act Congress, under the leadership of Livingston, of New York, and Gadsden, of South Carolina, adopted a series of resolutions echoing the spirit of those offered by Henry in the Virginia legislature, and addressed memorials to the king and to both Houses of Parliament.

Nine years later (1774), came the famous Continental Congress, so called to distinguish it from the Provincial Congress of several colonies. "The first call came from Virginia;" the first session of this Congress opened September 5, 1774; and the first president was Peyton Randolph, of Virginia. The South was nobly represented in these bodies. In the first, sat John and Edward Rutledge, of South Carolina; Samuel Chase, of Maryland; Edmund Pendleton, Richard Henry Lee, Patrick Henry, and George Washington, of Virginia. An eminent Northern historian, in naming the most prominent members, selects twelve,—the above seven, with five distinguished sons of New England, New York, and Pennsylvania.

VI

Virginia and Carolina

(1) TEA PARTIES

The Stamp Act was to go into effect November 1, 1765. When that day came, bells were tolled, business was generally suspended, and flags were raised at half-mast. When the stamps arrived, they were seized and burned. The stamp officers resigned. Lawyers agreed to consider unstamped documents legally valid. The woman of the colonies wore homespun cloth for clothing; English goods of all kinds were boycotted; the whole continent had risen in unarmed rebellion.

English merchants sent petitions for a repeal of the Stamp Act. Pitt and Burke, two great orators of parliament, opposed the law in the House of Commons. Pitt said, "I rejoice that America has resisted." On March 18, 1766, parliament repealed the Stamp Act, but asserted its right to "bind America in all cases whatsoever." This of course stirred the colonists to fury.

Shortly after this, an act was passed forbidding all trade between the colonies and certain West India islands. This greatly angered the New England colonies.

In 1767, were passed the Townshend Acts, laying duties on glass, lead, colors, paper, and tea. Then troops were sent over to see that these laws were executed, and, by the Quartering Act of 1765, our fathers were required to shelter and feed these soldiers. This monstrous demand led (1770) to the famous "Boston Massacre."

Meanwhile, the policy of boycotting went on. The noble women of the colonies showed their patriotism by boycotting tea. The Boston Tea Party is cool compared with some tea parties in which tea was conspicuous by its absence. Prominent ladies of Carolina "resolved" that they would not touch the tyrannical weed. A young lady of Williamsburg, Virginia, declined to drink tea with Lord Dunmore at a reception, and was warmly rebuked by him as a hot-headed scion of a fire-eating sire.

For refusing to shelter and feed the British troops, the New York assembly was forbidden to pass any laws. For its bold conduct, the assembly of Massachusetts was dissolved by order of the king. This body used to adjourn to Faneuil (Funel) Hall, afterwards called the "Cradle of Liberty." The Virginia House of Burgesses, when dissolved for its boldness, used to meet in the old Raleigh Tavern, so famous in colonial and revolutionary history.

What Grenville and Townshend could not do to anger the colonists, Lord North succeeded in doing. From 1768 to 1782, he and George III together left no stone unturned to alienate our fathers from the mother country.

Troops were sent to Boston to see that the Townshend Acts were enforced. In the state of feeling that existed, fights between the soldiers and the citizens were bound to occur. The most famous of these conflicts is the "Boston Massacre," which occurred March 6, 1770, and in which four citizens were killed and several wounded.

Meanwhile, the colonists were boycotting British goods of almost every kind. Agreements were made all over the country not to import goods of British manufacture. All were boycotted because of the principle of "taxation without representation." "Tea," about 1773, became a war cry of rebellion.

The Boston Tea Party of December, 1773, is famous in history. The boldness of a party of Bostonians who disguised themselves as Mohawk Indians and emptied more than three hundred chests of tea into the harbor, has been well chronicled by sons of New England. Not so well known, however, are the tea parties of Charleston, Annapolis, and other Southern towns and cities. It was in the same month in which the Boston Tea Party took place that the people of Charleston refused to buy or to handle the hated stuff, and the tea was left to moulder in the cellars where it was stored. In October, 1774, Annapolis gave her entertainment, the brig *Peggy Stuart* with her cargo of tea being publicly burned by citizens of that once-loyal town of Maryland.

These acts cannot be fully justified. Our fathers of that era were sometimes swept off their feet by passion and excitement, just as we are in our day; but their hearts were in the main right, and their occasional lawlessness must be forgiven if not justified.

All those bold acts infuriated King George and his henchmen. Instead of trying to appease the Americans, they poured oil on the flames. To punish the colonists, they passed the "Intolerable Acts," the worst of which closed up the port of Boston, thus paralyzing business and threatening starvation to thousands. This helped to unify the colonists; and the cry, "The cause of Boston is the cause of us all," rang from Georgia to New Hampshire. South Carolina sent 200 barrels of rice; North Carolina, $10,000 in money; Virginia, money and resolutions of sympathy. At a meeting of the freeholders of Fairfax county, Virginia, Maj. George Washington, the hero of Braddock's campaign, gave $250 to the poor of Boston, and offered to march 1,000 men at his own expense to resist English tyranny.

Meantime, North Carolina had poured out the first blood of the Revolution. In the spring of 1771, some of her brave sons rose up against the tyranny of Tryon, the royal governor, and at the river Alamance, on May 16 of that year, North Carolina patriots shed the first blood spilt in armed conflict between England and her colonies. The line, however, was not yet very closely drawn between the parties; for on Tryon's side fought Col. Richard Caswell, afterwards so famous as a patriot leader. The two hundred killed and wounded were American martyrs to liberty, and their names should be recorded on our annals.

Two years after this, that is, in 1773, Virginia suggested a plan of correspondence between the colonies. This had already been tried on a small scale in Massachusetts, where a system of correspondence between the various counties had been adopted through the influence of the famous Samuel Adams. Virginia's move was one of far-reaching importance. Hitherto, the individual colonies had stood separate and alone against George III and his tyrannical measures; now they are to stand shoulder to shoulder. The most eminent men were appointed on these committees of correspondence. Dispatched by swift messengers from colony to colony, the letters of these great men told of every new encroachment upon the rights of the Americans. A prominent colonist living temporarily in England wrote to friends at home that this system of coöperation on the part of the colonies had "struck a greater panic into the ministers" of George III than anything that had taken place since the times of the Stamp Act. Of Virginia's part in this great movement, the eminent northern historian Bancroft says,

"Whether that great idea should become a reality depended upon Virginia."

(2) MECKLENBURG AND ST. JOHN'S CHURCH

Two years later, met the immortal Virginia Convention of 1775. This convention ordered that steps be taken "for embodying, arming, and disciplining such a number of men as may be sufficient" to protect the colony against aggression—the first action taken by any colony looking towards armed resistance against England. This convention is likewise famous on account of the third great speech of Patrick Henry, the one known to every schoolboy in America. Old St. John's Church, Richmond, in which the convention met, is one of the most famous buildings in America and thousands of strangers visit it every year, and stand where Henry stood as he cried, "Give me liberty or give me death." An interesting incident of this convention is recorded. Edward Carrington, of Charlotte county, was standing in the churchyard, listening through a window, as Henry uttered those immortal words. "Let me be buried on this very spot," cried the enthusiastic and awe-struck man; and, thirty-five years later, his remains were laid on the very spot where he had stood as he listened to the orator.

The month of May, 1775, is famous for the "Mecklenburg Declaration," so dear to North Carolina. As to this declaration, historians differ; but the oldest of Virginia's living historical investigators says: "Beyond all reasonable doubt, the first actual declaration of independence was made by the people of the county of Mecklenburg, in North Carolina, on the 20th of May, 1775 . . . . In the immortal instrument of July 4, 1776, Mr. Jefferson is supposed to have been aided by this Carolina declaration." Mr. John Fiske, in arguing that the declaration is a mere "legend," and that no such paper was drawn up on the 20th of May, admits that, on the 31st of that month, the Mecklenburg patriots "ventured upon a measure more decided than any that had yet been taken in any part of the country." Though the day is disputed, most scholars accept the fact.

The people of Mecklenburg county established an independent county government. They threw defiance in the face of England. The only question of doubt is whether their independence was temporary or permanent; and this is one point on which historians differ.

Whatever this brave county undertook, no colony had as yet dreamed of absolute independence. Early in September, 1775, the Provincial Congress of North Carolina unanimously resolved, and called Almighty God to bear them witness, that it was the earnest wish and prayer of North Carolina to be honorably reconciled with the mother country.

The British called Mecklenburg county "the hornet's nest." It is the mother of patriots and heroes, the Polks being especially distinguished. Colonel Thomas Polk was very active in calling the Convention of 1775, and read the declaration from the steps. His son William, though a mere youth, distinguished himself in the Revolutionary War; and William's son, Leonidas, was an eminent general in the Confederate army.

Georgia had her revolutionary powder parties, which

should be known to all Americans. When the news of the battle of Lexington reached Savannah, a body of patriots, among whom Joseph Habersham and Edward Telfair were especially prominent, took possession of the royal magazine in that city, and seized more than five hundred pounds of powder for the defense of the people of Georgia. A little later a British powder ship, bearing 13,000 pounds of powder for the use of the royal troops, arrived at Tybee Island, below Savannah; again, the heroic Habersham was ready to serve his country. With a party of thirty volunteers, he captured this powder, stored 8,000 pounds in a magazine in Savannah, and sent 5,000 pounds to Boston, just in time to be of effectual use at the battle of Bunker Hill. In January, 1776, Habersham did a still bolder thing. The Committee of Safety in Savannah, believing that the royal governor was about to imitate the conduct of the infamous Governor Dunmore, of Virginia, determined to arrest him. This required a man of nerve and courage, and Habersham undertook to do it. Entering the council-chamber while the king's council was in session, Habersham laid his hand upon the governor's shoulder, and said, "Sir James, you are my prisoner!" The governor's person was secured, but he was treated with the respect due his rank and dignity. "Thus," says a Northern writer, "Colonel Habersham put an end to royal rule in Georgia."

The Northern historians themselves have immortalized the deeds of the revolutionary South: "The blessing of Union," says Bancroft, "is due to the warm-heartedness of South Carolina." Of Virginia, the same high authority writes: "In this manner, Virginia laid the foundations of our Union." Another eminent Northern man, Robert C. Winthrop, says of Virginia: "It was union which opened our independence; and there could have been no union without the influence and coöperation of that great leading Southern colony."

VII

Independence

(1) 1772 AND 1775

All the measures taken by the colonists were, thus far, purely in self-defense. Absolute and final independence of England was not dreamed of by any large number. Americans at first threw off the government of George III, just as an injured wife sometimes leaves her husband, and throws off his authority until he makes apology and reparation. The idea of complete independence took root slowly.

Meanwhile local governments were being organized. This was the result, in large part, of the battle of Lexington, which really precipitated the war long threatening. First came the Mecklenburg Declaration. A few days later, June 4, 1775, the Provincial Congress of South Carolina "organized an association which was practically a provisional government of the people." This is claimed by a distinguished Southern historian as "the first independent or revolutionary government set up in any of the colonies."*

---

*General Edward McCrady, of South Carolina.

This action of South Carolina was forestalled, however, by other Southern patriots, and their champion is Theodore Roosevelt, whose pen has done no little to glorify the South and its heroes. In his *Winning of the West,* Roosevelt tells us that the western pioneers of the Watauga settlement organized a government at the headwaters of the Tennessee river, in 1772, and that "they were the first men of American birth to establish a free and independent commonwealth on the continent." These men of Watauga were refugeeing from the tyranny of Tryon, the despotic royal governor of North Carolina. Their leader was James Robertson, of Wake county, North Carolina, who is known in history as "the father of Tennessee." Another eminent Southerner comes now upon the canvas. It is John Sevier, of Virginia, who, in 1772, joined James Robertson, and helped him to lay the foundations of the state of Tennessee.

Let us summarize briefly: In the matter of setting up an independent revolutionary government, Massachusetts was the first Northern colony; South Carolina was a month or more ahead of Massachusetts; but North Carolinians, led by a North Carolinian, were three years ahead of both Massachusetts and South Carolina.

We have gladly quoted Roosevelt, the Northern historian. As, however, the lamented J. L. M. Curry is better known in the South as an authority on such matters, we will say that he also makes this statement as to the priority of the Watauga revolutionary government.

The year 1775 was a critical year in the revolutionary movement. The battles of Lexington and Concord; the Mecklenburg Declaration; the establishment of revolutionary governments in some of the colonies; the fight with Dunmore at Great Bridge—all helped to precipitate actual independence. Virginia had been quite conservative until Dunmore seized the powder stored by the colonists in Williamsburg for defense against the Indians, urged the negroes to rise against their masters, and, on New Year's Day, 1776, burned Norfolk, the principal town of Virginia. Then, independence began to be discussed quite freely. "During the winter and spring, the revolutionary feeling waxed in strength daily." Still, no colony was willing to cut itself off from the mother country. They still called it "home," and hoped that terms of peace honorable to all might be agreed upon.

(2) THE YEAR 1776

On the 10th of February, 1776, a bold step forward was taken by Christopher Gadsden, of South Carolina. This fearless patriot said, in the Provincial Congress of his state, that he was in favor of the absolute independence of America. This, says the historian Drayton, "came like an explosion upon the members." John Rutledge, who later on came reluctantly and slowly to the side of total independence, rebuked Gadsden for his intemperate language, and the Provincial Congress refused to tolerate Gadsden's suggestion.

Early in 1776, however, matters approached a crisis. The efforts of England to hire troops from Russia and her success in securing mercenaries from parts of Germany infuriated all the Americans. About the same time an epoch-making book was published. Just as *Uncle Tom's Cabin* (1852) helped to fire the Northern heart against slavery and to inflame the South by its partisan treatment of the subject, so Thomas Paine's *Common Sense,* though containing much nonsense, had enough shrewd practical wisdom to produce a wonderful effect upon the people of all the colonies. Paine said nothing new and original. He anticipated the *Biglow Papers* by contemptuous ridicule of the other side, anticipated *Uncle Tom's Cabin* by a shrewd and plausible misrepresentation of the enemy's position, and put in caustic and catching style the arguments that such men as Samuel Adams had been for years advancing. The pamphleteers are mightier than the statesmen.

On the 12th of April, 1776, the "Old North State" spoke out. On that day, the North Carolina Congress authorized their delegates in the Continental Congress to "concur" with the delegates of the other colonies in throwing off allegiance to England; and this, say Northern historians, Fiske and others, was "the first explicit sanction given by any state to the idea of independence." Even South Carolina was behind her big sister. She had just sent delegates to Congress without any very definite instructions. Along with Georgia and Maryland, she, about this time, agreed to join in any movement for the general welfare. On the 15th of May, Virginia took a bolder stand than fearless old North Carolina. She declared in favor of total separation, and took steps to draft a constitution, which was adopted June 29, and was the first constitution of a free commonwealth on the continent.

Meanwhile, individuals were doing bold things on their

own authority. April 23, Chief-Justice Drayton, of South Carolina, told his grand jury that George III had abdicated the government, and that South Carolina was free and independent. Drayton and Gadsden moved too fast at this time for most of the South Carolinians. There were a great many Tory merchants and planters in the east of the state; while the Germans of the upper country had so much more liberty than they were used to at home that they did not become roused up until Tarleton went to Carolina and literally rode over the people.

The year 1776, then, was the year of independence. Many prominent South Carolinians took a bold position. North Carolina was the first colony to sanction independence, and Virginia, a month later, used still bolder language.

The vote for independence in Congress was at first far from unanimous. The Southern colonies were more outspoken than the Northern; but even one of the former had to be persuaded. Pennsylvania was slow in voting for the declaration. New York had given no instructions to her delegates, and they were very nervous; but, on July 9, New York ratified the declaration.

The Declaration of Independence was really a war measure. It was the triumph of a party, of the extreme liberty party led by the Adamses, Gadsden, and other fearless patriots. Some of the delegates had no idea of the seriousness of the step they were taking, but changed their votes as a man might do on any question of expediency. One prominent delegate, in writing to the president of his state, mentioned, parenthetically, that they had declared the independence of America. They builded better than they knew.

THOMAS JEFFERSON

Though the Continental Congress was nothing more than a vigilance committee of prominent citizens with no authority to bind the people, its acts of July 4, 1776, were ratified by all concerned, and all the members are now familiarly known as "signers."

The Declaration of Independence did not and could not create a nation. To say otherwise is to pervert history.

The month of June, 1776, is immortal. In that month Virginia adopted the Declaration of Rights, drawn up by George Mason. This great paper, commonly called the Virginia Bill of Rights, was the first declaration of rights ever passed on this continent. It placed George Mason, the Virginia planter, among the supreme political thinkers of the world. He has been called "the pen of the Revolution," a title which is also accorded Thomas Jefferson.

Most features of the Bill of Rights were familiar to all Englishmen. They were but concise rehearsals of clauses of the Magna Charta, and of the English Declaration of Rights of 1689. Mason was saying nothing new, but was saying it for the first time on the western continent. One clause, however, was magnificently new. If only the last clause of Mason's paper had been adopted by the Virginia statesmen, it would have made these men and Virginia famous throughout the ages. This was the clause in regard to religious freedom. Never before, says William Wirt Henry, had any civil government in the whole world allowed the claim of absolute religious freedom. Individuals here and there had suggested it. More, in his *Utopia,* told of the wonderful land where men might enjoy religious freedom; but men laughed at this as at other utopian visions. The Puritans of

New England persecuted Episcopalians, Roman Catholics, and Quakers. The Cavaliers of Virginia persecuted Quakers, Baptists, Puritans, and Roman Catholics. "Baltimore only professed to make free soil for Christianity."* Penn's laws of 1682 tolerated none but believers in God, and permitted none but Christians to hold office. "Williams's charter was expressly to propagate Christianity, and under it a law was enacted excluding all except Christians from the rights of citizenship, and including in the exclusion Roman Catholics."†

Williams was greater than laws and charter. He believed in absolute religious freedom. Rhode Island in his day became a house of refuge for men of all religions and of no religion. Williams was a great and remarkable man. He towered like a colossus above the other religious thinkers of his era. After all, however, he was but the leader of a small band of religionists, too feeble to affect the course of history. If we reject the opinions of Henry and Winsor, and say that the Rhode Island colony was more than a hundred years ahead of Virginia in time, what is the situation? Just this: Williams and his little band were a colony of religionists fleeing from persecution, and were in need of toleration. The Virginia Convention of 1776, on the other hand, was composed largely of churchmen, who needed no protection, and who saw, with prophetic statesmanship, that a great democracy must ultimately rest upon absolute freedom of religious opinion.

---

*W. W. Henry and Justin Winsor.
†Henry and Winsor.

No greater body of men ever sat in the Roman senate or met in the agora at Athens.

VIII

The South in the War of the Revolution

(1) HEROES AND HEROINES

(a) MARYLAND

The "Maryland Line" is famous in history. Throughout the whole of the Revolutionary War, this body of troops were famed for their gallantry. At the battle of Brooklyn Heights, "the highest honors" were won by the Maryland brigade under Smallwood; and, at the disastrous battle of Camden, almost the only honors fell to the men of Maryland. Again, at Eutaw Springs, they "drove the finest infantry of England before them with the bayonet."

One of the most eminent soldiers of Maryland is William Smallwood. At Brooklyn Heights, White Plains, and Fort Washington, the "Maryland Line" under his command distinguished themselves. At Germantown, they "retrieved the day and captured part of the enemy's camp." For his gallantry at Camden, where "Gates's laurels turned to willows," Smallwood received the thanks of Congress, and was appointed major-general.

Another popular hero is John Eager Howard. As a mere youth, he gallantly followed the noble Mercer at White Plains; distinguished himself at Germantown; and for his bravery and skill at Cowpens received a vote of thanks and a medal from Congress. It was the bayonet charge under his command that secured the victory of Cowpens and drove the vandal Tarleton from the field. "At one time of this day, he held the swords of seven British officers who had surrendered to him."

Though history has rather overlooked this hero, his own state crowned him with civic honors, still reveres his memory, and is erecting monuments in his honor.

We can of course name only a few especially prominent soldiers. In a rapid outline like this, however, we should not overlook General Mordecai Gist, one of the heroes of the Maryland Line at Camden, so enthusiastic as a patriot that he named his only two children "States" and "Independent;" Col. Otho Holland Williams, the hero of Eutaw Springs, to whom, at a critical moment in that battle, the commanding-general gave the order, "Let Williams advance and sweep the field with his bayonets;" and Col. Moses Rawlings, who led the Maryland riflemen at the storming of Fort Washington, when they, for several hours, withstood the attack of 5,000 Hessians.

(b) VIRGINIA

Though the battle of Lexington (April 19, 1775,) precipitated the War of the Revolution proper, bloodshed had taken place already. Of the battle of Alamance, North Carolina, in 1771, we have already spoken. In 1774, occurred the bloody battle of Point Pleasant, in which the men of West Augusta, frontiersmen of Virginia, defeated the

Indians under their famous leader, Cornstalk. The leader of the Virginians was the renowned Andrew Lewis. He is regarded by some as almost the equal of Washington, and his bronze statue has been placed by Virginia in the illustrious group near the state capitol at Richmond. Lewis, on October 10, 1774, builded better than he knew; for his victory of that day kept the Indian tribes of the northwest comparatively quiet for the first two years of the Revolution, and opened the way for the settlement of Kentucky and Tennessee, and for the acquisition of the great Northwest Territory, from which several states were afterwards carved and added to the Union.

It is almost certain that this Indian uprising was instigated by Dunmore, the royal governor of Virginia. In the next year (1775), we find him trying to stir up a slave insurrection. In this, however, he was almost as unsuccessful as John Brown, eighty-four years later, and for the same reason; namely, that the slaves in Virginia were so happy that they did not wish to rise against their masters.

At the Great Bridge over the Elizabeth river, Dunmore built a rude fort commanding the southern approach to the town of Norfolk. There, on December 9, 1775, his forces were overwhelmingly defeated by a body of patriots led by Colonel William Woodford, one of whose lieutenants was young John Marshall, afterwards chief-justice of the United States. Woodford was made a brigadier-general on February 21, 1777. At Brandywine, Germantown, and Monmouth, he served gallantly at the head of his brigade.

The "thunderbolt of the Revolution" is Daniel Morgan. Though born in another state, he is identified entirely with

Virginia, since he lived in that state for fifty years, commanded her troops, and is buried in her bosom.

Morgan rose from the humblest to the most exalted station. In Braddock's disastrous campaign, he served as a teamster. Later, he was made captain of a corps of ninety-six riflemen, which afterwards grew into the famous brigade that won the applause of both armies. In the summer of 1775, he appeared with his ninety-six riflemen before Boston, and brought a smile to the anxious face of Washington, just assuming command of the patriot army. He followed Arnold in his heroic march through the wilderness of Maine. At the great assault on Quebec, January 1, 1776, when Montgomery was killed and Arnold severely wounded, Morgan as commanding officer fought his way into the town, but for lack of support was taken prisoner with his whole detachment. After being released and exchanged, he returned to the army as colonel of riflemen. From that time, he and his corps became the "right arm of Washington." In the retreat through the Jerseys, he rendered eminent service to the commander. In the Saratoga campaign, he was a most important figure, and, along with Arnold, Herkimer, and Stark, won the admiration of the enemy. A standard Northern encyclopedia says that he was the "chief instrument" in the capture of Burgoyne. The British general gave most generous praise to Morgan and his Virginians. On being introduced to Morgan, he said, "My dear sir, you command the finest regiment in the world!" Gates and Washington contended for the honor of commanding him and his famous riflemen. They were lent by Washington to Gates for the Saratoga campaign, but the latter was loth to return them. Wherever he served, he was the "right arm" of his commander. He is the Stonewall Jackson of the Revolution.

An imbecile Congress slighted such men as the Arnold of Quebec and the Morgan of Saratoga. The former allied himself with Judas Iscariot; the latter, with Joseph E. Johnston. After the laurels of Saratoga turned to willows at Camden, and freedom shrieked, Morgan joined Gates in the South, Congress made him brigadier-general, and he was soon face to face with Tarleton, famous among cavaliers and chief among vandals. At Cowpens, Morgan, supported by Pickens, William Washington, and John Eager Howard, crushed an English army under Tarleton, depriving Cornwallis of all his best light infantry, and sent him limping to Yorktown.

Here ended the military career of Daniel Morgan: a physical malady that had been growing upon him soon compelled him to leave the service and return to his home in the Shenandoah Valley of Virginia.

In many ways, this great soldier prophesies of a later citizen of the Valley, and we are fain to call him brother to Jackson.

Two of the great cavalrymen of the Revolution were Henry Lee and William Washington. The latter was a kinsman of General Washington; the former, the son of Washington's old sweetheart, spoken of in correspondence as the "Lowland beauty." Henry Lee is known in history under the affectionate sobriquet of "Light Horse Harry." At the beginning of the Revolution, he was a mere stripling. On July 19, 1779, he surprised the British garrison at Paulus

Hook, where Jersey City now stands, and carried off about 160 prisoners, with a loss of only five in killed and wounded. For this brave deed he received a gold medal from Congress. In the Southern campaigns, he rendered valuable service to his country. When Greene made his masterly retreat through the Carolinas, Lee with his dragoons covered the rear of the patriot army.

The South will never let "Light Horse Harry" be forgotten. In romance and story, he is the Jeb Stuart of the Revolution; in history, he is immortal as the father of Robert E. Lee.

Col. William Washington deserves to be remembered. When Virginia sent her sons north to defend her sister colonies, Captain Washington, a mere youth, shed his blood in the battles of Long Island and Trenton. In the South, he coped with Tarleton, whom he resembled in all but his moral attributes. At Cowpens, under Morgan, he rendered distinguished service, and along with Morgan and Howard received a medal from Congress. In this battle, he and Tarleton had a sabre duel, in which both were wounded, and the latter had a good scar to show for the combat. The proud British dragoon ventured sometime afterwards to speak contemptuously of Colonel Washington to some North Carolina ladies upon whom he had thrust his society. "Who is this Colonel Washington?" he asked with a sneer; "I hear that he cannot read." "At all events," retorted Mrs. Wiley Jones, "he can make his mark." Again, he said to these ladies of Charlotte, "I should like to see this Colonel Washington." "If you had looked behind you at the battle of Cowpens, you would have had that pleasure," retorted Mrs. Ashe, of a noble family of Carolina.

A heroic figure is General Hugh Mercer, of Virginia. As a young surgeon, he followed in 1745 the ill-fated Charles Edward, the "young Pretender." Emigrating to Virginia, he identified himself wholly with that colony. In Braddock's expedition, he was severely wounded. The Revolution found him practising medicine at Fredericksburg, Virginia; but his military ardor was as great as when he followed the foolhardy leaders of his youth, and he offered his sword to Virginia. In June, 1776, at Washington's request, Congress made him a brigadier. He followed the commander-in-chief through the Jerseys, led the attacking column at Trenton, advised the famous march on Princeton, and commanded the advanced column in the battle. His men, mostly militia, began to waver, and in making a heroic effort to rally them, he fell, pierced with several bayonets.

Virginia has permitted a sister state, Pennsylvania, to outdo her in honoring the memory of the noble Mercer; and the United States has only recently erected a monument to commemorate his heroism.

Virginia should never forget Colonel William Campbell, one of the heroes of King's Mountain. In that battle, so momentous in its consequences, there was no ranking officer on the field, and the other colonels selected Campbell as their commander. He is entitled to a full share of the glory. Another one of these distinguished colonels, John Sevier, was born in Virginia; but we shall group him with the "Border Heroes." Colonel Campbell's men were Scotch-Irish of

Washington county, Virginia, and were of the same stock as the men who afterwards followed Stonewall Jackson.

To this distinguished list, we should of course add George Rogers Clark, "the Hannibal of the West." He gave the Northwest Territory to Virginia, and she, to the Union. Commissioned by Governor Henry, and leading hardy sons of the western counties, this brilliant young soldier set out to regain a very large territory which belonged to Virginia by original grant but which had lately been seized and garrisoned by England. His marches read like a chapter of romance, or a history of knighthood.

Clad in hunting shirts, carrying knapsacks, long rifles and horns of powder, these heroic men marched through the wilderness and the boundless forest, traveled in boats down the Ohio river, waded up to their arm-pits in the freezing water of the drowned lands of the Wabash river, holding their guns and powder above their heads to keep them dry, compelled the British to surrender, and sent the governor as a prisoner to Williamsburg, the capital of Virginia.

Thus this great area was restored to Virginia. In 1781, she ceded it to the Union. Afterwards, five states and part of a sixth were created from this Northwest Territory. Thus, in part, did Virginia earn her title of "the Mother of States." The grandsons of the settlers of these states were, in 1861, her fiercest and most indomitable foes on the field of battle.

Of Washington we need say nothing. To praise him would be like adding a grain of sand to the seashore or one drop to the falls of Niagara. We may say, however, to the young reader that even the illustrious Washington had his enemies, and still has his traducers. Shakespeare tells us,

> "Be thou as chaste as ice, as pure as snow,
> Thou shalt not escape calumny."

So it was with the "Father of his Country." During the war, he was assailed by the Conway Cabal, headed by an Irishman and encouraged by some prominent Americans; and one of the signers of the Declaration used anonymous letters to defame him. As president, he incurred the abuse of partisan papers and politicians, and was even accused of "looting" the treasury. In our day, a British historian would damn him as the murderer of André. These are but pigmies storming the rock of Gibraltar. The world now puts him with Alfred, regarding them as the highest products of the Anglo-Saxon race. To these, posterity will add a third—Robert E. Lee

(c) NORTH CAROLINA

Among the most eminent patriots of North Carolina is General John Ashe. As Speaker of the Colonial Assembly in 1765, he fearlessly denounced the Stamp Act, saying that the people of that colony would resist the execution of the law to the death. With an armed force, he compelled the stamp master to resign his hateful office. In 1771, however, along with Caswell and others afterwards eminent as patriots, he supported Governor Tryon at the battle of Alamance. So great, however, was his patriotic zeal in 1775 that he was publicly denounced as a rebel. During the war, he was captured and thrown into prison, where he contracted smallpox and died.

The Ashes were distinguished soldiers, and their name is justly perpetuated by North Carolina.

Two of the heroes of King's Mountain were Benjamin Cleveland and Joseph McDowell. They contributed no little to the brilliant victory which was a turning point in the Revolution. They led more than 500 brave North Carolinians, constituting over half the patriot army.

The most eminent of a prominent family was General Francis Nash. Though born in another state, he was identified with North Carolina. As captain, he served at Alamance (1771) on the side of Governor Tryon; but, when English tyranny became intolerable, he offered his sword to America. He was a member of Washington's staff. In leading a brigade at Germantown, he was mortally wounded. The city of Nashville, Tennessee, was named in his honor. In November, 1777, Congress voted $500 to erect a monument to his memory; but, like Mercer and others, he had to wait more than a century before this monument was finally completed.

Among the partisan leaders of the South, William R. Davie deserves honorable mention. When a boy, he was brought from England to South Carolina, but, at the outbreak of the war, was living in the "Old North State." Commissioned by her, he commanded a troop of dragoons in Pulaski's legion. A handsome estate he spent in equipping cavalry to protect the southwest portion of North Carolina. He distinguished himself at Hanging Rock and Rocky Mount; and at Charlotte, with a handful of men, he kept back for a while the whole British army under Cornwallis. He is the father of the University of North Carolina.

General Richard Caswell was both statesman and soldier. In the latter capacity he led the government forces at the battle of Alamance, but later on turned against King George and his henchmen. At Moore's Creek Bridge, February 27, 1776, he won a victory that greatly cheered the patriot cause in North Carolina. Most of his time, however, was given to civic office, and, in this sphere of usefulness, he left his impress upon the state of his adoption.

Two other soldiers of North Carolina worthy of honorable mention are Generals Griffith Rutherford and William Davidson. The former routed the Cherokees and Tories in 1776, compelling the Indians to sue for peace. General Rutherford, after the war, served both North Carolina and the new territory of Tennessee in high civic positions. General Davidson fought gallantly at Brandywine, Germantown, and Monmouth. Sent south, he lost his life obstructing the march of Cornwallis through North Carolina. The people of the state perpetuated his memory by naming a college in his honor, and Congress voted $500 to erect a monument to his memory.

If New England has her Putnam and his famous ride down the stone steps, North Carolina has her William Hunter and his rock. This Colonel William Hunter was a noble patriot, and his name was held in "holy horror" by the Tories and the British soldiers. Being captured by David Fanning, the notorious persecutor of his fellow-countrymen, he made his escape and hid under some corn in a farmer's wagon. Fanning captured him, and said: "I am very glad to see you, Colonel Hunter. How did you pass the night? You look tired. You shall be hanged at once." But Colonel

Hunter would not be hanged. Just as Fanning's men were getting a rope ready to hang Hunter to the nearest tree, he sprang upon Fanning's horse, famous for its speed, and rushed like the wind for Deep river, Fanning and his dragoons in hot pursuit. When Hunter reached the river, there was no ford near him. Just before him, there rose out of the water a large slanting rock too steep for a man to go down. Hunter dug his heels into the horse's flanks, dashed down the rock at lightning speed, swam the horse across the river, and made his escape.

The "Old North State" did nobly in the Revolution. Of her, Charles Pinckney, of South Carolina, said in 1779: "I shall ever love a North Carolinian, and join with General Moultrie in confessing that they have been the salvation of this country."

Not all the heroes can serve on the field of battle. Among civic heroes and martyrs, Cornelius Harnett, called by Josiah Quincy "the Samuel Adams of North Carolina," stands preëminent. He made his first reputation as an opponent of the Stamp Act; then served on the Intercolonial Committee of Correspondence; sat in the Provincial Congress of North Carolina; was for a while acting-governor of the state; exerted great influence in inducing North Carolina to declare for independence; was branded by Sir Henry Clinton as a rebel beyond the pale of foregiveness. On July 22, 1776, after he had read the Declaration of Independence to a great throng at Halifax, they bore him on their shoulders in triumph through the town. In the drafting of the state constitution in 1776, he became the father of religious liberty in North Carolina. He fearlessly dared the dungeon and the scaffold. When the British captured the Cape Fear region, Harnett was thrown into prison, and died in captivity.

In the War between the States, the women were the "biggest rebels." So was it in the Revolution. How Southern ladies could twit the notorious Tarleton, we have already seen; how they could fight like the Amazons of old, we see from the following story of Grace Greenlee McDowell. This heroic woman was the wife of Colonel Charles McDowell, an ardent patriot of the Revolution. She aided her husband zealously in his fight for liberty. When he was manufacturing powder afterwards used at King's Mountain, she made the needed charcoal in small quantities in her fireplace, and carried it to him at night secretly. When the time came, she could use the powder. Her house being plundered during her husband's absence, she called together a few neighbors, pursued the robbers,—Tories and British —captured them, and at the muzzle of the musket compelled them to restore her property.

(d) SOUTH CAROLINA

The first decisive victory of the Revolution was won at Sullivan's Island, South Carolina, by Colonel William Moultrie. Though most of his family were Tories, he from the first was an ardent patriot. He had won his first reputation in wars with the Cherokees. When the Revolutionary War began, he was made colonel of a regiment. On the 28th of June, 1776, he drove the fleets of Sir Henry Clinton and Admiral Peter Parker away from the city of Charleston.

A few years later, he was taken prisoner. While in captivity, he was offered a handsome sum of money, and a colonel's commission in a Jamaica regiment, to leave the American army. "Not the fee-simple of all Jamaica," he replied, "should induce me to part with my integrity." He was a typical gentleman of the South Carolina school.

In his honor, the name of the fort he defended was changed to Fort Moultrie.

His fame as a historian, also, is well established. His *Memoirs of the American Revolution* is one of the sourcebooks of American history.

No state has equalled South Carolina in the skill and daring of her partisan leaders. Virginia is proud of Mosby and his men, whom the Federal government threatened to hang on sight as brigands and assassins, in spite of the fact that Colonel John S. Mosby bore a regular commission from the Confederate government. Kentucky ought to glory in the fame of John H. Morgan, who, when captured, was confined in a felon's cell in the Ohio penitentiary, instead of being confined in a military prison. South Carolina can point to three famous partisans of the Revolution.

The greatest of these is Francis Marion. He served his apprenticeship in 1759 as a soldier in the Cherokee War. In 1761, he and a band of thirty performed a brilliant feat that aided materially in crushing the Cherokees. In the battle of Sullivan's Island, he rendered distinguished service as a major of a regiment. Gates, the great boaster, did not appreciate him. Accordingly, he raised a force known as "Marion's brigade." From this time, he practiced guerrilla warfare. With a force varying from twenty to seventy, armed with rude swords made from saws taken from the sawmills of his state, and using bullets made from pewter mugs and dishes, he would hide in the swamps and woods of the Pedee and Santee regions, and rush out and overpower much larger bodies of the enemy. His name was a terror to both Tories and British regulars. His enemies called him the "Swamp Fox."

He led Tarleton many a long and fruitless chase, and greatly annoyed that famous marauder. On one occasion, Tarleton, is said to have exclaimed to his men, "Come, boys, let's go back and find the 'Game Cock' (Sumter); as for this infernal 'Swamp Fox,' the devil himself could not catch him."

In the Southern campaign, Marion was intimately associated with "Light Horse Harry." The account of him given in that soldier's *Memoirs* of the war depicts him as a hero, a chevalier, and a gentleman.

An interesting story of General Marion will throw further light upon his character. An English officer sent to his headquarters on a special mission, was courteously invited to dinner. When the meal was brought in, it consisted of roasted sweet potatoes served on a shingle. "Surely, General, this is not all you have; is it?" said the Englishman. "Indeed, it is," answered Marion; "and it is uncommonly good on account of your visit." The Englishman then asked Marion what pay he got; to which he received the answer, "None." "Why do you fight for a government that gives you no pay and starves you?" he asked. "I am fighting for my ladylove," said the American. "Who is she?" "Liberty," replied Marion.

The officer, returning to his command, told his fellow-officers that it was useless to fight an army composed of such men as Francis Marion. Tradition goes on to say that this officer resigned his commission, went back to England, and said that he would no longer fight against a people with such motives and such leaders.

Thomas Sumter was called the "Game Cock" by Tarleton. In his fighting qualities and fearlessness, he resembles Hood, the Confederate. He was present at Braddock's defeat, and later served against the Cherokees. His great career, however, did not begin until after the fall of Charleston (1780). Shortly after this, he organized a band of partisan rangers, and entered upon a guerrilla warfare. At Hanging Rock, with Davie, the noted partisan of North Carolina, he routed a force of British and Tories. Sumter's men, however, did not like to fight in regular line and face artillery; they preferred irregular warfare and cutting communications, and revelled in surprises. In such things, he and his band were masters. Blackstock Hill is his greatest victory. There, November 20, 1780, he dealt a stunning blow to Tarleton, who retreated with heavy loss, and wrote Cornwallis of his brilliant victory. Sumter's irregular methods and his utter recklessness led to some unpleasantness with other patriot leaders.

Though his fame as a soldier was already secure, it has been freshened up by the "game cock" exploits of his namesake, Fort Sumter, in the War between the States. Cornwallis called him "the greatest plague in the country."

Along with Marion and Sumter, we group another noted partisan, Andrew Pickens. In 1761, he fought against the

Cherokees. In the Revolution he rose rapidly from the rank of captain to that of brigadier-general. He is one of the heroes of the Cowpens. For his nerve and daring in that battle he was voted a sword by Congress. He was allied by marriage to John C. Calhoun, the greatest of South Carolinians, and was the grandfather of Governor Francis W. Pickens, who in 1861 demanded that the Union forces should evacuate Fort Sumter.

Pickens, like Marion, was of Huguenot descent. Both belong to a stock that have ever known their rights and, knowing, dare maintain.

Dear to the South and to our whole country, should be the name of Emily Geiger, the noble daughter of South Carolina. Along with the brave Molly Pitcher, the heroine of Monmouth, she should be immortalized in the history of our country; for, when General Nathaniel Greene was resting his weary soldiers on the hills of the Santee and keeping them out of the sickly and malarial swamps of the lower country of South Carolina, and it was absolutely necessary that he should communicate at once with Sumter, who was many miles away, this noble girl of eighteen volunteered to pass through the British forces and the numerous Tories that swarmed the country and bear a message from Greene to Sumter. Both verbal and written messages were given her. Then she put spurs to her horse and galloped away on her patriotic errand—an errand which a man could not have thought of undertaking. On being stopped and searched by the enemy, she chewed and swallowed the written message, made her way to General Sumter's headquarters, and delivered the verbal message which produced such a movement of the patriot army as compelled Lord Rawdon, the British commander, to abandon his posts in the country and retreat to Charleston.

Another heroine of South Carolina is Rebecca Motte. Having married two patriot soldiers and being sister-in-law to a third distinguished soldier, Colonel Isaac Motte, one of the heroes of Fort Moultrie, she came well by her heroic character. After the British had seized her home, surrounded it with a parapet, and named it Fort Motte, Harry Lee and Marion laid siege to the fort, but were loth to destroy the property. Mrs. Motte soon quieted all their scruples, and showed the patriots how to dislodge the enemy. Bringing out her African bow and arrows especially adapted to the purpose, she soon set fire to the building, and compelled the British to come out and surrender. Then, with true Southern hospitality, she gave a banquet to the officers of both sides.

(e) GEORGIA

Georgia, in spite of her youth, of her small population of whites, and of the fact that many of her people were almost fresh from England, rendered no little aid in the Revolution. One of her finest soldiers was General Elijah Clarke. He fought the Indians and Tories on the frontiers; fought along with Sumter on the Catawba, with Shelby at Cedar Springs and at Musgrove's Mills; at Blackstock materially aided Sumter; and in June, 1781, aided by Pickens and Light-Horse Harry, drove the British out of Augusta.

General Lachlan McIntosh is the most prominent of a family of soldiers. His father had fought under Oglethorpe in Florida; seven of the family are said to have been prominent in the Revolution. Lachlan McIntosh was made brigadier-general in 1776, rendered valuable service against the Indians on the border of Pennsylvania and Virginia, took part in the attempt to drive the British out of Savannah, and was captured at the fall of Charleston. After his day, the family continued to produce fine soldiers. One of them distinguished himself in the Mexican War. In the War between the States, two brothers rose to prominence, one in the Federal, the other in the Confederate army.

General James Jackson was a distinguished soldier of Georgia. In March, 1776, he took an active part in driving the British away from Savannah; in 1778, took part in the defense of Savannah; fought with Colonel Elijah Clarke; was aide to General Sumter at Blackstocks; and fought under Pickens at Cowpens. He rendered valuable service at the siege of Augusta by Clarke, Pickens, and Henry Lee, and, after the expulsion of the British, was left in charge of the garrison. The Jackson family is eminent in Georgia, and has produced distinguished jurists, poets, and soldiers.

More famous than most generals is Sergeant William Jasper, a hero of Fort Moultrie. His name is embalmed in history and should be immortalized in literature. During the siege of Charleston in June, 1776, while the battle was at its fiercest, the flag was shot down and fell outside the ramparts. Sergeant Jasper sprang down, and, in spite of the galling fire from the British fleet, seized the flag, carried it back into the fort, put it on a new staff, and replaced it on the ramparts. This heroic soldier was afterwards killed in the siege of Savannah while acting as color-bearer (1779).

It does not detract from Jasper's fame to say that he has had many noble imitators. In the siege of Charleston in 1863-1864, during the War between the States, more than twenty cases like his occurred; but his, being the first, is greatest forever.

Among the heroines of Southern history is Nancy Hart, whom the Indians called the "War Woman." Various stories are told of her nerve and daring. On one occasion, a party of five armed Tories came to her house and ordered her to prepare them a meal. While she was carrying out the order, they stacked their arms within easy reach of the table. She shrewdly pulled the table into the middle of the room, so as to pass frequently between the men and their muskets. When the Tories asked for water, she sent her daughter to the well, with private instructions to blow the conch shell which summoned the men from the fields, and which soon brought her husband and neighbors to the house. Meanwhile, she had pulled a board from the house and slyly slipped two of the muskets through the hole. As she reached for the third, one of the soldiers saw her and gave the alarm. She raised a gun to her shoulder, threatening to shoot the first man that dared to come towards her. One took the risk, and fell dead; then a second; and the other three were captured, and, by Nancy's orders, hanged.

On another occasion, she went to the British camp disguised as a man, and gained valuable information, which she conveyed to Colonel Elijah Clarke, the famous soldier of Georgia.

Again, the Savannah river being high and all boats swept

away, she crossed from Georgia into Carolina on a raft improvised of logs.

The State of Georgia has honored Nancy Hart by giving her name to a county.

(*f*) HEROES OF THE FRONTIER

Among the famous sons of the South, we should never forget the heroes of the frontier. While the patriots in the old states fought a few vandals like Prevost and Tarleton, these brave frontiersmen contended with the relentless savage, who, when crazed with King George's whiskey, spared neither sex, age, nor condition.

Preëminent among frontiersmen stands Daniel Boone, the father of Kentucky. Though born in Pennsylvania, he is more intimately allied with Virginia, North Carolina, and Kentucky. In the same connection, we think of Isaac Shelby, a native of Maryland, but known to history as one of the founders of Kentucky. With several other Southern colonels, he won distinction at King's Mountain.

Of James Robertson, the "father of Tennessee," we have already spoken. With him we associate John Sevier, the first governor of Tennessee, and one of the heroes of King's Mountain. These two conquered the Cherokees at the Watauga in 1776, and thus helped to secure the ground won two years before by General Andrew Lewis and his men of West Augusta.

The fame of these men is assured: sectionalism has never attempted to belittle them. In the most recent volumes of Fiske and Roosevelt, their figures are thrown upon the canvas in proportions well-nigh colossal. Says the lamented Curry, one of Alabama's greatest sons: "These backwoodsmen were ardent patriots, and deserve to be classed with their fathers and brothers on the Atlantic coast." If Andrew Lewis "blazed" the way for Sevier and Robertson; if these in turn opened the way for George Rogers Clark, and if he added five great states to the republic, these five men, sons of the South, should assuredly be ranked among our national heroes.

John Fiske supports this claim most heartily.* He specifies "four cardinal events in the history of our western frontier during the Revolution." Three of these were the events named in the foregoing paragraph. So that Fiske clearly shows that the South deserves three-fourths of the credit for the fact that in 1783, when peace was declared with England, "the domain of the independent United States was bounded on the west by the Mississippi river."

(2) TROOPS AND BATTLES

The number of troops in the Revolutionary War can never be known accurately. The statements made in some books are totally unreliable. The chief basis of our knowledge is the official report of General Henry Knox, secretary of war in Washington's cabinet; but he says himself that the reports from the South were very incomplete; and we know now that many men were counted over again whenever their short terms ran out and they reënlisted. All statements as

---

*All this is ably brought out by Roosevelt in his *Winning of the West*, (I. pp. 240, 306) and by Fiske in his *American Revolution*.

to numbers in the Revolution made in this volume are therefore only provisional.

Pennsylvania, as said before, was rather lukewarm. If Knox's figures be taken as a guide, that state did little over half as well as Virginia; New Hampshire less than half as well as South Carolina; South Carolina did three times as well as Pennsylvania, and excelled even Massachusetts and Connecticut. Out of every 100 men capable of bearing arms, Massachusetts sent 76; Connecticut, 71; New Hampshire, 43; South Carolina, 88.

Neither section as a whole can claim to have done its full duty. According to Knox's report, the North sent about 44 per cent of its able-bodied men to the field; the South, 48 per cent. Of the rest, thousands fought bitterly for England. At King's Mountain, for instance, Americans slew each other; and it is likely that Ferguson, the Tory leader, was the only British soldier on the battlefield.

There were probably 500,000 men of military age in the country; Washington says he never commanded over 26,000 at one time. Contrast this with the 600,000 or more men furnished, between 1861 and 1865, by a white population of about six million. In 1861, parties and factions were wiped out in both North and South; in 1775, local jealousies, interstate feuds, differences in creed, and sectional feeling, wellnigh wrecked the cause of independence.

With good cause has it been claimed that providence, not man, freed America.

The South gallantly aided in defending her Northern sisters. At Long Island, "The highest honors," says Fiske, "were won by the brigade of Maryland men commanded by

Smallwood." At Trenton, Mercer, of Virginia, and Howard, of Maryland, with their "flying camps," led the column of attack; and, again at Princeton, Mercer led the advancing column. At Saratoga, as seen already, Morgan's Virginians turned the tide of battle, and this led to Burgoyne's surrender.

Besides taking an active part in the greatest victories won on Northern soil, Southern men were driving the invader from their own. The English were hurled back for two years by the victory of Fort Moultrie. King's Mountain, won by men of the South, is regarded by historians as one of the decisive battles of the Revolution. A little later, the Carolinians defeated Tarleton at Blackstock. A few months after that, Southern troops almost annihilated Tarleton at Cowpens, and thus deprived Cornwallis of his cavalry. At Yorktown, later in the year (1781), the matchless skill of Washington, the Virginian, closed the war of independence.

(3) MISCELLANEOUS

The Revolution was by no means a great popular uprising. Very few of the colonies were out and out in favor of fighting England. In 1771, for instance, when the battle of Alamance was fought, Richard Caswell, Francis Nash, and other great sons of North Carolina fought on the side of the royal governor Tryon against the "Regulators;" and that colony was not ready to rise as a whole till four years later (1775), when she heard of the battle of Lexington.

As late as July, 1776, a good many were very reluctant to separate from England. The Declaration of Independence had to be "lobbied" through the Continental Congress, and great persuasion had to be brought to bear upon some of the men now famous as "signers." Pennsylvania and New York were lukewarm in the cause of independence. "Pennsylvania," says one of her own historians, "fought in the Revolution like a man with one arm tied behind his back." Washington could not recruit his army in the Jerseys. Maryland was said to be full of loyalists. South Carolina did not rise to her feet until 1778, when Tarleton made his infamous raids into the Waxhaws. The mayor of New York was caught in a plot to seize General Washington, and either murder him or try him for treason. The British government counted upon the indifference of the Middle Colonies, and planned to detach them from the Confederacy, and thus cut it in half, and then kill the ends separately.

In those "times that tried men's souls," Massachusetts and Virginia stood shoulder to shoulder. Though the New Englanders and the Virginians mixed but little socially and, as said elsewhere, more or less despised each other, they united heartily in the cause of independence. A Massachusetts statesman selected and urged George Washington as commander-in-chief of the patriot army; and, while this was done largely from policy, it shows that great men could in those days rise above sectional prejudices, and give up personal preferences for the good of their country. Massachusetts passed by her own John Hancock, to honor the Virginian Washington.

In speaking of the Middle Colonies in the Revolution, we spoke without malice. Indeed, we spoke regretfully. Moreover, we are supported by eminent Northern authorities. We believe that those colonies were held back by circumstances that would have checked either Massachusetts or Virginia.

Nor do we claim that the South achieved American independence. We do say, however, that in what was done she played a conspicuous part, and that without her there would have been no independence. Of her part we are writing in this volume, the North's part being well told by her sons in thousands of volumes of history, of essay, and of poetry.

Bancroft, the Massachusetts historian, says, generously, that the men of South Carolina suffered more, dared more, and achieved more than the men of any other state. Charles Pinckney's opinion of the North Carolinians, we have already quoted. McCrady, the eminent South Carolina historian, says that South Carolina and Georgia overpaid their quota of expense, and that South Carolina in outlay vastly exceeded all other states save Massachusetts. General Joseph Reed, Washington's adjutant-general, said in 1776, "The gallantry of the Southern men has inspired the whole army." General Gates, in a letter which he wrote during the war to Washington, said that Burgoyne's army was most afraid of Morgan and his riflemen. Fiske's history of the Revolutionary period immortalizes many Southern soldiers.

The South bore the brunt of the suffering. Two of her principal cities stood long sieges, and one was burned by the enemy. Irregular warfare desolated her homes, and left

THE SOUTH IN OLDEN DAYS 77

her people without shelter. The vandals and hirelings of the British army plundered her people and desolated homes and firesides.

Probably one-third of the colonists sympathized with England. Thousands of the leading families of New York refugeed to Nova Scotia, Canada, and other places, to get away from the angry patriots. Many prominent families of the far Southern states took refuge in the Bahama Islands and the other English possessions. On the other hand, Massachusetts and Virginia were from the first practically unanimous against England.

Virginia had always been the most loyal of the old colonies. The tyrannical conduct of George III had, however, changed her sentiments. When Massachusetts was overawed and maltreated, Virginia nobly took her part. In all sections of Virginia it was boldly declared that "the cause of Boston is the cause of us all."

Most unnatural, therefore, was the long alienation between these two ancient commonwealths. Sad was it that two Massachusetts pens, Mrs. H. B. Stowe's and Mr. James Russell Lowell's, helped to increase this alienation. Better days, we trust, are coming. The kind words of Mr. Charles Francis Adams and of Hon. George F. Hoar, of that state, are doing no little to bring the two old sister commonwealths together and hasten the dawn of a better era. The small politicians, and the bomb-proof brigadiers of the editorial ink-pot, however, are still hurling their billingsgate in foul profusion, and postponing the day of reconciliation. If we could only hang these pygmies and let the voice of the giants sound from "Boston Plains" to the Rio Grande, these two sisters might soon meet at the old fireside and call a great family reunion.

IX

The South and the Constitution

(1) THE FEDERAL CONVENTION OF 1787

In your state histories, you read about your state constitutions. Most of the Southern states have recently adopted new constitutions, to meet the new conditions that have confronted our people within the last few decades. Of these state constitutions, we are not now speaking. Our present chapter has to do with the constitution of the United States, which was drafted in 1787, and which, with fifteen amendments, binds together the forty-seven sovereign states that form our Federal Union. Under this constitution without amendments, the Union was carried on from April 30, 1789, to December 15, 1791. The first ten amendments were declared in force on the date given. On January 8, 1798, the eleventh amendment was put into operation; on September 25, 1804, the twelfth; after the War between the States, three more amendments were added.

It is a most desirable thing for a people to have a written constitution. In this respect, our government is better than that of England; for her people have no such great written constitution, but a so-called "unwritten constitution" made up of charters, decisions of eminent jurists, compacts be-

THE SOUTH IN OLDEN DAYS 79

tween king and people—an undefined and indefinable something that is frequently called "the legal constitutional code of England."

The word constitution as used in this volume, then, generally refers to the constitution of the United States. In the drafting of this great paper, this compact between the states, the South was very prominent, two men that stamped themselves upon it very deeply being James Madison and George Washington, both, as you know, Virginians.

The convention that drafted this constitution met in Philadelphia, and sat from May to September, 1787. Its president was Washington. Among the members were Daniel Carroll, of Maryland; Edmund Randolph, George Mason, George Wythe, Madison, and Washington, of Virginia; Charles and Charles Cotesworth Pinckney and John Rutledge, of South Carolina; William R. Davie and Hugh Williamson, of North Carolina; William Few and Abraham Baldwin, of Georgia. Some of these were much more prominent in the convention than others; but history will show that Edmund Randolph and the Pinckneys were as influential as most of the Northern members, and that Alexander Hamilton alone among the delegates from the North was as influential as Madison and Washington.

A new and a strong constitution was the most "crying need" of our young nation. To this need, many good men shut their eyes deliberately. Some feared to create a Federal union stronger than the states. A few very wise men, like Madison, Hamilton, Charles Pinckney, and Washington saw that a strong general government had to be created.

The Declaration of Independence was adopted by the Continental Congress, which was a sort of standing committee of the thirteen states. By tacit consent, that is, by being generally endorsed all over the country, this declaration became binding upon the states. This same Continental Congress carried on war against England. It elected generals, sent ambassadors to Europe, and called upon the various states for money, troops, and supplies. It was utterly unable, however, to compel the states to carry out its orders; each state "did that which was right in its own eyes," and the result was confusion worse confounded.

In 1781, the states adopted the Articles of Confederation. This paper, also, proved too weak for purposes of government. It did not give the general government the power to carry out its orders, its mandates, and did not act upon individuals, like the constitution of 1787. These Articles were in force from 1781 to 1788, and these seven years are often called "the critical period of American history."

The young republic was drifting hither and thither. Her money was practically worthless; her soldiers and their families shivering and hungry; her credit gone; and European nations standing off, laughing at her calamity, and ready to devour her. A stronger government must be created. There must be power lodged somewhere stronger than that wielded by the old Continental Congress and by the Articles of Confederation.

No men saw this more clearly than Washington, Madison, and C. C. Pinckney, Southern representatives in the Federal convention. They wanted a strong Federal govern-

JAMES MADISON

ment, to act upon individuals and collect revenue, and to command the respect of foreign nations.

To the proposed constitution, many great men were violently opposed. Patrick Henry "smelt a rat," as he said, and refused to go as a delegate to the convention. He predicted that the new government to be created by the states would some day ride roughshod over the states; and we know how fully his prophecy has been verified, how it has been fulfilled to the very letter.

The constitution of 1787 was one of compromises, and, like most compromises, pleased no one entirely. It was, however, a wonderful paper, and puts the Americans of the 18th century among the greatest constitution-builders of the ages.

Various causes made it very difficult to frame a government for the thirteen sovereign states just separated from England. As already said, there were dislikes and jealousies between states and between sections. Very bitter was the jealousy of the small states against the large. Small states such as Rhode Island, Delaware, and Maryland were arrayed against large states such as Pennsylvania, Massachusetts, and Virginia. This sustains our statement made in previous paragraphs that in the early periods the lines drawn between parts of our country were not as sectional as in our era. This interstate jealousy came near preventing the convention from drafting a constitution. In the old confederation (1781-1788), the states had been on a perfect equality, the votes in Congress being by states. To give up this equality was a sore trial to the small states, as they feared that their representation in Congress would be utterly swamped by that of the larger states. This serious question was settled by giving all the states equal representation in the Federal senate. For this reason our Senators in Washington may be regarded almost as ambassadors from the states to the Union.

Other obstacles to a new government in 1787 were the negro questions continually presenting themselves for solution. A large number of people of the North and many statesmen of the South wished to abolish the slave-trade. This might have been done immediately but for the objection of a few states in each section. By a combination between these, the slave-trade was given a respite of twenty years, that is, till 1808.

Another perplexing negro question was whether the slaves should be counted in the population and help to fix representation in the lower House. This, like the two questions already discussed, came near preventing the adoption of a constitution. Here, again, compromise was resorted to. Under the leadership of James Madison, the South agreed not to demand full representation for her slaves, but to accept the three-fifths ratio, by which five slaves counted as three persons in the population. With these three compromises, the constitution was submitted to Congress and, afterwards, to the thirteen separate states, with the proviso that it should go into effect when any nine had adopted it and be binding upon the states so ratifying it.

In persuading the other states to accept these compromises, Connecticut and Virginia played a very prominent part.

(2) THE STATES CREATE THE UNION

The most casual reader must have seen that states were in the act of creating a Union. After the representatives of eleven states had drafted the paper now known as the constitution, it had no binding force whatever until ratified by conventions of at least nine states, and then only upon those ratifying it. Each state acted separately as a sovereignty through a convention. Three states reserved the right to withdraw whenever their interests were in danger. Two staid out of the Union for some time: North Carolina, till 1789; Rhode Island, till 1790. After the ninth state ratified the constitution, the other four might have staid outside as separate and independent republics; for, at that time, no such idea as that the states were created by the Union had ever been dreamed of in our philosophy.

Meantime, what became of the old Articles of Confederation? They were styled articles of "perpetual union," and yet, in seven years, they were coolly set aside as too weak for purposes of a strong Federal government, and a new paper substituted for them.

This was nothing short of secession. Nine states seceded and set up a new republic, and no voice was raised in protest. "Nothing secedes like secession" may be said of that movement, as well as of the secession of Panama from Columbia in November, 1903, the Roosevelt administration standing as godfather to the lusty infant nation as he yelled himself into the family of republics.

The word secede is not found in the constitution. To put it there would have been sheer folly; for doing so would have invited every discontented state to threaten secession. That the right of secession was held by all sections in 1788 is, however, now admitted by some of the most eminent Northern men, such as Henry Cabot Lodge and Charles Francis Adams. (In another chapter we shall show that secession was first threatened in New England.)

Bancroft calls James Madison "the chief author of the constitution." The "Virginia plan," outlined by Madison and presented by Edmund Randolph, was adopted in preference to plans outlined by Northern statesmen. Compromises on various questions had to be accepted. Problems were left for posterity to solve; some of them, unfortunately, to be settled on the field of battle. But might cannot make right, and gunpowder cannot determine moral questions. The South looks to posterity to prove that she has never violated the constitution.

James Madison is known in history as "the father of the the constitution." In this connection, we may quote the late John Fiske, of Massachusetts: "In the making of the government under which we live, these five names, Washington, Madison, Hamilton, Jefferson, and Marshall—stand before all others."

All but one of these five are Southern men. The name of Jefferson is a household word among men of all political parties. Both the great parties of our day use his name to conjure with, and claim him as their founder, their patron saint. Of Marshall we need only say that he is recognized both at home and abroad as the greatest expounder of the constitution. Both North and South have combined to glorify him; the former being swayed to some extent doubtless by the fact that he interpreted the constitution according to the view long popular north of the Potomac; the South being swayed by her admiration for his great abilities and by her confidence in his spotless character. While referring to this supreme chief-justice, we may pause to remark that, for nearly two-thirds of its existence, the Supreme Court of the United States has been presided over by Southern jurists, Taney and Marshall.

We have seen already that the idea of absolute religious freedom was born in Virginia. This idea was engrafted on the Federal constitution, the clause enacting that "no religious test shall ever be required as a qualification to any office or public trust under the authority of the United States," being moved by C. C. Pinckney, of South Carolina, and championed ably by James Madison. At this time and for several decades afterwards, England would not permit any one to hold office, or even to take a degree in her universities, unless he communed according to the rites of the established church. So that the statesmen and the legislators of the South blazed the way of religious freedom for the sages of Europe.

To the head of the new Federal government, all voices called George Washington. In his cabinet, sat Jefferson, Edmund Randolph, James McHenry, Charles Lee, and Joseph Habersham, Southern jurists and statesmen.

The foregoing paragraphs on the constitution are merely introductory. They are intended to show the part played by Southern statesmen in laying the foundations of our government. The conflicting views of the constitution, and the long, sad quarrel over its doubtful clauses, we reserve for later chapters.

X

The South's Part in Maintaining and Expanding the Union

(1) THE WAR OF 1812

Let us pass on to later eras. Let us study some statistics of the post-revolutionary and *ante-bellum* periods. In those periods, when sectional lines were less closely drawn than they were afterwards, the Southern states furnished nine out of thirteen presidents. Moreover, the only men elected to second terms were five presidents from the South: Washington, Jefferson, Madison, Monroe, and Jackson. Are those facts merely accidental?

To return to the great wars: Without Virginia and the Carolinas, the Revolution would have been a total failure. Let us consider the War of 1812. In this second struggle with England, sometimes called the Second War for Independence, the South again covered herself with glory. In bringing on that war, the lead was taken by Southern statesmen, because the warm blood of the young men of the South could no longer brook the insults of England, especially her stopping American ships on the high seas and dragging off sailors on the pretext that they were Englishmen. This war was very unpopular in New England, and was opposed by a few of the great leaders of the South, more especially the famous John Randolph, of Virginia. Clay, Calhoun, Crawford, Felix Grundy, Langdon Cheves, William

Lowndes, and other young leaders of the South determined to fight; and it is said that Mr. Madison thought of making Clay commander-in-chief of the army. The South furnished nearly all of the greatest soldiers, such as Isaac Shelby, Zachary Taylor, William Henry Harrison, Winfield Scott, and Andrew Jackson, and fully five-eighths of the private soldiers. Especially distinguished were Harrison and Jackson. Harrison, already famous as the hero of Tippecanoe, won the great victory of the river Thames, which, following the naval victory of Lake Erie by Commodore Perry, drove the British out of Michigan, and practically broke the power of the Indians in the Northwest. Jackson won the great battle of New Orleans (January 8, 1815), which showed the world that the fighting power of the Americans had not declined since the days of King's Mountain, Cowpens, and Yorktown.

Both Harrison and Andrew Jackson became national heroes. The former is known in history as "Tippecanoe;" the latter, as "Old Hickory." Both were elected to the presidency before the days of "dark horses," that is, in the times when both parties put their strongest men on the presidential ticket.

Even in a rapid sketch, we may pause to mention a few other men of Southern birth or Southern descent who distinguished themselves in this war. We again meet Isaac Shelby, of King's Mountain. Though sixty-three years of age, he fought under General Harrison, and distinguished himself in the battle of the Thames. In this same battle, Col. Richard M. Johnson, member of an illustrious family that had migrated from Virginia to Kentucky, led a cavalry charge that turned the tide of battle; and it is thought by many, and he himself thought, that he dealt the fatal blow to the great Indian chief Tecumseh, who was helping the British. In the Southwest, General Jackson was fighting the Creek Indians, who were allies of England; and in his army fought a gallant young soldier, afterwards idolized in Tennessee and in Texas, Sam Houston, the hero of San Jacinto and the father of Texas.

Another hero of this war is Major George Croghan (Crawn), nephew of George Rogers Clark. At Fort Stephenson, in 1813, Croghan, with one cannon and about 160 men, was besieged by the British general Proctor with 1,200 British and Indians. His gallant defense of the fort proved to be a turning-point in the war. Croghan received a gold medal from Congress, and was afterwards rapidly promoted. He afterwards served with great gallantry in the war with Mexico, being especially distinguished at the battle of Monterey.

The War of 1812 was, as already said, very unpopular in some sections of the country. The South and the West were eager for it, not because they had no interests at stake, as a well-known text-book says, but because they saw that the nations of the world would have no respect for us if we continued to bear the insults of England. The Middle and the New England States were as a rule bitterly opposed to fighting England. In Congress, the representatives of all these, except New Hampshire, Vermont, and Pennsylvania, voted against declaring war upon England. Says the same

Northern historian* just referred to: "Thirty-four members of the opposition joined in an address to their constituents in which they stated in substance that the United States was composed of eighteen independent sovereignties united by bonds of moral obligation only, and that, if we entered upon the contest with England, we did so as a divided people." A good many men volunteered from Massachusetts and Connecticut, but the governors of these states "refused to furnish their quota of militia." At that time (1812), the New England people evidently believed in states rights and in nullification.

From what we have said, it is clear that the people and the leaders of New England and of the Middle States were opposed to this war with England. In a later chapter, we shall have occasion to refer to the Hartford Convention (1814), in which such men as the Cabots, the Lowells, the Longfellows, and other leaders of New England, were protesting against the war, and taking steps towards seceding from the Union. All this is painful, but it is history. Our reason for telling these unpleasant facts is to show that other sections besides the South long believed in the right of secession, and that at a very critical period—in a life-and-death grapple with England—our country was threatened with disruption by some secessionists of other sections.

Greater and more patriotic than some of the leaders of New England at this crisis were her gallant seamen. How the young navy of our country met and worsted the navy of England, hitherto invincible; how the pride and arrogance of the English seamen were humbled; how the trade

---
*D. H. Montgomery.

of England was crippled, and marine insurance driven up to enormous figures; how such great sea-captains as Bainbridge, Porter, and Lawrence brought lustre to the name of the young republic—all this is a "twice-told tale," and need not be repeated in this volume.

Duing this war, the *Star Spangled Banner* was composed by Francis Scott Key, the most famous of a distinguished family of Maryland. This song and *America,* by Samuel F. Smith, of Massachusetts, are rivals for popularity. In the summer of 1903, the secretary of war announced officially that hereafter the *Star Spangled Banner* would be the national air for both army and navy.

During the period following the War of 1812, the only "doctrine" ever added by a president to the creed of the republic was proclaimed by President Monroe, of Virginia. In the famous paper referred to, President Monroe warned the nations of Europe that no more European colonies should be planted in America, and that the United States would not be indifferent to the interference of foreign nations in the affairs of any of the American peoples. This means "America for Americans." If accepted by the world as a part of the law of nations, it will make Monroe more famous than most of the kings and emperors of history, will make his name familiar to every schoolboy on five continents.

(2) THE MEXICAN WAR

In 1846, war again clouded the horizon. As in 1812, the brunt of it fell upon the Southern people, many Northern people, especially the New Englanders, regarding it as "a war of unholy aggression."

As in the case of most wars there were various causes, some remote, some nearer. Long-continued ill-feeling between the United States and Mexico had put the two countries into such a position towards each other that almost any disagreement might lead to armed conflict. This ill-feeling was due to American sympathy with Texas; the bitterness that made war likely to break out at any moment was due to the annexation of Texas to the United States (1845); the immediate cause, or the occasion, of the war was the question of boundary between Texas and Mexico.

Texas had rebelled against Mexico. The great victory of San Jacinto, gained in 1836 by General Sam Houston, led to the independence of Texas; but this independence had never been acknowledged by Mexico. She gave notice plainly to the United States that the annexation of Texas would be regarded by Mexico as an insult, and would lead to war between the two countries.

The abolitionists of the North were opposed to the annexation of Texas. They thought that it would increase the area of slavery, and probably add eight Southern senators. Massachusetts plainly said that she would not be bound by any such action, but would feel at liberty to secede from the Union. Twenty members of Congress, Adams of Massachusetts and Giddings of Ohio among them, published an address in which they said that the annexation of Texas would fully justify a dissolution of the Union.

In spite of such threats, however, the majority of the people of the United States voted in 1844 for "Polk and

Texas." Meantime, President Tyler had been very active in bringing on the annexation of Texas, and deserves a large part of the credit for the accession of that great territory. When Polk came into office, he found Texas in the Union, and saw a war with Mexico almost unavoidable.

As already said, a boundary dispute was the occasion of the war now threatening. Texas claimed that her western boundary was the Rio Grande; Mexico said that it was the Nueces river. Under ordinary circumstances, this question might have been settled by arbitration. It soon led, however, to armed conflict.

In the summer of 1845, Mexico sent an army to the Rio Grande. Thereupon, President Polk sent General Zachary Taylor with an army to protect American interests in the disputed territory, and also put an American fleet in the Gulf of Mexico. Soon the Mexicans crossed the Rio Grande and attacked the Americans. Thereupon Congress resolved that war existed between the two countries "by the act of Mexico." Again the abolitionists raised a great cry of "unholy aggression," Southern adventure, and slavery extension.

That the South wished to annex Texas, we cannot deny, and do not care to do so. That she hoped to see Texas added to the domain of slavery, we also admit with perfect candor. These two wishes, however, were both constitutional and honorable; whether they were expedient or not is another question, and depends upon the view one takes of the subject of African slavery. Slavery was an existing fact, recognized by the constitution, but its area had by this time been greatly limited by total abolition in many states and by prohibition in other states and territories. To extend slavery into Texas was the devout wish of the Southern people. The acquisition of Texas was the result of the election of Polk and Dallas, which was accomplished by the Democratic party, regardless of sections.

Here again, we see the South sticking to the constitution. Through thick and thin, through good report and evil report, this has been her record. Whether the constitution was out of date, a moral anachronism, an old skin which the new wine was obliged to burst—this is a question that only an inspired pen could answer with authority

General Zachary Taylor, as already said, had been sent to hold the disputed territory. Here began his distinguished career as a military hero. At Palo Alto (May 8, 1846), Resaca de la Palma (May 9), Monterey (September 19), Buena Vista (February 23-24, 1847), this great soldier brought lustre to his state and to his country.

Nor were all Northern soldiers idle in this great crisis. General Stephen W. Kearney set out in June, 1846, and marched from Fort Leavenworth, Kansas, to Santa Fe, New Mexico; thence, westward to California. There, in conjunction with Col. John C. Fremont and Commodores Robert F. Stockton and John D. Sloat, he snatched California from the Mexicans.

General Winfield Scott had been directed to assault Vera Cruz, the Gibraltar of Mexico. On March 29, 1847, he captured this old Spanish stronghold, and marched towards the city of Mexico, two hundred miles northwestward. At Cerro Gordo, Contreras, Churubusco, Molino del Rey, and

Chapultepec, the Americans won brilliant victories. On September 14, 1847, Scott entered the city of Mexico, and planted the American flag on the palace of the Montezumas.

General Scott says that his success in Mexico was largely due to the skill and the gallantry of Captain R. E. Lee, of the engineer corps. Other engineers worthy of praise are George B. McClellan, John B. Magruder, and G. P. T. Beauregard, men to be heard of in the '60's.

Two of the heroes of this war were Col. Jefferson Davis and Gen. John A. Quitman, both solders of Mississippi. To the former and his famous Mississippi Rifles, were largely due the victories of Monterey and Buena Vista; to Quitman, was largely due the victory of Chapultepec. South Carolina was represented by the gallant Major Pierce Butler and Daniel H. Hill, who was called by the young officers "the bravest man in the army," and whose native state presented him with a sword as a reward for his gallantry. The first body of troops to enter the city of Mexico was the Palmetto Regiment of South Carolina. Maj. Thomas J. Jackson, of Virginia, was promoted more frequently for gallantry than any other man in the army. Other Virginians worthy of special mention were Joseph E. Johnston and A. P. Hill, both famous in a later struggle.

Kentucky sent Theodore O'Hara, whose poem, *The Bivouac of the Dead,* has given immortality to the men that died in Mexico. North Carolina was represented by Capt. Braxton Bragg and his artillery, distinguished at Buena Vista. Maryland sent Samuel Ringgold, the artillery hero of Palo Alto, and Charles Augustus May, the cavalry hero of

Resaca de la Palma. Georgia sent General Henry R. Jackson, the poet-soldier, and Josiah Tatnall, whose little gunboat won great applause.

At least two-thirds of the troops were from the South; most of the others came from the states northwest of the Ohio. As said already, New England figured little; New Hampshire is said to have furnished one soldier. Had New England gone into the war, she would doubtless have furnished brave troops and famous generals. The statement of Mr. Theodore Roosevelt that her "military spirit" suffered a great "decline" about the middle of the nineteenth century, as the money-making spirit grew, will not make Mr. Roosevelt a popular author in New England.

The Mexican War was a great training-school for soldiers. Alongside of each other fought men that were afterwards to oppose each other in the war between the sections. Some of these we have already spoken of; others were Barnard E. Bee, Lewis A. Armistead, Ulysses S. Grant, H. W. Halleck, Joseph Hooker, A. E. Burnside, George G. Meade, Earl Van Dorn, and Irvin McDowell.

In this connection, we may recall an anecdote of General Winfield Scott. When the war of secession began, he was commander-in-chief of the United States army, and did all he could to capture the "rebel capital." He had to give up the idea of taking Richmond, however, and defend his own capital. Some one asked him why the man that had taken the city of Mexico could not take Richmond. His reply was, "Because the very men that took me into Mexico were keeping me out of Richmond."

Speaking of the Mexican War and its heroes, Mr. Percy Greg, the English historian, says: "As the Americans actually on the field were a little more than one to four, Buena Vista might well have been regarded as one of the most glorious names in the military history of the United States. It certainly entitles May, Davis, and Bragg to rank with the best and bravest soldiers of the Wars of Independence and of 1812—with Greene, Putnam, and Harrison." The heroism of Col. Jefferson Davis is frankly admitted by some Northern historians. Few writers of either section, however, have done justice to Ringgold, May, Bragg, Quitman, and Tatnall, but have given the lion's share of the glory to Scott and Taylor, while General Stephen W. Kearney is rarely given either his full name or his initials.

Of the "injustice" and "unholy character" of the Mexican War, we are being continually reminded. In a volume of addresses published by a recent cabinet officer, we are taught to censure our fathers of the South for going into this war of "unjust aggression."

(3) MISCELLANEOUS

If the South has had all of the censure, she has had also most of the glory of the War with Mexico. Two Southern presidents had brought about the annexation of Texas. Southern soldiers had done most of the fighting. To the South is due the credit for adding to the Union the great state of Texas, with New Mexico and California—in all more than 965,000 square miles of territory.

JAMES MONROE

What territory, indeed, has ever been added without Southern brains and Southern valor? Of George Rogers Clark's great conquest (1779), we have already spoken. The purchase of Louisiana by President Jefferson (1803) more than doubled the area of the Union. The same president's sending Lewis and Clark to explore the mouth of the Columbia river led later to the acquisition of Oregon territory. Monroe bought Florida, and thus greatly extended the national domain.

It is a well-known principle of human nature that men value what they pay for, that they appreciate what they suffer for. So the South loved the Union. It was her Union, the Union of her fathers, freed partly by the heroism of her fathers, enlarged and made glorious with the aid of Southern brawn and bravery. That she should love this Union was natural; that she did love it is undeniable. How can she ever leave it? How can she ever fire upon the flag which her Washington first flung to the breeze, and which her Key sang in immortal measures? The answer is written in later pages of this volume. In self-defense, she drew the sword against her Northern sisters. Against intolerable grievances, she protested long and fruitlessly, and in 1861 fought for the constitution, under the constitution, and against those who had violated the solemn guaranties of that constitution.

> " 'Tis better to have loved and lost
> Than never to have loved at all."

CHAPTER II

THE HOMES THAT MADE HEROES

I

"Truth Is Mighty and Will Prevail"

IN the foregoing chapter, we showed how our fathers resisted tyrants, wrote declarations, maintained them on the field of battle, and drafted constitutions. We now turn to more quiet scenes. In this chapter, we shall see them on the old plantation, and in the family circle. We shall watch them in their relations to the slaves. We shall refute the slurs heaped upon them up to the present moment by some ill-informed and by some malicious people. We shall learn why so many of our men became superb cavalrymen both in the Revolution and in the War between the States. We shall see the father in the family circle, with his sons around him, giving them ideals of honor that made Southern chivalry a phrase of glory among the nations.

Such is the theme of this chapter. Phases of social life not bearing upon these points, we shall leave to the magazine writer and the novelist.

This old Southern civilization has never been understood, but has been misrepresented, maligned, and travestied. The stage has caricatured it. Poets have prostituted their gifts to vilify it. The muse of history has been degraded from her high office and made the mouthpiece of the traducer and the slanderer. Fiction has lent her artful and seductive aid, and books, unfair and disingenuous if not purposely malicious, have made the Southern planter's name a byword and a hissing among the nations; while children in schools where the Bible was lying upon the table as the standard of life and of morals have been taught, by precept and by pictures, that a planter was a man whose daily business was to maltreat and lash the negro.*

Those misrepresentations have been sown broadcast, and borne upon the winds of heaven. The books that contain them are still found by thousands in private and public libraries wherever steam can carry them, and have been read as gospel truth by men, women, and children among all civilized nations. Oratory could not catch them. Statesmanship could not refute them. They went into the home of the mechanic, the merchant, the lawyer, the scholar, in the Northern and Western states, and in Europe, and taught them to hate and despise the Southern people; and their specious statements cut the South off from the sympathy of all mankind.

II

The South's History Written By Her Enemies

The South used to produce statesmen rather than writers. Nothing, for instance, is more remarkable than the vast array of legal talent shown by all the older generations of

---

*This refers to a text-book long used in certain schools; it defines a planter and illustrates by a picture of a man lashing a slave.

Virginia. The bar of Richmond was formerly made up almost exclusively of men that would have graced the Supreme Court of the United States or adorned the king's High Court of Justice.

Nearly every boy of promise wished to be a lawyer. Only thus could he hope for political honors; and political preferment was the goal of nearly every able man's ambition. If success came at the bar, it led him into prominence as a politician. Politics was both the glory and the bane of our civilization.

Few men had time for writing books. While Southern orators and jurists were thrilling listening senates, their enemies were writing books to prejudice the world against Southern institutions.

In this matter the enemies of the South got fifty years' start of her. They got the ear of the North and of all Europe, and did her an incalculable injury. The most that she can do now is to write the true story of her beautiful old civilization in essay, in fiction, in history, and in poetry, so that her own children and all others that care to do so can read it and tell it to those that are willing to listen.

Though most of her ablest men went into politics, the South had some very gifted writers. Her facilities for publication, however, have always been limited, and the works of her writers have had comparatively little circulation. Moreover, the ear of the North was poisoned, and Southern books defending the South were but little heeded. Such men as Thomas R. Dew, N. Beverley Tucker, and Abel P. Upshur, of Virginia; William Gilmore Simms and Samuel H. Dickson, of South Carolina, and Bishop Stephen Elliott, of Georgia, wrote ably in defense of Southern institutions; but their words fell upon unheeding ears, and their ink was wasted. *De Bow's Review* and the *Southern Literary Messenger* fought a brave fight, but could not stem the tide that had set in against the South. While *Uncle Tom's Cabin* sold by the million and was translated into several foreign languages, *Aunt Phillis's Cabin,* an able reply to it by Mrs. Mary H. Eastman, of Virginia, is known to none but antiquaries.

In this connection, let us quote the solemn warning of the late Dr. J. L. M. Curry, an eloquent defender of his people: "History, poetry, art, public opinion have been most unjust to the South. By perverse reiterations its annals, its acts, its inner feelings, its purposes have been grossly misrepresented. History as written, if accepted in future years, will consign the South to infamy." How true this is one can see every time he turns over the leaves of most of the encyclopedias and other reference books in our libraries; and the poetry of America is so filled with hostility to the South that we can hardly read it without throwing down the book in anger.

For instance, the *Encyclopedia Britannica* says: "Since the revolutionary days, the few thinkers of America born south of Mason and Dixon's line are outnumbered by those belonging to the single state of Massachusetts; nor is it too much to say that, mainly by their connection with the North, the Carolinas have been saved from sinking to the level of

Mexico and the Antilles." This slur could easily be refuted, but the scope of this volume does not permit our doing it. The Southern teacher and the Southern student, however, should be forewarned as to all such books. In the ponderous volumes of the work named above, we find all kinds of obscure foreigners and obscure Americans of other sections glorified; but it almost, if not entirely, ignores John Sevier and Isaac Shelby, heroes of the frontier; Cornelius Harnett, Richard Caswell, James Iredell, and Nathaniel Macon, heroes, statesmen and jurists, of North Carolina; Peyton Randolph, Edmund Randolph, George Wythe, William C. Rives, the Tuckers, and Light Horse Harry Lee, eminent men of Virginia; William R. King and William L. Yancey, of Alabama; William Jasper and Richard Henry Wilde, of Georgia; William Wirt and William Pinckney, of Maryland; King's Mountain, Guilford Courthouse, and Yorktown are buried in oblivion; and a reader has to scour the usual English editions to find out anything about General Daniel H. Morgan, one of the heroes of the Revolution, and J. E. B. Stuart and N. B. Forrest, two of the greatest cavalry generals of the English race.

An air of contempt for the South pervades, we think, the whole of this encyclopedia. After implying, in the passage quoted, that after the Revolution, the South sank into insignificance, it goes on in other places to underrate the most eminent men of that section. Take for instance, the statesmen of the period under discussion. The three men that stood preëminent in American public life were Clay, Calhoun, and Webster. This encyclopedia gives a tolerably

THE HOMES THAT MADE HEROES

complete outline of the career of Daniel Webster. It brings him out clearly as a statesman and an orator of commanding ability. Not so with Henry Clay and John C. Calhoun. No one would imagine, from reading the meagre sketches of these men, that they too commanded the applause of listening senates, solved the most complicated problems of international law, and became the idols of millions of their fellow-countrymen.

To see such men as Clay and Calhoun almost ignored in a great encyclopedia should bring every American to his feet. Who in the old *ante-bellum* days was not proud of these great senators? Clay, Calhoun and Webster! their names were always grouped together, and were household words in America. When Clay was to speak, the streets and the stores of Washington were deserted, and the whole city flocked to the capitol to hear that rich, sonorous voice reverberate through the senate chamber. Of Calhoun, the profound logican, the learned statesman, every schoolboy in our country is proud. These, with the illustrious Webster, made the American senate the delight and the wonder of two continents. Well may the South call for new encyclopedias to do justice to such sons!

Others besides the Southern people have suffered from having their history written by their enemies. No man has ever been more caricatured in history than Oliver Cromwell; no soldiers more ridiculed and burlesqued than his praying and fighting warriors. The facts are easily explained: the history of their era was written by their enemies, and it is only in our day that English historians are doing the Protector and his soldiers justice. In that respect, the heroes of the South have fared better than the Englishmen in question; for some eminent writers of the North now freely admit that the South produced far greater leaders than the North in the war of secession, and many Northern people regard Robert E. Lee as the greatest American since Washington.

III

Tired of Hearing Him Called "The Just"

A special object of hate and of derision was the so-called "effete aristocracy," played-out aristocrats, of Virginia. On these, the stage, the novelist, the poet, and the historian poured the vials of wrath and indignation. What had Virginia done? Why all this venom against the most ancient of the commonwealths, the mother of states and of statesmen? We have answered the question in asking it: She was the oldest of the commonwealths; she had produced too many statesmen and presidents, too many great soldiers in the Revolution and in later wars with England and with Mexico. It was the old story of Aristides reenacted on a new continent. The noblest of the Greeks was, you remember, stopped one day in the market-place by a man who asked him to write the name of Aristides upon his shell. "Why, my good fellow," said Aristides, "what has Aristides done that you wish to ostracize him?" "Oh, nothing, said the boor; "but I am tired of hearing him called 'The Just.'"

He who runs may read.

This "effete aristocracy" soon proved that it was not effete. At Manassas in 1861, it furnished a Johnston to lead with the noble creole of Louisiana, and a Stuart to ride like a Rupert carrying terror and dismay among the invaders of his dear Virginia. A little later, it produced a Lee, who, in seven days, made the deeds of the Confederate soldier read like a chapter from Caesar, or like an extract from the campaigns of Napoleon.

On the stage, the Virginian had been held up to ridicule and scorn. In fiction, he and his wife and daughter had been represented as vulgarians, speaking an English that would stamp them in any drawing-room of the North or of Europe as ignoramuses and provincials. Nothing could be less true. No greater misrepresentation was ever uttered. A good many old-fashioned Virginians, we admit, used a number of provincialisms that provoked a smile in other sections of the country and even from their own children and grandchildren; but, on the other hand, nowhere in the world has better and purer English been spoken than among the cultured classes of Virginia. So said the late Prof. George F. Holmes of the University of Virginia, an Englishman of finished culture, and Thackeray and Matthew Arnold, whose opinions will be accepted without question.

IV

Culture and Refinement

In pronunciation, we will admit, the Northern people are more exact, and talk more "by the book;" but in enunciation and intonation the South is far superior. Nothing is more musical than the voice of a Southern woman of culture and refinement.

The old Southern gentleman, in spite of an occasional provincialism, used racy, vigorous, idiomatic English. If he sometimes drawled, and often ignored his 'r's, he did not drop 'h's out of his 'which', 'white,' and other words in 'wh,' nor give a nasal intonation to nearly every sentence.

Culture and intelligence pervaded the old Southern society. Grammarians and philologists were not numerous; but well-informed, well-read men were plentiful. Home authors were not always encouraged; but the standard authors of England were read in thousands of families. Latin quotations fell from their lips almost unconsciously. In colonial days, "as Mr. Pope says, sir," was a familiar phrase; and, in recent decades, "Tennyson has well put it" clinched many an argument. The old tombstones of Virginia would prove that Pope was a household poet.

Private libraries were very numerous. Nearly every family of position had several hundred volumes, and they were not kept for mere appearance. They were well used by the purchaser, and went on a long visitation around the neighborhood. The whole society of the old states of the South was characterized by intelligence and culture. Questions of the day, questions of tariff, of revenue, of slave legislation, discussions of prominent candidates for office, the latest editorials of the leading Whig and Democratic papers—all came up at the table and in the general sitting-room. The father, usually a planter, would discuss all public questions with his sons, not interfering in the least with their opinions. While they were away at college, he would correspond freely with them, discussing politics and politicians, parties and platforms. The sons wrote with the greatest freedom. The father was not a dictator in matters of opinion. When the war between the North and the South was brewing, Col. R. E. Lee did not attempt to dictate the action of his sons.

The average of intelligence among Southern men was high. The great mass of citizens had well-formed opinions on public questions, and could express them forcibly. A churchyard on Sunday before and after "service" or "preaching," or a court green on "court day," heard animated discussions of many burning questions. The Southern man is a born politician. He can still discuss questions of the day, and his horse sense is often more useful to the state than the greater book learning of some other Americans.

Nor were schools and colleges neglected. A thoughtful writer* says that in 1850 the South sent eight boys to school or college where the North sent five. In the "olden days," the South, while employing numberless tutors for her sons, sent a great many young men to Northern colleges, such as Princeton, Yale, and Harvard. A few went to William and Mary. After the opening of the University of Virginia, the poor boys of Virginia flocked there. Later, it became more of a rich man's school, and its master's degree became the highest academic honor on this continent. Moreover, the "honor system," born at William and Mary, early

---

*Rev. J. M. Hawley.

took root at the University of Virginia. The ideal of absolute fairness and integrity fostered in Southern colleges was the Southern honor system in miniature, and has survived to a large degree to the present moment. It has both the virtues and the defects of the old Southern honor system. While not tolerating cheating, it too often permits idleness and shiftlessness. While demanding that students be first of all gentlemen, it too often winks at so-called "gentlemanly vices." We must admit, furthermore, that the college honor system is still very defective, and encourages things which, if done by a young man after leaving college, might soon land him in the penitentiary. The foundation, however, is solid, and should be used by us as the basis of a noble manhood. In spite of its defects, it is, we believe, far superior to the code of college honor prevailing in some other sections of our country.

V

Manliness and Self-Reliance

The whole trend of education was to develop manly self-reliance and independence. The honor system, as established in Virginia colleges and prevailing all through the South, was in thorough harmony with the training of the Southern home. While carousing and playing cards for money were sometimes regarded as rather gentlemanly accomplishments, to tell a lie, to cheat on an examination, to cheat at a game of cards—these damned a young man beyond all redemption. At home, he had been taught to despise a liar; and a man who got anything under false pretenses was regarded as a liar, and despised accordingly. The Southern youth, like the Persian, were taught "to ride, and to tell the truth."

The same honor system kept politics from being, as it is now called, "a dirty business." Bribery was practically unheard of. A gentleman could run for office without being asked or expected to use any money except the cost of printing circulars or "dodgers," paying his traveling expenses, and publishing notices in the local papers. Says the late Dr. J. L. M. Curry, in this connection: "Bribery and corruption in elections, when it occurred, made the place and persons a byword and a scorn."

Society was pure and elevating in its tone. Truth, courage, and honor were required of the men, and were their usual characteristics. Of the women, absolute purity was demanded, and no purer women ever became the mothers of heroes. Certain weaknesses and so-called gentlemanly vices might be tolerated in the men—especially drinking, playing cards, and dicing—but the women were like Cæsar's wife, above reproach. Nor was this confined to the higher classes.

On the point-of-honor, the Southern gentleman was scrupulously strict. So were the generations before him. The old Southern Cavalier has been ridiculed for his testy adherence to the point-of-honor, and much abuse has been lavished upon him. No doubt he had his faults; but he transmitted to his sons a sacred regard for truth, a chivalrous regard for women, fidelity to his friends, and a willingness to die for any righteous and noble cause that enlisted his sympathy and won his devotion. From such men, great civilizations may spring to enrich humanity.

A gentleman's word could not be questioned. The mere suggestion of "lie" or of "prevarication" would not be tolerated. Suit for damages was not brought inside of a court room, but in a field near by, with swords, or with "pistols and coffee." Even this so-called field-of-honor, however, was but an exaggeration of a great idea—the idea that honor is the greatest thing of all, and that life without honor is not worth living.

No Spartan mother ever trained soldiers more superbly than the Southern home. In the Revolutionary War, Southern troops rarely deserted their colors. In the War with Mexico, no Southern regiment disgraced itself. In the War between the States, the Spartan idea kept thousands of Southern men at the front long after they had lost all hope of independence. A gentleman could not afford to desert. Some men with nothing to lose did desert, and are pointed at to-day with the finger of scorn.

This high sense of honor was instilled into the boy from his very cradle. Along with this, he was taught to be self-reliant, manly. He was taught to think as a man, to act as a man, to be a man. When the great controversy between North and South waxed hot, every young man in the South had his opinion, and expressed it freely. When war seemed inevitable, each one asked himself the question, "What am I going to do about it?" and he answered it with his musket. He fought, not as a part of a great engine of destruction, but as an individual, as a citizen whose every blow helped to free his people from the invader. This individualism made him a superb fighter, though it sometimes interfered with his efficiency as a soldier. So was it with his sires of the Revolution.

VI

"Ole Marster"

No civilization has ever been more misunderstood than that of the *ante-bellum* South. Even some of our own people have unintentionally misrepresented it; while our enemies have caricatured and maligned it. The object of this chapter is to steer between these two extremes and tell the truth.

Some Southern writers have treated the life of the old Southern planter as a beautiful dream, or a realm of elysium; others, as an ideal of social and domestic bliss. Neither of these views is the correct one.

Enemies in America and in Europe have painted the *antebellum* South as a land of oriental ease and luxury, where the planter led a life of effeminacy and indolence, such as we read of in stories of the Persian kings and nobles, the planter reclining lazily on richly-embroidered divans and attended by retinues of trembling slaves, who fanned the haughty despot as he lay on his downy couch, and expected him at any moment to order them to execution. This is as true as the tales of the Arabian Nights or as the stories of Baron Munchausen.

The planter's life was neither a beautiful dream nor an ideal of social and domestic bliss. It had its beautiful, its charming features; and its social and domestic joys were many. It had some charms which can never be adequately described and which can never be seen again forever. It had also its shadows, its burdens, its responsibilities; and these shadows were so dark, and the burdens and responsibilities so heavy, as to preclude the idea of its being an "ideal of social and domestic bliss." Moreover, there were too many stern realities connected with it to permit us to regard it as a dream of any character. Furthermore, the responsibility of owning and of caring for so many human beings weighed heavily upon the planter and his family, so that emancipation was a glad relief to many.

A planter, in short, was a very real and a very practical man of business, a man of affairs, wide-awake, intelligently busy. To get food and clothing for his family and his servants, he must exercise the same habits of industry, watchfulness, and thrift that are required of business men in other callings. If he did not get up at daybreak, he had employees who were paid to do so for him; and he was out on his plantation earlier than most of the business and professional men of our money-making cities.

He kept his eye on the grain market, the tobacco market, and the cotton market. He studied his soil, knew the producing power of every field, exchanged ideas with his neighbors, and developed a wonderful sagacity. He led an earnest and "strenuous" life, but kept himself well and hearty by joining in the sports and diversions of his family. In whist, chess and backgammon, he was an expert, could lead a pretty girl handsomely in the Virginia reel, and was so full of "wise saws and modern instances" that young people often preferred to listen to his conversation rather than steal out on the porch and talk slang and nonsense to one another.

The great rendezvous were the stores and the churches. A country store was a sort of academy. There the planters met in groups—accidentally on purpose, as it were—and discussed the latest news, the questions of the day, the tariff, the slavery agitation, the last debate in Congress, and with great intelligence and discrimination exchanged opinions, and assessed the abilities of politicians and of statesmen. At church, before and after service or "preaching," the same scene was enacted.

A plantation was a veritable beehive. In many cases, the only drones were some negro slaves who would not work and who had such a bad reputation that no one would buy them, or some who were too old to work and were cared for by the master.

Idle planters there of course were. A good many wealthy men led very easy lives, and left most of the work to overseers and managers. But the statements made in the foregoing paragraphs of this chapter apply to untold thousands of men that had to work for a competent support for themselves, their families, and their dependents.

"Ole Marster's" sons inherited his business capacity. Being constantly thrown with inferiors, they learned the habit of command, of leadership. These facts help to ac-

8

count for the preëminence of the South in statesmanship and on the field of battle. On the other hand, the man that is thrown with inferiors continually is apt to become self-opinionated and dictatorial, even proud and arrogant. So was it quite frequently with the colonial Cavalier and his descendants, and with others of less noble lineage. Pride and haughtiness led to quarrelling and duelling. Duelling brought censure and even contempt. The whole generation of "first families" were ridiculed and hated in some quarters, and so the "root of bitterness" troubled the nation.

VII

"Ole Mistis"

The busiest body on the whole plantation was the "Missis," or "Ole Missis," or "Ole Mistis," as the servants called her. Busy? Yes, busy to the very elbows. Busy does not express it. No, busy is a trifling, impecunious word when applied to "Ole Missis." Busier than "Ole Marster;" for, if his "work was from sun to sun, her work was never done." Busier than "Mammy;" for, after the children were all asleep, she could go to bed and sleep all night, unless one of the children had the croup or a spasm. Busier than "Uncle Joe," "Uncle Henry" and the rest of the trusted field-hands; for they sat by the fire dozing and smoking and praying and humming hymn-tunes, while "Ole Missis" was busy with a thousand and one things that had to be attended to before the house and the "quarters" and the cows and the pigs and the chickens could settle themselves down for a good night's rest.

"Ole Marster" might know something; but "Ole Mistis" knew everything in heaven above and in the earth beneath and in the waters under the earth. From her opinion there was no shadow of dissent. Her decision on any point was absolutely final, more infallible than the pope's, more binding than that of any of the great councils of christendom. In the dressing, basting, and roasting of a turkey, her opinion was law. On mince-meat and pastry, she had a patent, left to her by her mother and inherited by her from bygone generations. As to how many eggs a pullet or an old hen ought to lay at such a season, her opinion was quoted all over the plantation with as much awe as a text of Scripture.

She was the *genius loci,* the goddess, or rather the queen of this little kingdom. In the domestic department, she was supreme, her husband being only Prince Consort, with no voice in the government. Her executive ability was equal to her husband's. They were like two monarchs living in the same palace, but ruling different kingdoms. He might call upon her to share the burdens of his administration, and even leave many matters to her decision; but he would not dream of interfering with her right of eminent domain in the culinary and domestic department. Thus she became a veritable statesman. She had the masculine abilities of an Elizabeth combined with the feminine graces of a Victoria.

From both parents, therefore, the children inherited executive ability, a talent for administration. The girls, too, were trained by the mother to assist in the affairs of state. The sons acquired habits of command, caught their father's methods, and learned to wield authority. Thus the daughters were fitted to become the queens of some younger planters, and the sons were equipped for writing constitutions, guiding cabinets and congresses, and leading armies on the field of battle.

VIII

The Planter Civilization

This activity on the lazy old plantation may be news to some readers. Let us supplement our statements with facts given by the late Henry W. Grady: "In material as in political affairs, the old South was masterful. The first important railroad operated in America traversed Carolina. The first steamer that crossed the ocean cleared from Savannah. The first college established for girls was opened in Georgia. No naturalist has surpassed Audubon: no geographer equalled Maury; and Sims and McDonald led the world of surgery in their respective lines. It was Crawford Long, of Georgia, who gave to the world the priceless blessing of anaesthesia. . . . . Though it is held that slavery enriched the few at the general expense, Georgia and Carolina were the richest states, *per capita*, in the Union in 1860, saving Rhode Island."

These facts are stubborn, and refute the charge of indolence and effeminacy. If mathematical facts will weigh more with some readers, however, let us give them a few statistics. The census of 1850 shows that in that year there were as many Southern whites as Northern engaged in laborious occupations. Between 1850 and 1860, the South, with only one-fourth of the white population, built 2,850 miles more of railroad than the New England and Middle States, her rate of increase in the ten years being 400 per cent; theirs, 100 per cent. In the same period of ten years, she made 24 per cent increase in manufacturing flour and meal; about 35 per cent increase in manufacturing lumber; in steam engines and machinery, gained over 200 per cent, while the rest of the country gained 40 per cent; in cotton manufacturing, gained $1,000,000 in the ten years.

Is this indolence and thriftlessness?

Again: the South, in 1850, had 30 per cent of the banking capital of the country; 44 per cent of the assessed property of the United States; 45 per cent of the live stock; she grew over half the total corn crop; had 56 per cent of the hogs and sheep. Besides producing all the cotton, sugar, rice, and molasses, she raised more than half of all the agricultural products. She slaughtered 33 per cent of all the animals killed. She did 67 per cent of the home manufacturing, owned one-third of the farm values, and increased their assessed value more than $1,300,000 in the decade between 1850 and 1860. The South was richer *per capita,* including slaves, who owned no property, than New England and the Middle States.*

So much for the mathematical and statistical argument. We, however, prefer the physiological and ethical argument, the "like-begets-like" theory of the subject. After water

---

*For most of these statistics, we are indebted to the valuable article of Gen. Stephen D. Lee, in the "Confederate Military History," Vol. XII.

rises above its level, after the pygmies of Lilliput produce the giants of Brobdingnag, and after men learn to gather grapes from thorns and figs from thistles, we may begin to believe that the heroes and the constitution-builders of the South are sprung from "butterflies of aristocracy."

"Look unto the rock whence ye are hewn," was said to them of old, ages ago. For us to-day, it is none the less wholesome counsel. We of the South are sprung from a race which providence seems to have chosen as the great torchbearers of civilization in the modern centuries. The great Anglo-Saxon race which settled the commonwealths of the South has, in a most marked degree, the capacity for civilization, and, since it stepped upon the arena of history, has never failed to produce leaders to meet the great crises of the ages. Egbert, Edgar, and Alfred the Great, in the Anglo-Saxon era; Henry the Second, the first and third Edwards in the Middle Ages; Henry the Seventh, Elizabeth, Washington, and Lee in the modern era—such men this race produces as they are needed. Put the Anglo-Saxon on an island in the sea, and he will soon write a constitution and build a commonwealth.

From this sturdy, potential stock, sprang the founders of Virginia, of Georgia, and of the Carolinas. Engraft upon this a twig of the Scotch-Irish, German, and Huguenot stock —men who, like the Anglo-Saxon, know how to suffer and be strong—and you have a race with an inborn love of freedom and a hatred of tyranny, a race that will plant commonwealths to stand forever.

The man of this race has the leaven that leaveneth the whole lump. He bears within him the fermenting power that buoys him up with a mighty frenzy, with an insatiable desire to go and tell all men the great message committed to his keeping. He will strike into the pathless desert, drive the panther from his covert, and expel the native denizens of the forest. A born ruler and organizer, nothing can stay his progress. Difficulties but whet his courage; obstacles but speed his march. Of the fathers of the South, all this is eminently true. Struggles with the Indian on the frontier, grim contests with jealous neighbors, fierce grapplings with the powers of nature yielding reluctantly to axe and hammer —all but tried his metal and trained his muscle.

IX

The Cavalier and the Puritan

In the settlement of the old Southern commonwealths, the Cavalier element was prominent. That all the people of the South are sprung from the gentle classes of England is claimed by no sane person; but we may say that many old families of the Southern states are of Cavalier ancestry.

And never have men been more caricatured and misrepresented than these Cavalier forefathers. Even some of our Southern writers have dubbed them "butterflies of aristocracy," and have thus played into the hands of our traducers. Many histories represent the "Pilgrim Fathers" of New England as a band of self-sacrificing missionaries leaving comfortable homes in England to christianize the savages of the American wilderness, and treat the early settlers of Virginia as idle adventurers coming to a new world to see the sights, and recoup their shattered fortunes by shipping turkeys and bogus gold dust to expectant multitudes in England. Both statements are untrue and preposterous.

The original settlers of Plymouth went from England to Holland, and came from Holland to America. In leaving England, they were refugeeing from royal tyranny and priestly despotism. After living in Holland a while, they found that their children were becoming weaned away from the customs and the language of the mother-country, and becoming tainted by the vices of the continent, and they realized that they themselves, the older generation, were at a great disadvantage in trying at their age to learn a new language, and to establish themselves in a new country where all avenues to prosperity were already crowded. Naturally, then, they looked towards the new colonies of England. In the virgin forests of America, they might breathe the air of freedom, worship as they pleased, and ship their surplus produce to the mother-country.* When opportunity offered, they would try to convert the Indians to Christianity.

These Puritans of New England were a brave, noble, indomitable people. During the era of Stuart tyranny, their numbers were greatly increased by immigration; they, too, hated tyranny and loved freedom.

After the overthrow of Charles I and his party, many Cavaliers flocked to Virginia. Between 1650 and 1670, the

---
*Lectures of the late Prof. Herbert B. Adams.

population of Virginia increased from 15,000 to 40,000. From some of these Cavaliers afterwards sprang George Washington, George Mason, the Lees, the Randolphs, Edmund Pendleton, James Madison, James Monroe, and other great patriots of America. These "butterflies of aristocracy" produced a race of giants.

Never has man been more travestied than the Cavalier. Because he wore a satin doublet, a slashed waistcoat, ruffles, and powdered his hair, he has been represented as a trifler and an adventurer, though under his slashed waistcoat there beat a loyal and noble heart, true to king and country; and though in the service of both—according to his views of duty—he fought brilliantly under Rupert, Bacon, Washington, and Lee. As a religionist, the Cavalier was, we admit, not as zealous as the Puritan. He loved his church, and would fight for it bravely and bitterly. In the details of Christian living, the sincere Puritan was no doubt superior; but the Puritan system, by adopting religion as a badge of office and as an avenue to social importance, put a premium upon hypocrisy, so that the class of men always despised in the South often rose to prominence in other sections. This sad fact, the genius of Hawthorne has heralded to unborn generations.

Both Puritan and Cavalier have much to be proud of. Both have a noble history. Both migrated to America, to escape tyranny and to breathe the air of freedom. Unfortunately, however, they brought their animosities with them, and on this new soil nursed the old grudge to keep it warm.

Neither by himself can make an ideal nation; the two

united can build an eternal commonwealth. In the blending of these two noble strains of blood lies the secret of our future greatness. The Puritan has the solidity, the stolidity, the seriousness, yes, even the moroseness of the Anglo-Saxon; the Cavalier has the buoyancy, the hopefulness, the vivacity of the Norman. Both have an inborn love of freedom, a sense of fair-play, and a hatred of tyranny. The two together could produce a people like that which gave jury trial to the world, and conquered the French nobility at Crecy, Poitiers, and Agincourt.

In the olden days, the sections as a whole did not know each other, though our statesmen, as already seen, met, deliberated together, and honored one another. It is time the past were dead and buried; but, before that can come to pass, there must be apology and reparation for insults and injuries inflicted. The dead—they shall arise at the last trump; we cannot bring them to life again; but we can follow Zaccheus,* the small of stature and the exceeding great of soul, who said, "If I have wronged any man, I will restore to him fourfold." Such apology and reparation is both manly and divine; who will make it?

There are signs of a better day. The light is even now breaking in the east. A Massachusetts senator† has said in print that, at the formation of the Union, "each and every state had the right peaceably to withdraw." Another Massachusetts leader‡ has said, more recently, that in the great war, "both sides were right." Mr. Roosevelt, some years

---
*See Luke 19 : 2-8.
†Henry Cabot Lodge.
‡Charles Francis Adams.

ago, said that the Southern soldiers were superior to the Northern, and that Lee was a greater soldier than Grant. Mr. Cleveland has very recently declared that the South alone can solve the race problem. Prominent men and leading journals are endorsing some or all of these statements, more or less vindicating the South's opinions and actions.

These are all hopeful signs, and an "era of good feeling" may be drawing near. Zaccheus is up the tree, and he will, we hope, soon come down and utter the noble words quoted in an earlier paragraph.

X

The Yeomanry of the South

The Cavalier element gave tone and elegance to Southern society. Below it in the social scale, but not separated by any impassable line and not in any cringing subjection to it, was the sturdy yeoman class, men of brains and of manly independence, who followed the Cavaliers against Berkeley, against George III, and, later still, against the encroachments and the invasion of former friends turned into enemies. In all these crises, this sturdy class have proved themselves worthy sons of the yeomanry of England. Both the Cavalier and the yeoman of the South have always known their rights and, knowing, dared maintain, and have taught, and still teach, their sons to face the tyrant, whether priest or potentate, king or cabinet.

The yeoman of the South has never been despised because he was a yeoman. From this stock have sprung many of the greatest soldiers and statesmen of the South, men whose names are household words from the Potomac to the Rio Grande.

Between the classes of society no hard and fast line has ever been drawn in the states south of the Potomac. Ability and genius, if united to character and gentility, have always been honored even in much maligned Virginia and South Carolina.

On no other point has so much stuff and nonsense been said and written. This or that city has been held up to scorn and ridicule for not admitting such and such a man into its *élite* society. In these charges, there is usually no scintilla of real truth. If an eminent self-made statesman, *littérateur*, or soldier has been coldly treated by any Southern community, it can be easily found out, on a quiet investigation, that there was some good and sufficient reason—something that would cause him to be coldly received by good and pure people of other sections.

Most of the talk about the haughty old aristocrats of Virginia is utterly without foundation. In Williamsburg, for instance, long famous as a centre of elegant culture and of the most refined society, there were the most pleasant relations between the classes. A respectable mechanic was on the most cordial terms with gentlemen of the best birth and breeding. The old Virginia gentleman "hobnobbed" with his more humble neighbors, and assumed no airs of superiority. In Virginia to-day the same state of affairs exists. A gentleman, sure of his position, is neither too proud nor afraid to be on the most pleasant relations with neighbors who move in spheres of society lower than himself. A few snobs look down upon honest workingmen, and assume an air and a tone of superiority; but they are soon labeled by all classes as "poor white trash" who have pushed their way into some position too big for their small dimensions.

While the most neighborly feeling existed between the classes, the gentry of the South rarely married out of their own circles. A self-made man might be received into the best society, but even to a man of unusual promise there often would be called a halt when he spoke of marriage. The old "first families" were in this matter very exclusive. "Since the war," however, a great change has taken place in such matters. Thousands of the best families of the South have intermarried with what are called "very plain" people.

The stout yeoman class is forging to the front rapidly. They are, in many cases, educating their sons and daughters, fitting them to become associates of better-born young men and women, and intermarriage between the old and the new families is very common.

In public life, also, the self-made men are taking the lead. Some of the most prominent public men in the South to-day are of humble origin. So is it in educational matters. Many of the rising scholars of the South can claim no connection with the old "first families." In many of the colleges and universities, the faculty are "making silk out of sows' ears," and the sons of the old families are either conspicuous by their absence or notorious for their idleness. Exceptions only prove the rule.

All these facts are attracting the notice of many thoughtful men and women. He who runs may read the signs of a great social revolution in the old Southern commonwealths, and in none is the revolution more noticeable than in the much-maligned state of Virginia. Merit, not blood, is now the measure of manhood.

Out of this blending of sturdy yeoman blood, refined by education, with the old blood, humbled by adversity yet retaining its self-respect and its great traditions, will spring a new and vigorous stock, to make the South blossom like the rose, politically, commercially, and mentally. History repeats itself. In ancient Rome, the blending of patrician and plebeian made a nation that conquered the then known world.

XI

Truth, Purity, and Piety

In the South of the earlier periods, purity in woman and honor in man outweighed blood, wealth, and social position. The purity of the women was required to be absolute. A divorce was almost unheard of, is not to this day permitted in South Carolina, and in most Southern communities is even now almost a social stigma. That a Southern lady should be divorced from one man in the morning and marry another in the afternoon is practically unthinkable. As soon think of a Southern girl's marrying her father's negro driver. One is illegal; both are monstrosities.

Every Southern boy was taught to tell the truth, to honor woman, and to respect religion.

Out of the old Southern honor system, by an exaggeration such as produced the knight-errant of the days of chivalry, sprang the "code duello," the so-called code of honor. While undoubtedly a perversion, duelling had its basis in the right soil, that is, in the idea that a gentleman must keep honor bright. Happily for all, it has now almost passed into oblivion.

How any man can read history and then abuse any one section is simply amazing. Our ancestors both in America and in England, if judged by present day standards, would have to be declared heartless and diabolical. As said elsewhere, the eighteenth century was very brutal. The very men that revolted against England and fought so bravely, permitted honest laborers to be shut up in loathsome prisons because they owed a bill to some merchant. While crying out against England for confining their countrymen in prison-ships and hulks, the Americans of the Revolutionary era tolerated in their debtors' prisons deeds of cruelty "in comparison with which the foulest acts committed in the hulks sink into insignificance." About this time, the Northern states were taking steps towards freeing the negroes. Because the South moved more slowly, some Northern people waxed warm with "righteous indignation," not sweeping their own house first of such things as the Newgate prison and the prisons at Northampton, Worcester, and Philadelphia, the stories of which, as told by the Northern historian McMaster, read like exaggerations of the worst chapters of *Uncle Tom's Cabin.* "Glass Houses"—you remember the proverb.

The South, too, had her debtors' prisons. She, too, was far less merciful than she is to-day. Though very often done mercifully, the whipping of slaves was sometimes cruel, the overseer being often of a class that has always disliked the negro worse than the higher classes have ever done.

If negroes were sometimes whipped to death in the South, they were sometimes burned at the stake in the North. If in our day, they are sometimes lynched in the South for crimes too heinous to discuss in this volume, the guilty ones alone are dealt with; while in the North whole negro settlements and communities are mobbed and burnt for the offenses or the crimes of individuals. The negro shows his preference by staying in the South. There he can make an honest living without interference, and is not punished for the sins of others.

In religious matters, the South was conservative and orthodox. Atheists and free-thinkers were almost unknown; the thousand *isms* of other sections were hardly dreamed of. All gentlemen respected religion and subscribed to its support. The South has always been a church-going people. The churchyard on Sunday morning was a rendezvous for all classes, and the slaves were welcomed to a special gallery. There were, we believe, more accommodations for public worship in the South than in the North, more seats in proportion to population.

Southern men hated hypocrisy and cant; and many a man staid out of the church because he was afraid he might bring discredit upon religion. Deception in any form was not tolerated by the despised Southern code-of-honor.

ANDREW JACKSON

Gambling used to be a national amusement in America. To play for money, for a slave, even for a house and lot, was good form for many generations. To cheat at cards, however, was a sin beyond forgiveness; and this neat distinction is still drawn in some quarters. In our day, playing for money is no longer common in the South, but ladies in some quarters have substituted prizes. The gambling propensities of the men find their outlet in the stock exchanges of the large cities, and buying "futures" is confined to no section. Who shall throw the first stone at the old Southern gentleman for gambling and betting? He who does so must be sure that he himself is not a worse offender.

The honor system applied to the card table also. A debt incurred there was regarded as a debt of honor, and was as promptly paid.

History shows conclusively that civil wars—and our great war was a civil war in its moral aspects—have a disastrous effect upon the morals of a people. This all students of history must admit, if they are candid. And yet what a sublime spectacle is presented by the old commonwealth of Virginia in her attitude towards her creditors! See how heroically she bends her shoulders to a burden that she might refuse to carry. With her schools and colleges needing hundreds of thousands, with her great heroes lying in unmarked graves, unable to make a good appearance among her sister states at national exhibitions or to advertise her resources adequately at the Tercentenary Exposition, she has recently (1901) obligated herself to meet an enormous increase in the annual interest on a debt which she might have repudiated, if the honor of her men had not revolted from such a measure.

"Still in our ashes live their wonted fires."

We do not, however, claim that our people are perfect. We must be candid enough to admit that the same fearful convulsion that so demoralized the men of the North and of the West had some bad effects upon the generation just before us, and also upon us and our contemporaries. If men of high standing in other sections could take our pictures, our pianos, and our family silver, and send them home under the name of "trophies," it is very probable that the war somewhat unsettled our moral vision; and all history proves that the moral effects of a civil war wear off more slowly than the material. After making all fair and truthful concessions, we still have a great deal to be proud of and to thank God for. The noble effort of Virginia to settle her old debt honorably has already been referred to. What grander sight has ever been seen than Wade Hampton's courteously but firmly declining to let the people that idolized him rebuild his house when it was destroyed by fire? Did General Lee sell his name to commercial concerns whose affairs he could not superintend in person? And noble beyond expression was the conduct of Gen. Dabney H. Maury, who, though aged and feeble, and impoverished by the war, refused a salary of $50,000 a year from a well-known lottery.

XII

Slavery in the South

No feature of Southern life has been more misrepresented and misunderstood than African slavery. For a long time, the enemy and the slanderer did most of the writing. They deluged the periodical press and the book market with tons of misrepresentation and abuse, while our Southern forefathers could not gain a hearing. The forum, the senate chamber, and the pulpit, also, rang with denunciation of the "peculiar institution," and, by gaining the ear of the world, stirred up a whirlpool of feeling against the system. The false impression produced by one book has never been eradicated.

Slavery had its sunshine and its shadows. The bright side has never been told; the dark side has been grossly exaggerated, and painted in colors blacker than the hinges of Hades.

No agricultural laborer has ever had food so nutritious and so plentiful as the plantation negro. He had, as a rule, a kind and considerate master, self-interest and humanity combining to make his master feed him plentifully, clothe him comfortably, see that he was not overworked, and look after him in sickness. His working days were from two to four hours shorter than those of European laborers.

In this connection, Bishop R. H. Wilmer, of Alabama, tells an interesting mule story. A thoroughly honest-hearted Northern man once asked him whether negroes were really harnessed to a plough and made to do the work of a mule, as abolitionists had told him. The Bishop asked him how much a mule cost, and he said one hundred dollars. Then he asked him how much an able-bodied slave to put to a plough would cost, and he said a thousand dollars. Then he asked him how many negroes it would take to draw a plough, and he said, "Eight or ten." "Then," said the Bishop, "apart from our good feeling towards the slave, do you think we would spend $8,000 or $10,000 where $100 would be sufficient?"

When the servants, as they were called, were sick, the doctor was sent for and "Ole Missis" went to "the quarters" with her scales, calomel, and rhubarb. When disabled by age, home, food, and clothing were still provided them. No wonder they loved "Ole Marster" and "Ole Missis," and would follow them to the ends of creation.

No such system of slavery ever existed elsewhere under heaven. Most writers of text-books for our schools and colleges do not feel called upon to make this statement, but prejudice our children against slavery in the abstract, and state no extenuating circumstances. They tell about Greek and Roman slavery, where the slave was often superior to his master morally and mentally, but do not tell how American slavery lifted the poor African out of his degradation, and fitted him to be the noblest character in the most famous of American novels.

A popular text-book on history tells us that, in ancient Rome, "sick and hopelessly infirm slaves were taken to an island in the Tiber and left there to die of starvation and exposure." A class brought up on *Uncle Tom's Cabin* and other specious books naturally thinks the poor, down-trodden slaves of the *ante-bellum* South were similarly maltreated. The Northern author, however, does not feel obliged to stop and vindicate his Southern neighbors, though a Southern writer would almost unconsciously defend his people against such base insinuations. He would tell the class how "Ole Marster" would go to old Uncle Henry and old Aunt Molly, thank them for their long and faithful service, point them to a new cabin just built by the plantation carpenters, and tell them to take that and enough land for a garden to work when they felt able, come to the meat house and storeroom regularly for their rations, and not worry about working any more as long as he and his boys had a home to give them.

In this connection, we shall quote Percy Greg, the English historian. He made a most careful and disinterested study of American history, among other things slavery, and came to the conclusion that the Southern negro was the happiest agricultural laborer in the world. Greg says: "Releasd from anxiety, transplanted to a healthy and congenial climate, the animal energies of barbarism combined with the advantages of a high foreign civilization would have ensured the rapid increase of the negro population. But their actual rate of multiplication during the first sixty years of this century bore witness to a combination of favorable influences such as have never been united save among the most favored classes of the highest, most civilized, and most energetic European communities. Abundance without luxury, labor which could not be made half as severe or effective as that of English operatives or Continental peasant-proprietors, the vigilant supervision of Anglo-Saxon intelligence, methods, and science, quickened by enlightened interest and natural humanity, prevented the infant mortality due to parental incompetence or neglect, protected the negro race from the waste of life caused elsewhere by overwork and underfeeding, by unwholesome habits, and by the thousand disorders that keep down the numbers of a proletariate left to its own guidance. Cruelty, hardship, discontent, mental or physical suffering, ill-usage of any kind, would have been, as they are known everywhere to be, powerful preventive influences. The vital statistics of American slavery alone are conclusive evidence of the material well-being and mental ease of the slaves. It does not follow that slavery was favorable to the mental or moral character of the negro, still less that it was economically, morally, or politically advantageous to the masters as a class or to the community as a whole. But no economist and no candid student of Southern history can doubt that as human chattels, as intelligent laboring machines, as valuable beasts of burden, the slaves were well treated and well cared for; that overwork, excessive severity, physical hardship, conscious suffering of mind or body, must have been rare exceptions."*

XIII

The Feudal Baron

The planter was a sort of feudal baron. "Vassals and serfs" at his side, might be said of him with more

---
*Greg's "United States," Vol. II, p. 352, American edition.

truth than poetry. The vassal was the overseer, and he was far more apt to be unkind to the servants than his employer. Of kind overseers there were many; but, oftentimes, they were either rough men of the South or brutal fellows from the North who hated the negro, and rode roughshod over him when the master could not catch them. Mean overseers helped to bring slavery into discredit. Such men, put in charge of cotton and sugar plantations by non-resident owners, brought a stigma upon the system that helped to overthrow it. Of such a type is Legree in *Uncle Tom's Cabin*.

Southern gentlemen dealt tenderly with their "servants," as they called them; they were often less lenient with their own children. The idea of a "lashing planter," as represented in the pictorial schoolbook already referred to, is utterly misleading. By the same reasoning, a 'father' might be defined and illustrated as a cruel man who whips his children.

It is estimated that about one Southern man in three was a slave-owner. A man would buy one or more servants and keep them as an investment and a convenience. A very small numbr of men, mostly planters, had large numbers; but the planters often hired laborers.

It is said that only one Southern soldier in ten held property in slaves; of course, many were the sons of slave-owners. It is probable, however, that seven-eighths of the Southern people were vitally interested in slavery; and its forcible and sudden abolition brought utter bankruptcy to the whole South.

The planter, while giving his servants food and clothing in abundance, looked after their moral and religious interests. The young girls were carefully looked after, to see that they did not go astray. If the overseer or his sons violated the planter's code of morals, great would be the latter's indignation. Aged colored people in the South say that the morals of the race have grown much worse since the days of slavery. The greatest curse to the colored man of to-day is his lack of friendly contact with the white race, the ill-feeling due to his unhappy use of the ballot. The colored man has no truer friends than his white neighbors would be, if scheming politicians had not turned him against them.

One shadow, as already said, was the maltreatment of slaves on the part of some overseers and a few masters. These, however, rarely belonged to the higher classes, where maltreatment of servants led to social ostracism. Hypocrites, liars, "nigger-traders," as they were called, and men that maltreated servants, were universally despised and hated.

Another shadow was the occasional breaking up of families. This, however, was comparatively rare. We know of a few old colored people that were separated from wife or husband; but, on the other hand, we know of many masters that would incur very great inconvenience and expense rather than permit such separation. Even hiring was avoided by many to keep family ties from being broken. Southern gentlemen were humane and tender in this matter, and the statements to the contrary in many books are to a large extent without foundation.

If the planter was a sort of feudal baron, he was also a

patriarch, a judge, and a lawgiver—the Abraham, the Othniel, and the Moses of his people. He often dispensed justice and settled their disputes in a biblical and patriarchal manner. In cases beyond his jurisdiction, he went with them into the courts, sometimes using his means and his influence to save them from the law, if he thought they should not be punished. At times, however, he would let the law take its course; and in this case the jury, seeing the slave apparently deserted by his master, would mitigate the punishment.

An industrious, frugal slave could by making extra time buy himself from his master. Sometimes they would hire themselves from their masters, set up for themselves in some trade or business, and pay the sum demanded. By having gardens and selling the vegetables, by the skillful use of tools, by spinning and weaving, the industrious slave could earn no little money, and often lent money to his master. These happy conditions, however, were rendered less possible by the abolition movement. In self-defense, the South had to curtail the number of "free negroes," as they were made tools of by the abolitionists.

As said already, a gallery was set aside in the churches for the servants. In addition to this, churches were built for them by their owners. Where there were only a few, they were often brought into family prayers. No slave class, no agricultural laborers, ever had their religious interests more carefully attended to. The younger generation, however, have little use for the white man's church or his religion.

Of course there were cruel masters, just as there are cruel fathers and cruel husbands. No one despises fathers and husbands as a class. Why, then, should slaveholders have been held up to the odium of the world, because some were unkind and cruel?

Elderly colored people talk now with deep emotion of their old masters. If they could write books, the world would burn *Uncle Tom's Cabin,* and curse it as a libel. If half the tales of cruelty palmed off on a long-suffering public had been true, the torch and the axe of the slave would have disbanded the Southern armies; but, led by the gentle hand of woman, the dark battalions moved out, day after day, winter and summer, to make the crops that fed the masters at the front of battle.

The atrocious acts that now lead to lynching in the South are emphatically the freedman's license. Before the war and during the war, if he did not love, he at least looked up to his master and his family, and would not have dreamed of laying his hands upon them, save to fondle his "little mistis" and "little marster."

XIV

The "Lazy" Planter

Possibly we have turned aside a little from our main argument. In this volume, however, no paragraph, no chapter, is really a digression, if it either directly or indirectly, pleads the cause of the South, sets forth her great part in the making of our country, refutes any slur made against her in history, encyclopedia, literature, by editor, poet, or professor.

Let us now return to the old plantation, to the throngs of servants that used to love "Ole Marster." These great companies and regiments of slaves had to have good officers; and such were found in the planter, his sons, and the overseer. The habit of command thus acquired by the men of the South developed leadership, and, as already shown, the planter civilization furnished in all crises statesmen and soldiers and great military leaders.

The indolence-and-ease-and-luxury theory was not invented in any recent period. When the troubles between England and her colonies were waxing serious, some Englishmen predicted that there would be slight resistance from the Southern colonies. How little they knew of the mettle of our colonial fathers! With far greater wisdom and insight did Edmund Burke, the philosophic orator of parliament, read their character. He told England that the people of the Southern colonies were much more strongly and stubbornly devoted to freedom than those of the Northern, and that all history would show that, in "all masters of slaves who were not slaves themselves, the haughtiness of domination combines with the spirit of freedom, fortifies it, and renders it invincible."

Proofs of this in abundance can be found in Southern history. Who defied the Crown in the Parsons' Cause in 1763? Who passed the Five Resolutions two years later? Who poured out their blood at Alamance in 1771? Who adopted the Mecklenburg Declaration, drafted the first constitution of a free American commonwealth, moved and penned the Declaration of Independence, and led the armies of the united colonies? The answer rises to your lips: "Masters of slaves who were not slaves themselves," the indomitable and patriotic Southern planters, our forefathers of a sturdy era.

Nor did time enfeeble this mighty stock. In later periods this planter civilization furnished political and military leaders for several decades, fought England in 1812, conquered Mexico, added Louisiana, Florida, New Mexico, California, and Texas to the Union; and in 1861 furnished a half a million of the greatest soldiers the world has ever seen, and leaders such as Hampton, Beauregard, Forrest, Sidney Johnston, and Stonewall Jackson.

Their sons and grandsons had to fight the battle of freedom again at a later era. The declaration that their forefathers of 1776 had drawn no longer protected them. The constitution of 1787, which the genius of their sires helped to perfect, was turned against them. The right of secession, which was so glorious when used against England, was an unpardonable crime when used against sister states that had violated their solemn compact. Instead of the impressment of sailors on the high seas, they suffered the impressment of servants on their own soil. Instead of maltreatment from an unnatural mother, they have that of brothers in whose defense they had staked their lives, their liberties, and their sacred honor in the War of the Revolution, and whose commercial interests they had protected at the cost of blood and treasure in the second war with England. They will ask to be "let alone" and to be permitted to "depart in peace," but the answer will be the sword and the fagot.

Yes, the lazy planter has saved this country and must save it in future eras. But for him, there would have been no King's Mountain, no Cowpens, no Saratoga, no Yorktown. To him we owe New Orleans, Monterey, Buena Vista. His intelligent grasp of public questions has made him a patriot and a soldier. His hours of rest in his library give us Masons, Madisons, and Washingtons. When the old planter civilization becomes effete, the "traveller from New Zealand shall sit upon a broken arch" of Brooklyn Bridge "and sketch the ruins" of Manhattan.

That there were some lazy planters, we admit readily. That too many of them left their plantations to overseers and managers, we shall not deny. But, while lingering around the fire at the "Old Raleigh," the "Red Lion," and other taverns, they were discussing questions of matchless importance, and were fitting themselves to write out declarations and constitutions, and to maintain them on the field of battle.

The lazy planter was not idling. Even when lolling at the courthouse or at the tavern, to talk with his cronies on the questions of the day, he was but following the bent of his genius, his inborn talent for government. Thither nature herself led him. Thither he went spontaneously as the young swan to the pool or as the bird to the air; and from his inborn love of public affairs, of politics, if the word must be written, was evolved the great Southern supremacy in the government—a supremacy which was both the wonder and the hissing of some other sections of the Union.

XV.

Uncle Tom's Cabin and Other Slurs

A beautiful and sturdy civilization, we see, was that of the *ante-bellum* South. If a tree may be judged by its fruits, we may well be proud of that era in our social history. Let us present it in its true light to our children and our children's children. That it was perfect, we do not say; no civilization is perfect. That it had some dark sides, we may admit readily. We must not, however, let those that come after us read, unrefuted, the hostile books that describe the effeminate, indolent Southern gentleman—your grandfather; the proud, haughty, brutal "slave-holder"—your grandfather again; his trifling, immoral sons—your father among them. Let us put our everlasting condemnation upon the books that have made the South a byword and a hissing among the nations, especially that most plausible and most misleading of all books, *Uncle Tom's Cabin*, in which an ideal and almost impossible "Uncle Tom," an overseer, Legree, who could not have kept his place on a gentleman's plantation,— a Northern man by the way—and whippings such as were rarely permitted, and cruelties never tolerated are held up as types, instead of as figments of the imagination or as monstrosities. These things let us teach our children and their children. For the stranger that comes with butter in his mouth and war in his heart, let us have ready the retort with which the good Bishop Richard H. Wilmer, of Alabama, silenced a slanderer: "Uncle Tom, who was, you say, one of the finest characters you ever read of, was a slave. Africa did not produce him, does not now produce him. Does not the book go to show that, if you want to find the best specimen of honesty and piety among servants, you must seek him among the slaves? Eva, you say, is one of the most lovely of her sex, gentle and refined, a beautiful character indeed; was she not a slave-holder? Legree, you rightly say, was the worst character in the book, a vile and cruel man. Was he not a Northern man that came South, trafficked in slaves, and maltreated them?" "A profound silence ensued," says the good Bishop.

Uncle Tom we have pronounced an almost impossible character. One, and only one, slave measuring up to Mrs. Stowe's hero have we ever heard of; and it would be utterly misleading to take such a rare and almost miraculous character and use him as representative.

Many true and faithful old slaves there doubtless were, and some of them we have been thrown with. Their very virtues are due to their contact with a higher civilization. Slavery lifted the African race from paganism and barbarism, and made thousands of them true to their fellow-men and to their Creator. For this reason, men like Stonewall Jackson gave it their approval, and men like Jefferson Davis defended it in the senate.

Some colored people are, undoubtedly, better than many white people. Colored men and women of fine character there are among us. As a race, however, the negro does not measure up to any high standard, either intellectually or morally, and as a race he seems to be lacking in moral responsibility. His great need is domestic purity and personal chastity.

XVI

"Of the Old School"

We trust that the young reader has caught a view of our beautiful *ante-bellum* civilization. A few representatives of that era are still among us: you have known some; the writer, many. Courtly old gentlemen they were; noble and queenly women. To sit in their presence, hear their musical voices, listen to their talk about "old times before the war" was a benediction. Dear old grandfathers and grandmothers, venerable great-aunts and great-uncles, even now pass before the mind's eye, and smile graciously upon us. Let us, my young reader, imitate their virtues. If faults they had, let us try to avoid them; yet we rather think that ours are a thousandfold more in quantity and worse in quality.

Some phases of their life and character do not come within the scope of this book, and will be found in the charming volumes of Thomas Nelson Page and other novelists. A few points we may mention in connection with our treatment of the *ante-bellum* period.

The highest compliment that is ever paid a man in the South is to call him "a gentleman of the old school;" that includes everything. It means that he is honest in business, is refined in his tastes, is courteous towards his inferiors, is chivalrous toward woman, has great respect for religion.

Let us state our recollections of some of these men.

These gentlemen were polite, but not bootlicking, like some of their modern imitators. They were so sincere as to seem at times brusque in their manners. They paid their debts at the rate of a hundred cents on the dollar, and many of them were more than impoverished by paying security debts for other people. They hated "short cuts" in business. They despised sneaks, hypocrites, negro traders, deserters, scalawags, and carpetbaggers. They looked with suspicion upon the soft, velvety, smooth-tongued fellow that can get into your office, glide noiselessly across the floor, and slip his hand, glistening with seal rings, into yours before you know that anyone has entered. They were "open and aboveboard" in all their dealings. If they played cards for money, it was in a gentleman's parlor, not in a secret chamber protected by a bribed policeman. They took their toddies and their juleps, but were not drunkards. They talked more sense in one evening than we do in a month. They knew more of Horace than we do of Tennyson. They had the polish of Chesterfield without his vices. After reverses came, they wore sleek, shining broadcloth coats left over from old times, because they did not wish, like some of us, to owe for a new one —forever.

This writer, you see, believes in the past. He loves and treasures its hallowed memories. He longs for "the tender grace of a day that is dead," and feels with the poet:

> "It is not now as it hath been of yore;—
> Turn whereso'er I may,
> By night or day,
> The things which I have seen I now can see no more."

CHAPTER III

THE HUNDRED YEARS' WRANGLE

I

Early Causes of Estrangement

(1) LIGHTS AND SHADOWS

LIFE is made up of lights and shadows. As with men and women, so it is with states and with nations. The joys of the South in the period already outlined were great; but her sorrows were sometimes well-nigh insupportable. She felt at times like an orphan, a foundling, like a stranger in her father's house. The Declaration which her Richard Henry Lee had "moved," which her Jefferson had drafted, and which her Washington had maintained with the sword, no longer seemed to protect her in the Union. The constitution which her Washington, her Madison, her Mason, her Pinckneys, her Davie, her Williamson, her Rutledge, her Baldwin, and other great sons had helped to draft, no longer seemed to protect her and her institutions. Let us inquire the reasons.

We often hear that the war between the North and the South was "inevitable." The phrase "irrepressible conflict" was coined by a Northern statesman, and soon became popular in some sections. All such phrases are utterly misleading. There is no good, substantial reason why the North and the South should have felt a dislike so deep as to poison for years the life of the republic and make them stand more or less aloof even at the present moment.

We may admit that there were two distinct civilizations on this continent. We may admit that the two peoples differed in political ideas, in religious beliefs, in social customs; but such differences did not have to be settled on the bloody field of battle, with its years of agony and its centuries of hatred. If differences in civilization led to armed conflict, the United States would be in civil war incessantly. The so-called "gulf" between the North and the South of the earlier periods is nothing compared with the yawning chasm which at this moment separates the West from all the old centers of civilization.

The ill-feeling between the North and the South is one of the oldest, and is the deepest, of sectional animosities. It began in the colonial era, and has lasted to some extent to the present. Differences in climate, in views of government, in pursuits, in religion, do not explain it. In colonial days the Pennsylvania Quaker and the New York "churchman" hated the New England Puritan, and in the troubles with England rallied but slowly to his assistance, but in later eras all three combined against the Southern planter. After independence was achieved, "Pennsylvania discriminated against Delaware and New Jersey; Connecticut and Pennsylvania quarreled over the Valley of Wyoming; New York and New Hampshire, over the Green Mountains;" but later on these dislikes were forgotten in the common dislike for the "slaveocracy" of the South. To-day, as a consequence, we have the Solid South following the lead of a handful of Northern and Western politicians.

Why, then, this old sectional feeling? Why did Puritan New England dislike the planters of Virginia so violently that the animosity swallowed up so many local jealousies and lasted till the present?

Various solutions have been offered. Many think that the Puritan and the Cavalier, in emigrating from England, brought their old grudge with them in the *Mayflower*, the *Discovery*, the *Godspeed*, and the *Susan Constant*. Fiske tells us that the New Englander and the Virginian disliked each other, the Virginia Cavaliers looking down upon the people of New England as a race of shopkeepers, and the New Englanders despising the Cavaliers as haughty, domineering, purse-proud aristocrats, like Squire Western in Fielding's *History of a Foundling*. That this feeling existed all history shows us. That the antipathy still exists to some extent, we admit candidly. That it alone would have produced a war horrible in its proportions, we do not believe for a moment.

A thoughtful scholar of our day puts "spatial separation" —that is, distance—among the elemental causes of sectional feeling. No doubt better acquaintance might have helped matters. Had our earlier generations been better acquainted with each other, they might have judged each other less severely, and been more willing to bear each other's burdens and help to solve each other's problems.

Another reason often given is "differing social antecedents" in the old country. This presupposes that the whole North and the whole South came from different ranks of society in the mother country. We know, however, that only a minority of the Southern people claimed descent from the gentry and the nobility of England. The great mass of the Virginians and the Carolinians sprang from the yeoman classes. Only a select few were so aristocratic as to excite jealousy and hatred. The average Southern family had no reason to look down upon the masses of New England.

Another cause often given is the "difference in local administration;" that is, the New Englanders held to township government, government by town meetings, while the planters of the South, living in remote country neighborhoods, adopted the county system. That this political difference led to social differences, we of course know. The fact that the Virginia planter "ran his course remote from men," lived in isolation, and ruled his dependents as a sort of feudal baron, did tend to make him lordly and overbearing; but the contact between the old Virginia Cavalier-planter and the New Englander was in those days too slight to mention. Only the leaders took the long tedious journeys across Mason and Dixon's line; the masses never met each other.

These explanations do not explain. We must seek further for a solution.

Many writers speak of "climatic causes." Not that the likes or dislikes of races and of peoples depend directly upon the thermometer, but that climate largely determines occupation; that difference in occupation leads to difference in interests; and that these in turn lead to a demand for laws that injure some portion of the country.

Most of these causes may have helped to alienate the North from the South. Not all of them combined would, we think, have brought on a bloody conflict. It was secession that caused the war. It was to save the Union that the whole North rose to its feet and marched across the Potomac. Only a few Northern soldiers were fighting to free the slaves; and President Lincoln himself did not interfere with slavery until he thought that such action should be taken as a war measure to strengthen the North, weaken the South, and excite the sympathy of foreign nations.

(2) VIEWS OF THE CONSTITUTION

(a) THE LEAGUE OR COMPACT THEORY

One most unfortunate thing was that the two sections came to take opposite and conflicting views of the constitution. We say "came to take;" for at first there was no strictly sectional division as to the unsettled questions of the constitution. At first the New England statesmen were as zealous for states rights as the Southern; and we shall see later that New England was a stronghold of secession and of nullification.

In 1789, both sections believed that the states were independent sovereignties, and that the Union was a league, a compact. Massachusetts so regarded it. In 1804, her legislature, in asserting the right of secession, refers to the Union as a compact. About thirty years later, John Quincy Adams, one of her greatest men, so regarded it. In a memorial to Congress by several Northern members, who were vehemently opposed to the proposed annexation of Texas, Adams, the head of the committee, said that annexation would be "a violation of our national compact" and "would be identical with dissolution." Webster, also, in his riper years, used the word compact. After a while, this view became almost entirely localized in the South, and the North adopted the consolidation view of the government. No union could have been formed, if the idea of an indissoluble union had been emphasized. As we shall see later, both sections believed that a state might secede whenever she, not others, thought that her rights were violated or her interests endangered.

After a while, the North dropped the league or compact theory, except when it suited some state like Massachusetts or a group of states—New England, for instance,—to go back to it. The South, on the other hand, held on to this theory consistently. She argued that thirteen sovereign and independent states had carried on war with England; that these same sovereign states had drawn up the Articles of Confederation, under which our fathers lived from 1781 to 1788; that thirteen separate states had been recognized as free and independent in 1783 by England, France, and other nations; and that nine of these states, acting as states, withdrew or seceded from the union of 1781, and set up the new union of 1789. So that the South knew that the states were older than the Union, and believed that a man's first loyalty, his "paramount allegiance," was due his state, not the Federal government.

This led to a state pride for which the older Southern states have ever been distinguished, which few Northern states except Massachusetts have ever understood, and of which two-thirds of the states know as little as they do of Sanskrit. This state pride is still very strong in some Southern states. In earlier periods it was very intense, especially in South Carolina and Virginia. It pervades the literature of the South, and influenced the views of the people beyond all calculation. It led John Randolph of Roanoke to scream in his shrill tones across the halls of Congress, "When I speak of my country, sir, I mean Virginia;" led the noblest men of the South, with few exceptions, to "go with their states" in the great war between the sections; and lent keenness to the sword of Lee, as it flashed "forth from its scabbard, pure and bright," "beneath Virginia's sky."

In believing that the states are older than the Union, Massachusetts was not behind her Southern sisters. As late as 1845, a prominent committee of the General Court (legislature) of Massachusetts said: "She (Massachusetts) cannot forget that she had an independent existence before the Union was formed." This fact, however, was long denied by the politicians and the publicists of New England; but occasionally a candid writer of that section admits it. George Bancroft, the eminent Northern historian, says, "The states, as they gave life to the Union, are necessary to the continuance of that life." George Clinton, the eminent soldier and statesman of New York, said: "The sovereignty of the states, I consider the only stable security for the liberties of the people against the encroachment of power."

The young men of the South were taught to watch the Federal government. There was a deep-seated fear that the general government might assume so much power as to reduce the states to mere counties of the Union, as Lincoln actually regarded them. This feeling was very strong in the South, and was confined to no political party. Jefferson Davis was trained under this nervous dread of encroachment upon the rights of the states. For the sake of his state, Mississippi, he was willing to crucify personal ambition. In 1846, for example, when the war with Mexico began, Congress authorized the president to appoint two new major-generals and four brigadier-generals, and Mr. Davis, already well-known as a soldier, was offered one of the appointments. He, however, declined on the ground that such appointments were unconstitutional and that state troops mustered out for the national defense should be commanded by officers either elected by the troops or appointed by the governor.

"A bargain broken on one side is broken on both sides," said Webster in speaking of the compact between the states. For decades the whole South and a large part of the North believed in the league or compact theory and in its corollary, the right of secession. When the North broke her "bargain" by interfering in many ways with the rights and the property interests of the South, the South accepted all kinds of compromises, instead of fighting forty years earlier than she did. When she did fight, the North and the West united solidly against her. The odds and the world were against her.

(b) THE PARTNERSHIP VIEW

Again, the South regarded the Union as a partnership, as

what is called in the business world a "limited partnership." Each state contributed a part of her sovereignty. She reserved all such rights as were not specified in the terms of agreement, these terms being set forth in a paper already familiar to the reader as the Federal constitution, adopted in 1787. "Reserved rights" was a common phrase in Southern political language. Foremost among these reserved rights, but to be exercised only as a last resort, was the right of secession. The South did not wish to secede. She always loved and honored the Union which she had done so much to create and to defend. The right to secede, that is, to withdraw from the Union, she reserved as a last desperate measure of self-defense, just as every man feels that, in some great emergency, to save his own life, he might possibly use a pistol against some human being.

So it is in a partnership. Men do not contribute their capital and their services to go into a partnership that cannot be dissolved. If the partners differ so widely on questions of management that they cannot coöperate pleasantly, they dissolve. If one partner continues to overdraw his share of the profits, they dissolve. If one partner adopts methods that injure the standing and the reputation of the others, a dissolution can be demanded. So with the sovereign states that formed the Union in 1789. Our fathers believed that, if the powers granted by the states to the Union should be used to the injury of the states, the states themselves being the judges as to the extent of the injury, they might secede from the Union; and many eminent Northern authorities admit that on no other terms could the constitution of 1787 ever have been ratified. Three states, Virginia, New York, and

Rhode Island, adopted it on those express terms, and others inferred that there was no objection to the proviso, as no state made such objection.

Nor was the partnership view of the Union confined to any one section. For instance, Josiah Quincy, the famous statesman and publicist of New England, applied the term partnership to the Federal government in a speech in Congress in 1811. This, by the way, was the first secession speech* ever heard in that body.

The states, then, were thirty-four partners. Fifteen of them held property in slaves; the rest had sold out their holdings. The nineteen not only condemned the fifteen, but declared that owners of slaves should not take their slaves into the common possession of the partnership—that is, the territories acquired by the blood and money of all the partners.

Again: the nineteen passed laws declaring that, if any partner traveled with his slaves through the land owned by any partner not holding slaves, the slaves thereupon became free. This law was upset by the Supreme Court of the United States.

The nineteen went still farther. In 1860, they elected as president a man who had said in his speeches that this country could not remain half free and half slave, regardless of the fact that the institution was recognized in the terms of partnership, or constitution, and that the Union had been for nearly seventy-five years cherishing it and protecting it.

All these things were palpable violations of the equity that underlies all partnerships, and were regarded by the

---
*See page 183.

"cotton states" as justifying their withdrawal from the Union. Four other states waited, hoping for a reconciliation. In the spring of 1861, however, when Mr. Lincoln called for troops, these four refused to march upon their Southern sisters, and, rather than do so, joined the Southern Confederacy. It is clear then that there were two separate secession movements.

(c) FEDERALISTS AND ANTI-FEDERALISTS

Very soon after the adoption of the constitution (1787), there sprang up two parties holding opposite views of that paper. One believed in consolidation, centralization of power, at the Federal capital; the other wished to guard carefully the rights of the states, make the Federal government the "general agent" of the states, in order to collect revenue, to keep the states from trespassing upon each other's rights, and to present a united front against interference from foreign nations.

The party last referred to was especially strong in the South. Among its earliest leaders were Henry, Mason, Monroe, and Jefferson; and later this party, led by Jefferson, swept the country and held sway for over half a century. In still later periods, its leaders were such men as John Randolph of Roanoke, John C. Calhoun, and Jefferson Davis.

This party believed firmly in the right of secession. Some of them, Jefferson, Madison, and Calhoun, for instance, believed in nullification, that is, the right of a state to set aside a law of Congress trespassing upon her rights as a member of the Federal Union.

The other, or consolidation, view of the constitution was very strong in the North. There it was learned by thousands of European settlers, and by them was spread throughout the Western and Northwestern states, until it became the prevailing view of the American people, and put the states-rights people in a minority. Thus the South came to stand politically almost alone, cut off from the rest of the Union. The North also forgot that thirteen separate colonies had rebelled against England, declared themselves independent, sovereign states, been recognized as such by European nations, established a confederacy in 1781, seceded from that in 1788, and adopted a new constitution by the votes of separate state conventions. Forgetting all this, the North came to ridicule the idea of state sovereignty, and her overwhelming numbers have enabled her to make this idea seem now almost ridiculous.

The two parties referred to above were called Federalist and Anti-Federalist. They were by no means sectional or geographical. There were no more zealous Federalists anywhere than John Marshall, Charles Cotesworth Pinckney, and George Washington.

In 1801, the Anti-Federalists made Jefferson president. Their name about this time was changed; they called themselves Republicans, while their opponents nicknamed them Democrats.

When elevated to the presidency, Jefferson was well known to believe in nullification, that is, the right of a state to declare a Federal law null and void within her borders, and also to be in favor of limiting slavery to the old states in which it already existed. His doctrine of nullification was never popular. His other doctrine was afterwards adopted by the abolition, free-soil, antislavery, and South-hating politicians, and did a great deal to bring on the war between the sections.

John Marshall, also, unconsciously forged chains to bind his state and his people. Selected as chief-justice by John Adams, the retiring Federalist president, this great Virginian interpreted the constitution in such a way as to make himself one of the few Southern men that have never been abused by billingsgate orators of the North, and claptrap professors of history. Alas, how limited is human vision! If this august Virginian could have foreseen that he was to be quoted by men hurling scorn and contempt at Virginia, he would have rejected the seductive offers of Adams, and like Moses of old would have refused to be called the son of Pharaoh's daughter.

II

Later Causes of Estrangement

These different views of the constitution were, as already said, by no means entirely sectional. Some of the ablest men of the South were Federalists, that is, believed in a strong centralized government; but the anti-Federal ideas of Thomas Jefferson were far more popular, swept the country, and in 1801 put him into the presidential chair.

These differences of opinion alone might not have led to sectional bitterness. Soon the question of tariff thrust its-self into politics, and the agricultural interests of the South were seriously overlooked by Congress in legislating for the commercial interests of other sections. This produced an intense feeling, and led South Carolina to threaten in 1832 to "nullify," that is, to declare the tariff laws of Congress null and void in South Carolina. The planters of the South wanted a low tariff. The manufacturers of the North wanted a tariff high enough to protect their manufactures, that is, to keep them from being undersold by foreigners shipping to this country. These opposing needs helped to create bitterness between the sections.

In this connection we should mention the scheme of many Northern statesmen to surrender the right of navigating the lower Mississippi in exchange for a favorable commercial treaty with Spain, then our next door neighbor to the southward. This angered the South beyond expression, and very naturally. Mr. Theodore Roosevelt, in his *Winning of the West,* tells us that the statesmen of the North "thought more of our right to the North Atlantic fisheries than of our ownership of the Mississippi valley." So we see that commercial jealousy helped to increase sectional animosity.

Territorial expansion, also, caused no little jealousy between the sections. The manufacturing states were not willing to see new territory added to the agricultural sections of the country, and very loud threats of secession were made by New England when Louisiana, Texas, and New Mexico were added in that direction. This, however, was partly due to other causes. It was due partly to the "balance of power" between the sections. It was feared that, when these territories were made states, the South might have too much power in the senate. Moreover, when Texas was admitted to the Union, there came in another very warm question to complicate matters and make some sections bitterly opposed to annexation; *viz.*, the slavery question.

The South, after a while, found herself in the minority on most great questions. Immigration did not seek her shores at all generally. New states began to fill up with foreigners and with settlers from the old states of the north Atlantic seaboard. In Congress, the South was outvoted on many important issues. The majority vote seemed to her to be unfriendly to her interests, to work against her and for other sections, not only in the tariff question, but in "bounties" of various kinds, encouraging other sections in their favorite schemes to her injury; in selling the public lands for the benefit of other sections; in establishing more dockyards in the North than was equitable; in giving Southern states a very small proportion of the money voted for coast defenses; and in many other matters calculated to make her feel like the stepchild of the republic.

Again, another danger threatened her. As foreigners filled up the new states and adopted the national, the consolidation, view of the government, held so generally by the Northern men they were thrown with, the South felt that her Union, the Union of the fathers, was passing away; and that she would be far happier if she could have a republic of her own and not be lost as a part of a consolidated nation.

Such sorrows the South had in those *ante-bellum* days. Yet many of our people loved the Union too dearly to think

JEFFERSON DAVIS

of leaving it. Nearly all these questions were, from time to time, adjusted or compromised by statesmen of the two sections. There was one question, however, which would not be settled, which, like Banquo's ghost, would not down; or if compromised at this or that time would, like the ghost, appear at the feast to bring terror to the guests. This was the slavery question. It was this that proved to be the occasion, the precipitating cause, of the great war between the North and the South.

This subject we reserve for our next section. Just here, however, we pause to say that the North, not being able to make much use of slave labor, was sometime ahead of the South in the idea of abolishing slavery; and fanatical abolitionists and scheming politicians dragged the question into politics, insulted and vilified the slave-owners of the South, and thus brought estrangement between the sections. Thus, various causes were adding to the bad feeling between the North and the South, until it culminated in the great war of secession (1861-1865).

Another cause of sorrow to the South was the continual violation of the constitution on the part of many states. The South stuck to the letter of the constitution. Most of her great leaders were "strict constructionists;" and, as long as the Southern states belonged to the Federal Union, as long as they were members of this great partnership, most of her people felt that the several states should enforce the laws passed by Congress and not declared unconstitutional by the Supreme Court. A few people believed differently; but the doctrine of nullification was never popular with the South as a whole. She saw many Northern states, however, disobeying the constitution, nullifying acts of Congress, that is, refusing to enforce laws of Congress, and even passing bills of their own in direct opposition to acts of Congress. Many of these bills were aimed at the South and her domestic institutions, their special object being to get rid of African slavery by any means whatsoever. After 1850, no less than fourteen states thus nullified one bill based upon the constitution.

III

The Greatest Cause of Estrangement

(1) SLAVERY IN THE NORTH AND THE SOUTH

A few slaves were landed at Jamestown in 1619 and sold to the planters. These excited little interest and no ill-feeling. At that time, slavery was common in the whole civilized world, even kings and queens being partners in the slave trade. In 1650, there were only 300 negroes in Virginia.

Meanwhile, in New England slavery was becoming well established. Indians captured in the Pequot wars were sold into slavery, husbands and wives being sold to different masters, often at remote distances. Some were burned at the stake, says Morris,* the Northern historian. In 1641, when the first Massachusetts code of laws was drafted, there was enacted the first statute establishing slavery in America.

Slavery spread slowly in Virginia. White "indented

---

*History of the United States, page 472. (Edition of 1898.)

servants," redemptioners, and apprentices were numerous and cheap, and African slaves were not especially welcome. In 1663, however, the English government chartered the Royal African Society, of which James, Duke of York, afterwards King James II, was president. This society, supported by the English government, forced the African slaves upon the unwilling Virginians, who then and afterwards made noble efforts to stop the traffic in human beings.

Says a well known Virginia writer:* "Virginia, as a colony, passed twenty-three acts to stop the slave trade. She was the first nation (*sic*) in the world to prohibit it. In 1782, she passed the act permitting the manumission of slaves. It was under her presidents that the slave trade was declared piracy. It was C. F. Mercer, a Virginian, who secured the passage of a resolution that proposed to concede to Great Britain the mutual right of search of vessels suspected of slave trading. Throughout the period from 1776 to 1832, the subject of emancipation engaged the attention of Virginians. Judge St. George Tucker and Thomas R. Dew, among others, proposed schemes for emancipation before the Legislature. And, that same year, John Tyler proposed to abolish the slave trade in the District" (of Columbia.)

The noble efforts of colonial Virginia were balked by England. Some English noblemen and kings were waxing rich on the traffic in slaves, and the acts of the Virginia Burgesses were vetoed by royal governors and by monarchs.

South Carolina was more willing to receive the Africans. Her fields were so malarious that white men could not work

---
*Lyon G. Tyler in his *Tylers*.

them without great risk to health and life, and no one thought of blaming her for buying slaves from the English and New England dealers.

In the eighteenth century, slavery took deep root in America, both north and south. By 1740, about 130,000 Africans had been brought over; by 1776, more than 300,000; by natural increase, they numbered probably 500,000 at the time of the Declaration of Independence. At that time slavery existed in all the thirteen colonies. A feeling against the slave trade had long existed in some quarters, and in 1769 the Virginia House of Burgesses had made an effort to stop it in so far as it affected Virginia; and George III, in the interests of English commerce, commanded the royal governor of Virginia to veto the measure. The slave trade was very objectionable to the people of Maryland, Virginia, North Carolina, and South Carolina. While there was no widespread objection to slavery, yet the whole world was rising up against the slave trade. This "infernal traffic," as George Mason called it, led to the kidnapping of negroes in Africa and of whites in Europe, and excited the sympathy of mankind. In 1815, the congress of European nations at Vienna declared against the slave trade, and denounced it as piracy. Against it, too, many American statesmen of 1787 raised their voices, and wished to prohibit it in the constitution. Alas! "self is all in all." By a combination between some Northern men who wished to encourage the carrying and the selling of slaves, and some Southern men who wished to stock Southern plantations, the slave trade was given twenty years' extension; and "thereby hangs a tale."

(2) THE NORTH SELLS OUT

After the Declaration of Independence was adopted, a good many Americans began to favor emancipation. The Northern states, which had only 40,000 of the 700,000 slaves, were especially willing to free the negro. Some of the states freed their slaves at one time; others, gradually. All of the Northern states freed the slaves between 1777 and 1804; but a great many owners sold their slaves to Southern planters in full time to avoid all financial loss by emancipation.

The 18th century was, as said elsewhere, heartless and brutal. In England, parliamentary votes could be bought easily and cheap for cash or for titles. Sir Robert Walpole, the first prime minister, invented the phrase, "Every man has his price;" and he had good reason to believe it.

In America, in that century, there was much brutality in the treatment of slaves. Even in New England, slave families were often separated. Young infants interfered so much with the usefulness of the mothers that they were given away just as puppies are in our day.* New England stopped rearing slaves because it was cheaper to buy them. White bondmen, "redemptioners," were a drug on the market. They were sold into slavery for a term of years to pay their passage across the ocean.

In the 18th century, there were several slave insurrections. In 1712, some of the slaves of New York city rose up against their masters. They were punished very severely, some very

---
*Dr. Guy Carleton Lee.

cruelly, twenty-four being executed. In 1740, an uprising in South Carolina had to be quelled by force of arms. The slaves there were always more dangerous than those farther north, and the influence of barbarous negroes from the West Indies made the Carolinians exceedingly nervous and anxious. In 1741, the slaves in New York city again attempted an uprising. Thirty-three of them were executed, thirteen by burning.*

Emancipation ideas began in 1688 with the Quakers of Pennsylvania. These ideas did not spread quickly to Virginia or New England. Between 1767 and 1774, however, many people in Massachusetts tried to abolish slavery; but the royal governors would not sanction the movement. In 1769, as seen already, a like movement was suppressed by the governor of Virginia acting under explicit orders from George III. England would not give up so valuable a branch of commerce.

When independence was brewing, Congress made a move towards abolishing the slave trade. On April 6, 1776, the Continental Congress resolved "that no slaves should be imported into any of the thirteen colonies." It is needless to add that this law was constantly evaded by English and Northern slave importers.

In 1784, after independence had been achieved, Congress again discussed the slavery question. It came within one vote of deciding that after the year 1800 slavery should be excluded from all the territory west of the states then existing, and above 31 degrees north latitude. This, if passed,

---
*Charles Morris's *History of United States.*

would have nipped the slavery question in the bud; but, if the war was "inevitable," as some say in their books, the contest would have come on some other issue.

In 1787, Congress passed the ordinance for the government of the Northwest Territory, in which slavery was forever excluded from that section. Not only did Virginia surrender a queenly domain conquered by George Rogers Clark and other sons, but she voted for the exclusion of slavery from the territory, so great was her desire to please her sister states of the Union. Maryland and Georgia likewise ceded their claims to the general government. One clause of this ordinance guaranteed the seizure and return of runaway slaves. This same clause was, as said elsewhere, incorporated in the Federal constitution of 1787; and its continued violation was, as said already, one of the South's sorest trials for three-quarters of a century.

This "self-denying ordinance" did not satisfy the Pennsylvania Quakers. In 1790, they petitioned Congress to suppress the foreign slave trade, and to take steps towards emancipating the negroes. As to the first, Congress referred them to article 1, section 9, paragraph 1, of the constitution. As to the second, Congress resolved that the question of domestic slavery must be left to the individual states to settle.

(3) "WHO DID SIN?"

In 1787, the slavery question came near breaking up the Union. Many Northern men said that they would not take their states into the proposed Union if the slave population of the South was to be counted in fixing representation in Congress. This led to the so-called "Federal ratio," by which five slaves were counted as three persons in the population. Another trouble was the strong desire among both Northern and Southern members of the convention to put a stop to the slave trade. This was settled by giving the traffic twenty years' respite; during which time, Northern owners sold out to the Southern planters. The third burning question was how to get runaway slaves back to their masters. To meet this, article IV, section 2, paragraph 3, was put in the constitution; and Fugitive Slave laws based upon it were afterwards passed by Congress, only to be ignored or violated.

All these compromises proved disastrous. The "three-fifths clause" continually tempted the South to encourage the importation of negroes, so as to give larger representation in Congress, and it lent wings to the numerous slave ships owned by English and Northern slave traders. The twenty years' respite, accordingly, saw an enormous increase in the number of Africans brought to America. The "runaway" clause led to untold bitterness between the sections, because of its continued and flagrant violations.

Very few people of those earlier eras regarded slavery as morally wrong. Jonathan Edwards, the great theologian, owned slaves. Whitefield, the great Methodist divine, left seventy-five to a devout sister of his communion. Gen. Anthony Wayne, of Pennsylvania, had a plantation in Georgia stocked with negroes. In colonial New England, a "godly Newport elder always returned thanks, on the Sunday following the arrival of a slave ship in the harbor of Newport, that an overruling Providence has been pleased to bring to this land of freedom another cargo of benighted heathen to enjoy the blessings of a Gospel dispensation!" At a later day, some of the leading thinkers of all sections were in favor of getting rid of slavery, among them Thomas Jefferson, George Washington, John Marshall, Hugh Williamson, George Wythe, Luther Martin, and William Pinckney.

Among later leaders of thought, we find such men as Francis Scott Key, John Eager Howard, Bishop William Meade, James Monroe, G. W. P. Custis, Wm. C. Rives, Henry Clay, and John Randolph. All these men were, however, ahead of public opinion. Neither the North nor the South as a whole condemned slavery just after the Revolution. We may add, also, that the leaders referred to could never solve the great problem as to what should be done with the slave after he had his freedom. The Colonization Society sent a few to Africa; but they were a mere drop in the bucket.. The North got rid of her slaves by selling them to negro traders who bought them for the Southern planters.

To censure our ancestors for not abolishing slavery before 1800 would be preposterous, would be a moral anachronism. As well censure Washington for not using the telegraph or the telephone. England did not abolish slavery at home till 1772; and in her colonies, till 1834. If it took her a thousand years, how shall America be blamed for not doing it in two hundred?

The idea of emancipation took root slowly. As already

said, the leaders were far ahead of the people. If left alone, Virginia might have shown her Southern sisters the way to settle the slavery problem. Her constitutional convention of 1829, one of the greatest bodies that ever sat in America, came very near voting for "prospective emancipation." In 1831-1832, the legislature debated the slavery question, and came near taking some decisive measures towards emancipation. In 1827, North Carolina had a strong leaning in the same direction. Georgia was the first state to prohibit the slave trade in its constitution. Many earnest people in the South longed to see slavery abolished. Great problems, however, presented themselves in that connection; and, before the South had time to think, there came a shriek from the fanatics, that slavery must be abolished immediately, regardless of property rights, regardless of the constitution, regardless of the fearful convulsions that would come upon the whole fabric of Southern civilization. Of these anarchists of freedom, we shall speak in a later chapter. They and their followers urged the slaves of the South to rise and slay, watch their masters turn pale and tremble as the smoke of their dwellings ascended to the skies; and these modern crusaders hailed the dawn of a political and moral millennium which they saw approaching.*

The attacks of the abolitionists enraged the South. The idea of emancipation and of colonization soon vanished. Instead of discussing these any longer, the South fell back upon her rights under the constitution, where slavery was clearly recognized.

---

*From a speech made in Congress.

Two things postponed indefinitely the day of peaceable emancipation. One was the invention of the cotton gin (1793); the other was the rise of the Abolition party (about 1832). Up to 1793, it took a negro a whole day to clean one pound of cotton ready for market. In the year named, Eli Whitney, of Massachusetts, invented the cotton gin, which would clean a thousand pounds in a day. The effects of this invention were incalculable. By one man's labor, the planter could clean for market one thousand pounds where he had cleaned five or six before. Cotton exports increased prodigiously. They rose from 189,500 pounds in 1791 to 41,000,000 pounds in 1803. Southern lands trebled in value. Negroes increased in value proportionately. Southern capital went into cotton plantations; Northern capital, into cotton factories, and into vessels for carrying the cotton to the markets of the world. Eli Whitney thus laid the basis of the wealth and preëminence of America. Unfortunately and innocently, however, his inventive genius laid the basis of the South's wealth in negro slavery; for, from this time, untold thousands of the Southern people, and many Northern people interested in handling the cotton, closed their eyes to the moral side of the slavery question. This is human nature. This is the same human nature we see around us every day. In our day, it is ruining children in factories, grinding the faces of the poor widow and of the orphan by paying starvation wages, and in a hundred ways calling down the wrath of a righteous Heaven.

Other evils followed Whitney's great invention. Among

them was the increased violation of the law against importing African negroes. Instead of stopping in 1808, as the constitution prescribed, it went on, more or less openly, for years afterwards. Both sections were equally guilty.

When President Jefferson bought Louisiana in 1803, trouble resulted. The Northeast objected to adding so much territory to the South, and thus increasing her influence and her prestige. Thereupon, threats of secession came from New England. That section feared that the addition of so much territory to the South would endanger the commercial supremacy of New England, and create a great trade emporium at New Orleans. Some conscientious opponents of slavery, moreover, feared that the area of slavery would be greatly widened. This, however, was rather a minor interest.

Meantime, the number of slaves was increasing in the South and diminishing elsewhere. The climate of the North was too severe for them. They did not have the intelligence to render skilled service in the factories. Under these circumstances, it was very easy to dispense with them, and to condemn others for not doing so. It is easy to do right when it involves no sacrifice: "Self is all in all."

By 1820, slavery was no longer "a sleeping dog," but very wide-awake. When Missouri applied for admission into the Union, the slavery question convulsed the nation. Finally, a compromise was adopted, admitting Missouri as a slave state, but forbidding slavery north of 36° 30' north latitude. This quieted matters somewhat till 1854; but it doomed the South to Egyptian bondage.

(4) "THE HIGHER LAW"

Meanwhile, the antislavery sentiment in the North was growing. First gradual emancipation was advocated; then (1832) absolute emancipation of every slave in the country. This movement met with bitter opposition even in the North, but Garrison and his party of abolitionists were undaunted. In 1832, was founded the Antislavery Society; in 1833, the American Antislavery Society; later, nearly two thousand abolition societies. Congress was flooded with petitions. This movement is the second of the two things that postponed the day of peaceable emancipation.

In connection with this movement, sprang up the so-called "Underground Railroad." By means of spies and emissaries in the South, especially teachers from the North, large numbers of servants were taken from their masters every year, Virginia being a heavy loser. About 1840, several states passed Personal Liberty bills aiding and abetting runaway slaves, and making it a crime to aid in their capture—all this in the very teeth of article IV, section 2, of the constitution, and of the Fugitive Slave laws standing on the statute books of the United States. To meet the charge of unfairness and of violation of compact, the phrase "higher law" was devised, and soon became a political catchword in some sections. When the South pointed to the constitution, the abolitionists said that there was a law higher than the constitution. Between 1850 and 1860, fourteen states flagrantly nullified the Fugitive Slave law re-enacted in 1850. To argue with such men was a waste of breath. There stood the constitution recognizing domestic slavery and providing for the return of fugitive slaves; but in vain did the South plead for justice and protection.

(5) A NEW GOD DEMANDED

We can even now hear the yells and the shrieks of the fanatics. The problems that had baffled Jefferson, Marshall, and other giants were settled with perfect ease by these pygmies; and the means proposed by them was the same used by Alexander when he untied the famous knot at Gordium—that is, the sword.

When the Supreme Court decided that slavery was recognized by the constitution, they hooted this august tribunal, and cried, "Down with the Supreme Court; down with the constitution; we appeal to the 'higher law.' The constitution is a league with death and a covenant with hell."

When Webster, the idol of New England, dared to say that the South had some rights in the matter, many denounced him, saying that he was a Judas Iscariot selling himself for Southern votes for the presidency; and the God-given art of the poet was used to hand this great man down to eternal infamy wherever American literature is read by countless millions. Some blasphemous fanatics boldly said, "The times demand, and we must have, an antislavery constitution, an antislavery Bible, and an antislavery God."

These fanatics abused and vilified the South, using the words "slave-owner," "slave-holder," as synonymous with thief, robber, blackguard. What cared they that Washington himself had been a slave-holder, and that, until quite recently, some of the best men of their own section had belonged to the hated "slavocracy?"*

Our fathers, however, still hoped for better things; they still stood on the rights guaranteed them by the constitution.

Soon, too soon, these fanatics made a league with the politicians. Some of the latter saw that the slavery issue might be used in some quarters as a "bloody shirt" to conjure with, and stir up their lukewarm voters. In 1848, a very prominent public man of the North said that the slavery question was an "irrepressible conflict," and by that fearful utterance not only inflamed the South, but encouraged the fanatics to make war upon Southern institutions.

(6) THE PLOT THICKENS

The Southern people still hoped for fair treatment, and gave up a part of their rights in the interests of peace and harmony. Some of their leading statesmen, Senator Jefferson Davis among them, followed Henry Clay in his second compromise bill of 1850, which prohibited slavery in the new state of California, settled largely by Southern people, but left to other territories the power to decide the question for themselves. This compromise act, however, was violated by many, and Mr. Lincoln in 1858, in his famous debates with Douglas, said that "this country could not remain half free and half slave." If a man of his ability could thus ignore the rights of the South, what could be expected of ordinary people?

---

*It may be stated on high authority that General Grant himself owned slaves after General Lee had sold or manumitted all under his control.

Meantime, *Uncle Tom's Cabin* had been published (1852). Its one-sided presentation of slavery infuriated the South, stirred the North to fever heat, and cut the South off still more from the sympathy of mankind. Of this book, we shall speak quite frequently. Just here we pause to say that its author, Mrs. Harriet Beecher Stowe, disclaimed any intention of misrepresenting the South or of denouncing all slave-holders. She thought that slavery ought to be abolished, and used the so-called "purpose novel" to aid in its abolishment. Whatever her intentions, her method was wrong, and unfair to Southern civilization. The world inferred that the noble and holy Uncle Tom was a typical slave, and that the cruelty practiced upon him was common in the South, rather than a monstrosity which would have been denounced by every man, woman, and child south of the Potomac.

Two years later (1854), another spark was thrown into the magazine. That was the fearful Kansas question. Congress decided that Kansas should enter the Union unrestricted, and that the slavery question should be decided later by its inhabitants. This has been characterized by a distinguished writer as "local option" applied to slavery; and it stirred up as much bitterness in the country at large, as "local option" always does in small communities. Both sides proceeded to induce settlers to migrate to Kansas. The abolitionists were very successful in their efforts, and filled the new state with a population that voted for an anti-slavery constitution. This produced bitterness indescribable.

In 1856, another scene in the drama was enacted. In

HENRY CLAY

that year a new party, avowedly hostile to Southern institutions, polled a vote large enough to make the South fear that her rights under the constitution would no longer be respected. It was the large vote cast for John C. Fremont, the Republican antislavery candidate for president, that compelled the South to believe that she was soon to be deprived of the right of taking slaves into the territories, the common property of all the states—which would unquestionably be a clear violation of the terms of compact or partnership made in 1787.

In the next year (1857), the North felt that she had a great grievance. In that year, the Supreme Court of the United States decided that a slave-owner might take his slaves into the territories just as he took any other property. For this decision, the court was abused by fanatics and loaded with execration. Especially hated was Chief Justice Roger B. Taney, the distinguished son of Maryland. This decision, which was delivered in the famous Dred Scott case, added fuel to the flame. In discussing this matter, even Mr. John Fiske prejudices the young student against the South and against the majority of the justices.

In this contention, the South was still clinging to the constitution. Though her claims were usually legal, the South was in regard to slavery lagging in the rearguard. All the world seemed against her. The whole North believed that slavery was as bad as Mormonism. The laboring men of Europe were against her. The higher classes of Europe, not realizing the difficulties of the problem, and not knowing how the proud, high-strung temper of the South had been tried by years of abuse and misrepresentation, withheld any open sympathy. She was now, instead of Greece, "the Niobe of nations."

In the year 1858, as said already, Abraham Lincoln, then rising into prominence in Illinois, declared that "this country could not remain half free and half slave."

In 1859, John Brown's raid stirred the South beyond expression. This fanatic, supported by a band of desperadoes armed with pikes and other weapons, crossed the Potomac at Harper's Ferry, Virginia, seized the arsenal, entrenched himself there, and shot down several inoffensive citizens, among them the mayor of Harper's Ferry. His object was to stir up an insurrection among the slaves, but he met with slight encouragement among the negroes. Captured by the United States and Virginia forces, Governor Wise, Colonel R. E. Lee, Thos. J. Jackson, and J. E. B. Stuart being prominent, he was turned over to the courts, tried by a fair jury, and hanged under the laws of Virginia. What followed? Denunciation of Brown throughout the country? On the contrary, he was in many quarters glorified and lauded as a martyr; bells were tolled in his honor; and pulpit, press, and platform denounced Governor Wise as a Judas Iscariot, and added Brown's name to the calendar of saints, some even comparing him to Christ himself.

The last statement is sometimes denied by Northern writers; but none can deny that the name of John Brown was used as a charm to conjure with, and that great armies sang him into glory as they marched across the Potomac into Virginia.

(7) THE LAST STRAW

This "glorification" of John Brown reduced the South to desperation. She did not know what to expect next. Accordingly, many of her principal statesmen and numbers of her other citizens began to believe that she would never be happy again in the Union. Few, however, were as yet in favor of secession.

The patience of the South was not yet exhausted. She still hoped against hope. She did not wish to leave the Union. It was her Union, and why should she be driven out of it as long as life was worth living under its starry banner?

There is a limit to human endurance, and a time comes when patience ceases to be a virtue. The next year, 1860, this time came to many noble Southerners. The election of a sectional president on a sectional platform, that is, the election of Abraham Lincoln, who had said in 1858 that "this country could not remain half free and half slave," and that by a strictly sectional vote hurled against the South and her institutions—this was regarded by seven states as an overt attack upon the South; and, rather than wait to see what the new president would do to carry out the policy of his party, they fell back upon the right, always reserved and never surrendered, of withdrawing from the Union which now threatened to use against the states the powers lent it by the states; in other words they determined to exercise the right of secession.

Slavery, we see, was the greatest cause of alienation between the sections. Many books and thousands of honest but mistaken men persist in saying that the war was fought on the slavery issue; this is entirely erroneous. The Southern soldier was not fighting for slavery, and the Northern soldier was not fighting to abolish it. The Southern soldier was fighting for his state, at her summons, heeding the call of her to whom he believed he owed his first allegiance; and, if there was any mistake, any crime, he was not responsible; "his but to do and die."

The Northern soldier was not intentionally fighting to abolish slavery. The politicians had tricked him into thinking that he was fighting for the Union, now assailed by "rebels" and "traitors;" that he was defending the flag, lately insulted by "hot-headed South Carolina" and her minions.

The Southern soldiers owned very few slaves, though most of them were more or less directly interested in slave property. The Northern soldiers cared little for the negro, and few would have made war in his behalf. Slavery, then, was but an important incident of the war; the real causes lie much deeper.

The same politicians that deceived the soldiers influenced Mr. Lincoln. He, too, started out with a high sense of duty towards the Union, saying that he had sworn to see that the laws of the United States were executed in all the states, and that he had neither the wish nor the authority to interfere with slavery. Erelong, however, he made a complete somersault. After the brilliant victories of Lee and Jackson in 1862 had depressed the North beyond expression, he issued his famous Emancipation Proclamation

(Jan. 1, 1863), which was a mere war measure, and would have been declared utterly unconstitutional by any Supreme Court referred to in this chapter. The United States still owes the South two billion dollars for her negroes.

IV

The Right of Secession

(1) NEW ENGLAND PIONEERS OF SECESSION

In our day, no one ever mentions the possibility of secession. No matter what unjust laws Congress enacts, no man, no newspaper, seriously threatens secession. The last suggestion of such a possibility came, we believe, from some Western people during the presidential campaign of 1896, when William J. Bryan almost swept the country.

Not so with the generations immediately before us. With them, secession was always a possibility, and oftentimes a probability. As the ill-feeling between the sections increased, the probability of secession became greater and greater. The South being in the minority in Congress and being the injured party, secession became more distinctly a Southern doctrine; but we shall show clearly that the right of secession was held by eminent men, and by whole communities, in other sections of the country.

Secession was first threatened in New England. While the thirteen states were living under the old Articles of Confederation (1781-1788), threats of a New England confederation were loud and deep, and prominent men declared that, if the Mississippi river were not closed up for twenty-five years, the New England states would secede from the "perpetual Union" and establish a confederation for themselves. In 1792 and 1794, secession movements began to take definite shape. In 1793, Timothy Dwight, the eminent theologian and the president of Yale, speaking of the threatened war with European powers, said: "A war with Great Britain, we, at least in New England, will not enter into. Sooner would 99 out of 100 of our inhabitants separate from the Union than plunge themselves into an abyss of misery." In 1796, Governor Wolcott, of Connecticut, declared that, if Jefferson should be elected president, he (Wolcott) would heartily favor a separation from the Southern states. Governor William Plumer (Plummer), of New Hampshire, one of the most famous publicists and writers of the early part of the 18th century, names many prominent New Englanders that were in favor of a dissolution of the Union—the second "perpetual Union" (1789). Among them were Timothy Pickering, George Cabot, Harrison Gray Otis, Josiah Quincy, Roger Griswold, the Lowells, Stephen Longfellow, and many other fathers of New England. In 1804, Colonel Timothy Pickering said: "The principles of our Revolution point to the remedy: a separation. . . . . . A Northern confederacy would unite congenial characters, and preserve fairer prospect of public happiness . . . . . It (the separation) must begin in Massachusetts." Some may say that these are the views of individuals. In 1804, the legislature of Massachusetts resolved: "That the annexation of Louisiana to the Union transcends the constitutional power of the government of the United States. It formed a new confederacy, to which the States united by the former compact are not bound to adhere." Where was the right of secession ever more clearly stated? The reader will notice, also, that the legislature of Massachusetts in 1804 regarded the Union of 1788 as a compact, and as dissoluble for cause satisfactory to one of the parties thereto.

The high priest of secession was the eminent Josiah Quincy, of Massachusetts. In the Congress of 1811, while the bill for admitting the Louisiana territory to statehood was under discussion, this distinguished statesman—afterwards president of Harvard,—said: "If this bill passes, it is my deliberate judgment that it is virtually a dissolution of this Union; that it will free the states from their moral obligations; and, as it will be the right of all, so it will be the duty of some, definitely to prepare for a separation—amicably if they can, violently if they must." Quincy was called to order by Mr. Poindexter, of Mississippi territory; but the House, on appeal, decided that a suggestion of secession was not out of order. Then Mr. Quincy proceeded to argue that the Union was a partnership consisting of thirteen members, and that, if ten of them admitted a fourteenth not acceptable to the other three, the three could demand a dissolution.

Hildreth, the Massachusetts historian, says that this was the first mention of secession ever heard in Congress.

Eighteen years later, Quincy was elected president of Harvard College. There he served with great usefulness and great distinction for sixteen years; and we may imagine that he taught his views as to the right of secession to thousands of the brightest young men of New England. The same may be conjectured as to Dr. Timothy Dwight, the learned and eminent president of Yale, quoted in an earlier paragraph. We shall not be surprised then if secession views were commonly held in New England from about 1810 to about 1850.

John Quincy Adams says that a secession scheme was formed in 1803-1804, and that a military man was selected to lead the armies that might be needed. In 1839, this same statesman and ex-president said that separation was better than an unhappy and unwilling union. In 1842, he presented in Congress a petition from citizens of Haverhill, Massachusetts, for a dissolution of the Union.

Horatio Seymour, the eminent New Yorker, said in a public address, October 8, 1880: "In 1812, while the walls of the Capitol were blackened and marred by the fires kindled by our foes, and our Union was threatened with disasters, the leading officials and citizens of New England threatened resistance to the military measures of the administration!" How Massachusetts and Connecticut refused to send their quota of troops, we have seen already.

John Fiske says: "John Quincy Adams, a supporter of the Embargo, privately informed President Jefferson that further attempts to enforce it in the New England states would be likely to drive them to secession." This was in 1809.

The "storm center" of New England secession was the famous Hartford Convention. Let us quote Mr. Fiske

THE HUNDRED YEARS' WRANGLE 185

again: "In December, 1814, some of the Federalist leaders met at Hartford and passed resolutions. Among other things, they demanded that custom house duties collected in New England should be paid to the states within whose borders they were collected, and not to the United States. This would have virtually dissolved the Union." Mr. Fiske puts it very mildly.

Mr. Fiske says, "Some of the Federalist leaders." Horatio Seymour says, "A convention of delegates appointed by the legislatures of three of the New England states, and by delegates from counties in Vermont and New Hampshire." John Quincy Adams believed firmly that the convention was called to dissolve the Union, and that it would have met again and done so, but for the closing of the war with England (1815).

(2) LATE NEW ENGLAND SECESSIONISTS

In 1844 and 1845, the state of Massachusetts again threatened secession. When the annexation of Texas was pending, the legislature of Massachusetts resolved that "the annexation of Texas might drive these states into a dissolution of the Union." Notice the language, "these states." This implies clearly that Massachusetts knew of other Northern states that believed in the right of secession. We are not attacking Massachusetts and her sisters. If they believed that their interests were endangered by the annexation of Texas, they had a right to leave the Union. We simply wish to prove that belief in secession was not confined to any one section of the country.

We have shown that New England leaders believed in secession. We have proved that a convention representing three New England states and parts of others took strong secession ground in 1814. We have shown that the most influential state of New England threatened to secede in 1844 and 1845. How, then, can any one say that the North did not believe in secession after 1830? Even if this could be proved, why should the South be condemned for believing in it in 1861? Let us, however, trace Northern opinion to a later period. In 1860, Horace Greeley, the famous editor of the New York *Tribune,* said: "If the cotton states shall become satisfied that they can do better out of the Union than in it, we insist on letting them go in peace. The right to secede may be a revolutionary one, but it exists nevertheless. . . . . We hope never to live in a republic whereof one section is pinned to the residue by bayonets. . . . . If the Declaration of Independence justifies the secession from the British Empire of 3,000,000 colonists in 1776, we do not see why it would not justify the secession of 5,000,000 Southrons in 1861."

The New York *Herald,* in 1860, admitted the right of secession, and said, "Coercion . . . . is out of the question." The Cincinnati *Commercial,* one of the great *ante-bellum* Republican papers, favored the recognition of a slave-holding republic. General Winfield Scott, the commander-in-chief of the United States army in 1861, was in favor of letting "the wayward sisters depart in peace."

From all we have said, there is but one fair inference: the South had the right to secede if she wished to do so.

Why she wished to do so has been already told, and need not be repeated.

For many years after the war, Northern writers rarely admitted the right of secession as ever having existed. Mr. Charles Francis Adams says that up to about 1830 this right was universally admitted; but we have shown that his own grandfather and his own state believed in this right after that time, and that his state threatened to exercise it. More recently, candid students of history have been more outspoken. In 1889, Mr. Henry Cabot Lodge, sprung from the best secession blood of New England and now (1906) senator from Massachosetts, said that originally "each and every state had the right peaceably to withdraw." When was this right surrendered prior to 1861?

In the face of such facts as those given, writers of high repute in the North are still telling us in their books that the South had no warrant for the doctrine of secession. A well-known Northern text-book says: "For fifty years, no man, or set of men, possessed of political influence had so much as hinted at the possibility of Northern secession."

This Northern scholar is quite sarcastic towards John Quincy Adams and his constituents of 1842, referred to in a foregoing paragraph, the Massachusetts legislature of 1844 and 1845, and various congressmen and senators who presented petitions in Congress between 1820 and 1860. Of ignorance, we dare not accuse him; for many of his statements as to the treatment of slaves in the North have been quoted in this volume.

Some of the so-called histories are filled with bold statements of opinion, palmed off as history on unwary readers. One of them bearing an eminent name on its title page says: "The doctrine of state sovereignty thus put every man in the South on the wrong side, and kept him there." From these two books and others like them, the student would never suspect that the idea of secession had ever had any serious foothold in New England; for neither of them speaks candidly of the Hartford Convention and its plans for secession; and one of them varnishes it over so that a casual reader would hardly know of its importance.

Some writers, however, are more candid in their statements. Prof. Goldwin Smith, of Canada, though far from friendly to the South, recently said: "Few who have looked into the history can doubt that the Union originally was a compact dissoluble on breach of the articles of union." Professor Smith does not tell us when the South ever surrendered the right of dissolving the Union in case of a breach of the articles of union. We say that this right was not surrendered until the fearful war of the '60's, and only then at the point of the bayonet.

Very recently, Mr. Charles Francis Adams, the Massachusetts free-lance and the "morning star of reconciliation," said, "Both sides were right in 1861." This is magnanimous, but the Confederate veterans cannot endorse it. If the South was right, the North was wrong, and *vice versa*.

To the same fearless son of a race that fearlessly speaks out, we are indebted for the valuable fact that, from about 1825 to 1840, the right of secession was taught at the West Point Military Academy. The author of the text-book used there was William Rawle, one of the most distinguished legal writers of Pennsylvania. Mr. Rawle was appointed to high positions by President Washington, and declined a seat in the cabinet of that great president. His lectures on constitutional law attracted large numbers of law students to Philadelphia, where his influence was incalculable. In the book referred to, *A View of the Constitution of the United States,* Rawle says plainly, "The secession of a state from the Union depends on the will of the people of such state." No Southern writer ever stated it more clearly.

While this doctrine was being taught at West Point, Jefferson Davis, Albert Sidney Johnston, Joseph E. Johnston, Leonidas Polk, Robert E. Lee, and other Southern cadets afterwards distinguished were graduated from the academy. The right of secession they learned, then, from the Federal government. How that government punished them for their proficiency as students, we shall learn in later chapters.

(3) NULLIFICATION IN THE NORTH

If facts mean anything, we have proved that secession was first threatened in New England. We now pass on to show that nullification was not only believed in but actually practised in New England long before South Carolina ever made her reputation as a nullifier.

In 1809, when the Embargo Act of 1807, passed by Congress to protect the United States against England, injured the commerce of New England more than that of England, Massachusetts declared that "the act was not binding upon her citizens." This was nullification. In 1812, while the country was at war with England, "the leading officials and citizens of New England threatened resistance to the military measures of the administration." This is quoted from a speech by Horatio Seymour, of New York.

Mr. Fiske, you will recall, said that the Hartford Convention, composed of the flower of the New Englanders, "passed resolutions." That is putting it mildly. One of these resolutions was: "When emergencies occur which are either beyond the reach of judicial tribunals or too pressing to admit of delay incident to their forms, states which have no common umpire must be their own judges and execute their own decisions." This is nullification. This statement of the fathers of New England is as clear and as strong as anything ever said by John C. Calhoun or the state of South Carolina. In 1832, South Carolina said that, if the pending tariff law passed, she would be her own judge and execute her own decision—which was that that law would not be binding upon her people.

That the Embargo Act of 1807 led New England to threatened secession and to actual nullification, we have already seen. The War of 1812 produced the same results. Of the refusal of the two largest New England states to furnish their quota of troops for national defense, we spoke in the chapter on the War of 1812. That was nullification. Again, in 1844-1845, the legislatures of several New England states resolved that those states were not bound to recognize the annexation of Texas. What is this but nullification? It makes South Carolina turn green with envy.

The right of a state to nullify an act of Congress was

always held by a respectable minority in the South. Belief in secession was, on the other hand, almost universal. To stay in the Union, however, and attempt to nullify a law of Congress, the great mass of the Southern people did not consider logical. The Virginia and Kentucky Resolutions of 1798-'99, passed at the time of the Alien and Sedition Acts, by the legislatures of Virginia and Kentucky, show that the doctrine of nullification was popular at that time in those two states, but this doctrine was never generally popular. No Southern state ever nullified; South Carolina in 1832 only threatened; while Massachusetts, as we have seen, several times acted.

The decade 1850 to 1860 was the great era of Northern nullification. In that period, as already shown, fourteen Northern and Western states nullified both the constitution and a law based upon it. That is to say, after the passage of the Omnibus bill of 1850, one clause of which was a stringent act for the return of fugitive slaves, these fourteen states passed Personal Liberty bills in the very face of the new Fugitive Slave law of 1850. In every possible way, slaves were helped in escaping from their masters. The constitution and the Fugitive Slave law were nullified openly and boldly. As said already, this was one of the South's sorrows in the period just before the war between the sections.

The greatest Southern exponent of nullification was John C. Calhoun. His influence was very great, but not great enough to make this doctrine popular. In 1832, Virginia did not believe in it. She sent a commissioner to urge South

Carolina to withdraw her threat of nullifying the tariff acts of Congress.

It was reserved for the oldest of the Northern states to take up this doctrine in 1844, twelve years after South Carolina had dropped it, and for thirteen others to "out-Herod Herod" after 1850.

Are these facts stated in the histories? Would a Southern youth ever dream that South Carolina was far behind many Northern states in the matter of nullification?

We turn to the indexes of several standard Northern text-books. Under the word "nullification," we are almost invariably referred to the South Carolina matter of 1832; very faint intimation do we find that the North taught South Carolina how to nullify. Fiske is one of the few frank and candid Northern writers, and he puts it very mildly. The *Encyclopedia Britannica,* in its discussion on the subject, leaves us under the impression that the whole thing was born in the "fevered brain" of South Carolina, and that she had no warrant for her action of 1832.

V

"The War"

To the last and extreme resort—secession—then, the South was finally driven. The "straw that broke the camel's back" was the election of Abraham Lincoln, an avowed enemy of slavery, but objectionable to the South rather because he was the candidate of a party born out of the hostility to her and her institutions. As soon as he was

JOHN C. CALHOUN

elected, the secession movement began. South Carolina seceded December 20, 1860; Mississippi, January 9, 1861; Florida, January 10; Alabama, January 11; Georgia, January 19; Louisiana, January 26. On the 8th of February, a convention of delegates from these states met at Montgomery, Alabama, and formed a temporary government for the Confederate States of America, and elected Jefferson Davis, of Mississippi, president, and Alexander H. Stephens, of Georgia, vice-president. February 1, Texas seceded and applied for admission to the new republic.

Other Southern states held back, hoping that some compromise might be made. Virginia called a Peace Convention, but this effected nothing. President James Buchanan, a Pennsylvania Democrat, did not believe that his oath of office required him to coerce the seceding states, and left the question to be settled by the incoming president. The latter, Abraham Lincoln, an Illinois Republican, believed that his oath of office compelled him to call out armies to see that the laws of the United States were duly obeyed in all sections of the country. His call for troops was indignantly met by Arkansas, Tennessee, Virginia, and North Carolina. Seeing armies mustering to march against their Southern sisters, these states seceded from the Union—Virginia, April 17; Arkansas, May 6; North Carolina, May 20; Tennessee, June 8. Kentucky, Missouri, and Maryand were divided in their sympathies, but all furnished some great generals and some fine troops to the Confederacy.

The Southern leaders seem to have expected a peaceable secession. For this reason, few preparations had been made for an armed conflict. Only a few very far-sighted men, like Jefferson Davis and Robert E. Lee, foresaw that the Northern states would not permit any state or states to secede peaceably. Senator Davis got little thanks when he told his constituents and others that a long war would follow secession. When many talked about a three-months' war, Col. Robert E. Lee predicted that the struggle would last seven years, and be immense in its proportions.

For this war between the North and the South, several names are more or less common. The Northern people used to call it the "Rebellion;" and this title defaces the published records of the government, grating day after day upon the feelings of the Southern reader, because it is associated with conquest, contumely, and perversion of history. The war was not a rebellion. If the states created the Union, how could the creators rebel against the thing created? If the Union was the general agent of the states, how could the principals rebel against their agent? If the Union was a partnership, and if some of the partners wished to withdraw, how is that a rebellion, even if the other partners forcibly drag them back into partnership?

Many writers of both sections now use the term "Civil War;" but this, while not offensive, is logically and historically inaccurate, and has been repudiated by the Confederate veterans; for a civil war is a struggle for supremacy between two or more opposing parties or factions in the same nation, while the war of 1861-1865 was a war fought by a large section of the people of our country for total separation and independence. It was really a war between two nations, and General Lee so regarded it.

Some call it the War of Secession, or the War for Secession. These are better than the two names discussed above, but are not satisfactory.

Many old Confederates like the name War for Southern Independence; but this is too long to gain any general acceptance. A good many Southern books call it the Confederate War; but this would imply that it was instigated and brought on by the South—which is totally erroneous. For many years, the Southern people called it "the war," but, after the war with Spain (1898), another name was felt to be necessary.

Around the "camp fires" of the veterans or over their pipes, some good old fathers and grandfathers call it "our war;" but this, while sociable and endearing, will never spread among the masses.

The name "Great War" has recently been proposed, and is used frequently in the *Confederate Veteran,* the organ of the various associations for preserving the records, memories, and traditions of the struggle. That title, however, would not do in general history, for we might have at any time a great war with some strong nation. The name War between the States has the high authority of Jefferson Davis and of Alexander H. Stephens, two of the most prominent Southern statesmen, and has been officially adopted by the Grand Camp of Confederate Veterans. It is, however, rather longer than busy people are apt to fancy, but is logically correct, and can be used without wounding the feelings of any reader. At this time, we prefer it to any other name, and shall use it frequently in the following pages.

Mr. Lincoln should never have used the term "Rebellion." Of all men in the North he should have called the war "The Revolution of 1861"; for he declared in Congress, January 12, 1848, in a debate about Texas that any portion of a people may "revolutionize", and take possession of the territory they inhabit. His exact words are: "Any people anywhere, being inclined and having the power, have the right to rise up and shake off the existing government, and form a new one that suits it better. This is a most valuable and most sacred right, a right which, we hope and believe, is to liberate the world. Nor is the right confined to cases in which the whole people of an existing government may choose to exercise it. Any portion of such people, that can, may revolutionize and make their own of so much of the territory as they inhabit."*

Whatever its correct name, the storm long brewing burst in 1861. For four years, the South waged a heroic contest against enormous odds, and had to surrender April 9, 1865.

Slavery was extinguished. Secession, as an actual fact, was given up. A whole race had citizenship thrust upon it. Then the fearful era of "reconstruction" followed; and, since that time, all kinds of small men in all kinds of big places have been trying to solve, in a day or a month, problems that would baffle the wisdom of Washington, Hamilton, Jefferson, Marshall, and other sages of the republic.

---

*Morse's *Lincoln*, vol. I., p. 76.

CHAPTER IV

THE PRIVATE SOLDIER AND THE SAILOR

I

The Real Hero

FOR forty years, the South has glorified her generals. While they were living, she heaped honors upon them, and, since their death, has built lofty monuments to their memory. May their names grow brighter with the ages! May the names of Beauregard, Hampton, Hill, Forrest, Pickett, Stuart, the Johnstons, Lee, Jackson, and others be held in everlasting remembrance!

The real hero, however, is the private soldier. It was he who won the victories that distinguished his commanders. It was he that stood sentinel at the lone midnight hour; faced cold, hunger, nakedness, peril, with no hope of promotion or of fame; pointed the rifle, wielded the sabre, fired the belching cannon; defied overwhelming odds; shivering, barefooted, starving—all for the sake of loyalty to his state and to the flag of the young republic.

His history has never been written. His day is just breaking on the horizon. In these rapid sketches, we can give but a slight hint of his greatness and of his achievements. Suffice to say that no grander, no more tragic, figure has ever trodden the arena of history. To the future we must leave an adequate portrayal of his character. When the poet, the historian, or the orator of coming ages needs inspiration, he will turn his eyes to Manassas, Shiloh, Chancellorsville, and Richmond.

II

Who?

Who was this Southern private? Was he a loafer, wharf-rat, "bruiser?" Was he a laggard and a dastard, driven by a despot's whip, like the soldiers of Xerxes? A few such men are found in every army. Even the South had some such; but they soon deserted, and went home, to be pointed at and despised to the present moment. Very different, however, were the great mass of the Southern army. They were the pick of the South, the *crème de la crème* of her chivalry, the flower of her young manhood. The merchant closed his store. The mechanic laid down his saw and his hammer. The lawyer closed his office, and the physician gave up his practice. The teacher left his schoolroom, and the professor resigned his chair, gladly putting themselves under the instruction of some old pupil who had had some military training. David went forth to meet Goliath. The so-called "effete aristocracy" of Virginia and other states went out to fight for constitutional government, for home and fireside. Not even Athens in all her glory sent forth such an army breathing such a spirit.

III

Why?

Various motives actuate the ordinary soldier. Some fight for the money that's in it; some, wishing to see the world, join the army; some long for adventure, and so dare the cannon's mouth. Of money, the Southern private saw but little; his month's wages, when paid, were very meagre, and, after the second year of the war, were almost nothing. As to fame: the private knew that his name would never be heralded to the world, and that he would, if killed, probably be buried in an unmarked grave.

The question "Why?" has been already answered. The Southern soldier and sailor fought for his state; went with her out of the Union; answered her summons after she seceded and called upon her sons to repel invasion. Possibly he was not in favor of seceding from the Union. If not, he still felt it his duty to obey her summons; and this was the feeling that led Alexander H. Stephens, Sterling Price, Jubal A. Early, Stonewall Jackson, Robert E. Lee, and many other eminent men to throw themselves into the cause of the Southern Confederacy.

Mr. Stephens, for instance, was opposed to secession. He spoke strongly against it in the secession convention of Georgia. After his state decided to leave the Union, he went with her, and soon became vice-president of the Southern Confederacy. Mr. Stephens was a typical Southerner. He represents the Southern soldier, both private and officer. The state had acted as a sovereign state, with the right of secession as one of her reserved rights, and the soldier's duty was but to obey her summons. This is the whole story in a nutshell.

Some say that the South was fighting for slavery, and we cannot deny that without slavery there would probably have been no war. The private soldiers, however, were not fighting for slavery. Probably not over one-third of them owned slaves; few of them owned enough to be worth fighting for; and yet we must admit that fully seven-eighths of them were more or less indirectly interested in slavery as the economic basis of Southern institutions.

IV

"Gideon's Band"

The Southern soldier believed that his cause was just. He felt that he was fighting for local self-government, the same battle that his ancestors had waged in 1776 against George III and his ministry. The odds against him did not affect him. He did not count the enemy. As to the overwhelming numbers opposed to him, let us quote a prominent Northern authority, General D. C. Buell, of the Union army: "It required a naval fleet and 15,000 troops against a weak fort, manned by less than 100 men, at Fort Henry; 35,000 with naval coöperation, to overcome 12,000 at Donelson; 60,000 to secure a victory over 40,000 at Pittsburg Landing (Shiloh); 120,000 to enforce the retreat of 65,000 intrenched after a month's fighting and maneuvering at Corinth; 100,000 repelled by 80,-

THE PRIVATE SOLDIER AND THE SAILOR   201

000 in the first Peninsular campaign against Richmond; 70,000, with a powerful naval force, to inspire the campaign which lasted nine months, against 40,000 at Vicksburg; 115,000 sustaining a frightful repulse from 60,000 at Fredericksburg; 100,000 attacked and defeated by 50,000 at Chancellorsville; 85,000 held in check two days by 40,000 at Antietam; 43,000 retaining the field uncertainly against 38,000 at Stone River (Murfreesboro); 70,000 defeated at Chickamauga, and beleaguered by 70,000 at Chattanooga; 80,000 merely to break the investing line of 45,000 at Chattanooga, and 100,000 to press back 50,000, increased at last to 70,000, from Chattanooga to Atlanta, a distance of 120 miles, and then let go an operation which is commemorated at festive reunions by the standing toast of 'One hundred days under fire'; 50,000 to defeat the investing line of 30,000 at Nashville; and, finally, 120,000 to overcome 60,000 with exhaustion after a struggle of a year in Virginia."

V

Mr. Roosevelt Explains

We have quoted General Buell. We have proved by this prominent Northern general that it took four well-fed, well-equipped Northern soldiers four years to whip one half-starved, ragged, barefooted Confederate. Let us inquire the reason.

Did the South fight a race of cowards? This writer will never admit that. Had the Northern soldier no convictions to fight for? Hundreds of thousands of them were fighting heroically "to save the Union." Mr. Roosevelt offers a partial explanation. He says that the "militant spirit in the Northeast declined during the first half of the nineteenth century, in proportion as the so-called upper classes developed along the line of a wealthy and timid *bourgeois* type, measuring everything by a mercantile standard"—that is, the fighting capacity of the Northern people declined as the love for money grew. To this he adds another reason: the men of the South kept up their warlike spirit by their habits of hunting, riding, and handling weapons and horses.

We cannot agree with Mr. Roosevelt. His explanations do not explain. The men of the Northeast, if they had declined in military ardor, soon regained their spirit; for we soon find them fighting heroically at Shiloh and other places under Sherman, Grant, and Thomas. His statement about the Southern soldiers, also, is open to serious question; for thousands of the Southern troops had lived in stores, offices, banks, and factories, and had had little training in outdoor sports and in the use of firearms; no more glorious rosters illuminate the pages of history than those of the Mobile Cadets, the Richmond Blues, Company F, and the Washington Artillery.

There are better explanations. There are reasons already intimated or stated in these pages. Without repeating too much, we may say: the Southern soldier was fighting for constitutional liberty, for state, for home, to repel invasion; and every man felt that individually he had an important part to play in the great drama.

VI

Wearied Out By Their Own Victories

There is a limit to human endurance. Even this superb body of men had to surrender. After a heroic struggle of four years, the 174,000 starving, half-clad men could not stand before the million well-fed, well-equipped men that the North had under arms in the spring of 1865.

Can history show another army like that? Where shall we find it? Call ancient Sparta from her tomb and she will say: "With me, war was a trade, an occupation; but with the South a mighty principle." Ask Athens why she fell; she will reply: "I forsook the great principles of Marathon, and fought for spoils at Syracuse: the South is greater than I."

Greece has her Marathon; the South, her Chancellorsville and Cold Harbor.

But for his victories, the Southern soldier would have died of cold or of hunger. By capturing food, clothing, and equipment, he fitted himself to meet the enemy. By leaving so many supplies behind him, General N. P. Banks earned the nickname of "Jackson's Commissary." Guns, the soldier captured on the battlefield. Overcoats, he threw away, relying on taking new ones from the enemy when the weather made them necessary.

Well has Charles Francis Adams said that the Southern armies succumbed to sickness, exposure, starvation, but not to defeat.*

---

*From a speech made at Lexington, Va., Jan. 19, 1907.

VII

The Soldier's Joys

We have called the Southern private a tragic figure. In some aspects he is certainly tragic. In other respects, however, he is a bright and happy figure. No merrier fellow ever sat at the camp fire, sang in the parlor, or picked the banjo at an evening party. Even now, his bosom swells as he tells us of the "good times" he had when he was in the army.

Why, then, was he happy?

In the first place, he believed in his cause. He believed that the South was right, and that God was with her. Again, he believed in his commanders. He trusted them, honored them, loved them, and thought that they were almost infallible.

Another source of joy was their unity of purpose. They were controlled by one great idea, love of state and loyalty to her summons. This held them together as a band of brothers. If some had been fighting for slavery, some for the navigation of the Mississippi, some for money, adventure, promotion, they would have disbanded after the dark days of Gettysburg and Vicksburg.

Of the camp life we have already spoken; the soldier's accounts of it are very entertaining. Songs, jests, anecdotes, reminiscences, stories of adventure, hairbreadth escapes—more or less adorned according to the temperament and imagination of each story-teller—all brightened up his life, and helped him to bear his separation from his loved ones.

A great bond of fellowship was the mess. To have eaten at the same mess during the war still binds men together in warm affection; "messmates" is almost a synonym for sweethearts.

All soldiers have some of these pleasures, and some of the foregoing paragraphs would apply to almost any army. A few of the statements, however, apply more particularly to the Southern soldiers. No body of men on earth ever believed more firmly that they were absolutely right. No body of men, except the Japanese, ever rose so unanimously to fight for their country. And, last but not least, they were, as we have said, banded together like brothers and equals; and they treated each other with courtesy and consideration.

VIII

"What Is Life Without Honor?"

These are the words of Stonewall Jackson. In them the South breathed forth her burning question. Honor, as seen in an earlier chapter, was the watchword of our *ante-bellum* fathers.

The Southern army was an army of gentlemen. Its ethics were the ethics of gentlemen. Even its errors were the errors of gentlemen; and the very brotherhood and equality already spoken of interfered very seriously with the discipline and morale of the Southern armies.

The Southern private treated woman with deference. He was considerate of his nurses, and rarely forgot himself in their presence. Ladies who served in the hospitals tell us that drunkenness and profanity were almost unheard of.

The average intelligence of the Southern soldier was very great. He was a good judge of character and of ability, and soon took the measure of his generals. His opinion of war questions is well worth having, even after forty years have passed over him.

The number of educated men in the Southern army is remarkable. Nearly all the colleges and universities poured forth both students and professors. Five hundred students of the University of Virginia joined the army. All but one at William and Mary College enlisted. In the Rockbridge Artillery, there were seven A. M.'s of the University of Virginia, forty-two college graduates, and nineteen students of theological seminaries.

Remember the home the soldier came from. Recall the picture of the father training him in ideals of truth and of courage. Take this man, then, the blood of the Anglo-Saxon tingling in his veins; give him a great cause, a mighty principle to fight for, intolerable grievances to redress; stir him to fever heat with a spirit of devotion, so that he shall "shut his eyes to untold odds and close his ears to every warning of policy or of calculation;"* then give him leaders that he trusts, loves, and honors—and you have a picture of the soldier and sailor of the Southern Confederacy.

---

*Gen. E. C. Walthall, of Miss.

IX

Christ in the Camp

Of earnest Christians, there were large numbers in the Southern army. The Southern soldier came from a Christian home, and was, as already seen, taught to respect and honor religion. Probably no army since that of Cromwell ever had so large a proportion of devout Christians both in the ranks and among the generals. Large numbers of the best ministers of the South entered the army as chaplains, preaching on Sundays, holding services during the week, and following the soldier to the front of battle, to hold the cross before his closing eyes and tell him of the great Captain of his salvation.

Prayer meetings, often conducted by private soldiers, were frequently held, both in camp and when the troops were moving. Such leaders as Stuart, Lee, and Jackson often joined devoutly in these services. Irreverent and utterly irreligious soldiers there of course were, and thousands of them. Gambling would often go on within sight and hearing of the prayer meeting, and many privates and officers used to gamble freely when they visited the cities. We do not say that the army was made up of saints without sinners, but we do say that the moral tone of the Confederate army was remarkably high.

Great religious movements used to sweep through the Southern armies. The soldier, cut off from his dear ones at home, felt very keenly at times the need of divine love and divine companionship, and found both in the God whose praises he had heard so often in the dear cottage on the Tennessee or the Rappahannock.

The Southern soldier, as already said, believed that God was with him, and would give him the victory. Great was his disappointment and his grief in April, 1865. For a time he felt as if God "had forgotten to be gracious," as if "his mercy were clean gone forevermore." Soon, however, he brushed away his tears, opened his Bible at another verse, and started out with determination to rebuild his home, till his land, and redeem his state from the carpetbagger and the scalawag.

To-day, the Christian veteran is the pillar of our public worship. He often stands in the pulpit, and tells us how to suffer and be strong. His courage and his wisdom have laid new foundations for the South to build upon.

Among her Christian leaders, the South fondly remembers, not only Lee, Jackson, and Stuart, but Polk, the bishop-general, who laid down his pastoral staff and took up the sword because his people needed his West Point training, and Jefferson Davis, who, when he heard that Richmond must fall, was engaged in the most solemn ordinance of the Christian religion.

X

"Pirates"

We have spoken incidentally of the Southern sailor, but he richly deserves special mention. What a halo decks his brow! What lustre hangs around his memory! Under

J. E. B. STUART

such leaders as Semmes, Buchanan, Catesby Jones, Tatnall, and others, he won a glorious immortality.

"Pirate," Raphael Semmes was branded. "Should have been hung at the yardarm" was the verdict often hurled against him. If so, why was John Paul Jones's body not hanged on a gibbet, instead of being brought across the ocean and buried with national honors at Annapolis? Jones and Semmes were "pirates" of the same order.

Some stigmatize Semmes and his crew as privateers, using the word as a contemptuous epithet. Semmes, however, was not a privateer, but was regularly commissioned by the Confederate government. Suppose he had been a privateer, it was preposterous to denounce him; for privateers were long popular with the United States government. Of John Paul Jones, the Revolutionary hero, we have already spoken. In the war of 1812, privateers played havoc with the commerce of England. In 1856, when the great nations drew up the Declaration of Paris, the United States flatly refused to accept the clause which declared that privateering was piracy.

There never lived a braver hero than the Southern sailor. History, poetry, and eloquence may turn to Hampton Roads for inspiration. What is more sublime than the *Virginia?* When she steamed out of Norfolk on the 8th of March, 1862, to dare the Federal fleet, her crew expected the vessel to sink at any moment; they had no idea that she would carry them across the harbor. They simply braved the waters. See them ram the *Cumberland,* fire the *Congress,* and drive the *Minnesota* into shoal water where the *Vir-*

ginia could not follow her! The world wondered; the North was panic-stricken.

This victory of the 8th of March was due to the superiority of the Southern vessel, and not to any lack of bravery on the other side. It was a one-sided affair: wood on one side; thick iron, supported by a powerful battering-ram, on the other. The heroism of that day consisted in the Southern crew's risking the sea in a totally untried vessel, of entirely untried mechanism; while the Northern crew deserve great admiration for fighting such a creature.

Early on March the 9th, appeared the "little *Monitor*," as she is fondly called in many volumes. She stood between the *Virginia* and the stranded *Minnesota*. For three or more hours, these two ironclads engaged in a colossal duel. The *Virginia* had size, weight, a much larger battery, and a ram; the *Monitor* had the most powerful guns ever launched up to that time, and she could be much more easily maneuvered. Both crews expected their ship to sink at any moment: each was a novelty in warfare, a mere experiment. The two vessels fought like hyenas; but neither could hurt the other seriously. Both crews became exhausted, physically and nervously. The *Virginia* had her funnel and smokestack shot away, and was otherwise more or less wounded. About 12:30 or 12:45 P. M., both combatants stopped fighting. Just as the officers of the *Virginia* were conferring as to continuing the fight, the pilots said that they would have to take the vessel up to Norfolk right away or wait another twenty-four hours for a tide that would float her into the harbor. When the *Virginia* steamed toward Norfolk, the electric wires flashed numerous messages North claiming a great victory for the *Monitor*.

The *Monitor* deserves our highest admiration. The fight of March the 9th was rightly pronounced by the Federal Congress "a remarkable battle."

The *Monitor* did stand in the way of the *Virginia*, and save the Federal fleet from total destruction. She, however, did not save Washington, Philadelphia, and New York; for the *Virginia* could not have gone up there to shell the White House, as the Federal cabinet so nervously dreaded.

The *Virginia* staid at the Norfolk navy yard a month for repairs, especially waiting for her shutters. On the 11th of April, she came down to look for the Monitor and her twenty-five wooden consorts; but they could not be found. Again, early in May she renewed the challenge. Orders had been issued by President Lincoln and Hon. Gideon Welles, Federal secretary of war, "that the *Monitor* be not too much exposed."*

Some months later the crew of the *Monitor* applied to the Federal Congress for prize money for disabling the *Virginia;* but their claim was not allowed, the *Virginia* having been destroyed by her own officers on May the 11th, 1862.

The South is greatly indebted to the United States government for volume 7, series I, of the so-called War of the Rebellion records, as a casual reading of the first hundred pages will convince any reasonable man that the *Monitor* won no victory except in so far as she saved the Federal fleet from annihilation.

Records of the Rebellion, vol. 7, series I.

The charge made by some Northern people that the South stole the *Merrimac* is too puerile to notice. The Gosport navy yard was abandoned by the United States government, and the *Merrimac* was scuttled and sunk by the Federals. The Confederates raised the vessel, fitted it up with armor, and called it *Virginia*.

CHAPTER V

THE WOMEN OF THE CONFEDERACY

I

The Truest Patriots

OF the great generals of the South, much has been said and written. In the following pages, we ourselves shall make some attempt, though utterly inadequate, to outline the career of Lee, Jackson, and Albert Sidney Johnston, and to give some idea of the great deeds of Stuart, Beauregard, Forrest, Joseph E. Johnston, and other heroes of the Southern Confederacy. Of the private soldier and sailor, also, some record is found in history; and the present writer has attempted, though all in vain, to throw upon the canvas the outlines of that noble and tragic figure.

The women of the South, however, are but little noticed in our histories. They patiently await the historian's pen, the poet's song, and the sculptor's chisel; and all these will find in the women of the Confederacy a fit subject for their art and a theme fraught with inspiration; but history, art, and poetry alike will shrink in dismay from attempting a picture at all complete; for to do full justice to the subject is utterly beyond the power of historian, poet, painter, and sculptor; is, indeed, beyond the reach of human imagination.

President Davis said that the Southern women were "better patriots" than the men; and Stonewall Jackson in a letter to one of them said, "They are patriots in the truest sense of the word." No reflection upon the true men of the South was intended by these great leaders; but they no doubt meant that all the women were patriots, first, last, and forever, and that they had more unshaken faith in their cause than the men, and suffered more willingly for it.

If there were few spies and traitors among the men, among the women there were still fewer. If a woman ever led the enemy over bypaths to the rear of a Southern army, tradition is silent about it. While some men here and there are still spoken of as having sent information to the enemy, the women are far less numerous. The name of such a woman is a hissing and a byword, more execrated than that of Benedict Arnold; and her very house is still pointed out, almost as an object of execration.

The Quaker poet, Whittier, has immortalized the mythical Barbara Frietchie. For some Southern poet, the real Hettie Cary, Belle Boyd, and other heroines of the South offered abundant inspiration.

II

Wives and Mothers of Heroes

Willingly, gladly, though tearfully, the Southern woman gave her dear ones to the Confederacy. Filled, thrilled with "patriotic zeal," the maiden bound on her warrior's sash, the wife girded on her husband's sword, the mother pressed her son to her heart, breathed a few brave words in his ear, kissed him a hundred times—sending them forth to fight for state, for home, and for loved ones. In their vocabulary, there was no such word as fail. Hopeful, buoyant, confident, assured that their cause was just and that a just cause must succeed, they never dreamed of failure. Men might reason and calculate the chances of defeat; women, never. A man might argue that one ill-fed, half-clad, half-shod, ill-equipped soldier could not hold out long against four well-fed, thoroughly-equipped men; but the women closed the argument with an incredulous smile, and reminded him that Lee was at the head of the armies and that God was in heaven.

The Southern woman was thoroughly informed as to the movements of troops, and as to the details of battles. She read the newspapers eagerly and greedily, would prefer a paper to a good dinner if called upon to choose between them; and, after the second year of the war, when both were scarce, she had less trouble in getting the paper than in getting the dinner, but bore her loss of dinner with Spartan fortitude.

On all subjects connected with the war, she always had her "opinion." She "lambasted" poor President Davis for not permitting "our" army to take Washington! She thought Beauregard was the "handsomest creature" and "so brave," and wished that he and Joe Johnston had let Jackson take "old Lincoln" prisoner in the White House. She still shakes her head wisely, and tells us what Southern generals "ruined the Confederacy." These opinions she is handing down to her children and her children's children.

III

The Recruiting Officer

No fellow with a sore thumb and his arm in a sling could deceive a Southern woman. She would soon inquire where his regiment was, and sing him back to the army. If some admirer of hers was looking for a bombproof position when able to be in the field, she would make it warm for him at the next "starvation party." Just as he was hanging over the piano and ogling her with devouring glances, she would strike up a song somewhat as follows:

> "Wouldst thou have me love thee, dearest,
>   With a woman's proudest heart,
> Which shall ever hold thee nearest,
>   Shrined in its inmost part?
> Listen, then! My country's calling
>   On her sons to meet the foe!
> Leave these groves of rose and myrtle;
>   Drop thy dreamy harp of love!
> Like young Körner,* scorn the turtle,†
>   When the eagle screams above!"

The young swain might not know who Körner was, or what kind of turtle he must scorn; but, by the time Arabella sang

---

*A young poet of Germany killed in the war of liberation.
†Used by the poets for "turtle-dove."

the rest of this well-known Alabama poem,* Jack would hear a good deal of snickering among the girls, and see the soldiers present nudging one another. Among a small class of men, Arabella was one of the regular recruiting officers of the Confederacy; the other army had "bounties" for the present, and pensions for the indefinite future.

At church on Sundays, Arabella continued her work of recruiting. If some young fellow that neighborhood gossips said ought to be at the front but was dodging duty, tried to be polite, and came to help her off her horse or out of the carriage, she would hardly give him time to get near her before she asked him, "Why aren't you with your regiment?"

IV

"The Uncrowned Queens of the South"

Woman's battlefield was at home, amid the cares and the drudgery of domestic life. While change and excitement helped to keep up the soldier's spirits, an eternal sameness of anxiety and of dread weighed upon his wife, his sisters, and his mother. While he was filled to intoxication with "the rapture of the strife," as the poets call it, she was bowed down with the cares and the responsibilities of the home, by wild rumors from the front, and by a constant dread of terrible news from the hospital or the battlefield.

No bugle, no drum, called her to her daily battle. Day after day, she arose from alarming dreams "tired by her

---
*By A. B. Meek, of Alabama.

night's rest," to begin the humdrum life of the farm or of the workroom, and saw her means of subsistence growing more and more precarious. No Joan of Arc was needed to lead the armies of the South, and none made her appearance. Few opportunities for fame or distinction came to the Southern woman; her chief glory was to be queen of the home, and to write to her husband or son that all were well and strong, and that he must feel no uneasiness about them. Often these words were penned with trembling fingers, and blotted with tear drops. In quiet and seclusion, she passed her days, craving no publicity, and not wishing to see her name heralded to the nations.

Occasionally, however, some heroine would all unconsciously "wake up some morning and find herself famous." Some patriotic song sung by beautiful lips, with a chorus of blushes, would send a young girl's name ringing through the Southern army; or some Emma Sansom,* showing a great soldier the way to surprise the enemy's cavalry, and riding in front of him on the saddle, ostensibly as a guide, but really to shield him from the Federal bullet, would flash all unconsciously into fame and immortality.

A war heroine of Virginia is Belle Boyd, of Martinsburg, now a town of West Virginia. She rendered such valuable service to the South as to receive the special thanks of Stonewall Jackson and the special hatred of E. M. Stanton, Federal secretary of war. She made her *début* in public life by shooting a Northern soldier that addressed her mother and herself "in language as offensive as it is possible to con-

---

*The young Georgia girl that showed Forrest where to find Streight's cavalry. See *Confederate Veteran*, May 1895.

ceive," and she was completely exonerated by the commanding officer. Later she was confined in Northern prisons, condemned to hard labor in jail, and, as a special favor, was banished to the far South. After a while she was allowed to go to Canada, with the threat that, if ever caught in the United States again, she would be shot.

V.

"Stitch, Stitch, Stitch"

All this anxiety and this responsibility, without companionship, would have driven our mothers and our grandmothers to insanity. Instinctively they sought each other's society. Those that lived in towns and cities, or in the country within reach of county courthouses, used to meet frequently to sew and knit for the soldiers. Coats, overcoats, pantaloons, and havelocks were made in great quantities. The socks that were knit by "saints of all ages," an unabridged arithmetic could not number. Click, click, click, went the busy needles, day after day, all day long, with hardly a minute for pea soup and corn bread at dinner time. Click, click, click, went the busy needles again at night, till the "Confederate candle"* burned to a frazzle, or till old grandmother's spectacles fell off as she dozed in her chair,

---

*A "Confederate candle" was made of porous cord of various sizes, saturated in beeswax and wound on a spool or on a stick. The spool could of course stand on one end; the stick was put on a wooden stand. The end of the string had to be manipulated with the fingers at short intervals, making the whole matter very troublesome. Sometimes the whole apparatus would catch on fire and go up in smoke, leaving the family in Egyptian darkness for the rest of the night.

and Mother and Auntie said it was time to go to bed and get a good night's rest.

Along with these socks, went oftentimes a pretty necktie, a handkerchief, a pair of knit gloves, and a piece of paper carefully folded, on which was written in a smooth, ladylike hand—not the great big hand now in vogue—some message of love or a text of scripture; such as,

"The Lord is my shepherd; I shall not want."

Oftentimes, the hands that made these garments milked the cows, planted and hoed the vegetables, and made crops to feed the family. In numberless cases, these women superintended the work of the servants on the farms and the plantations, and thus furnished food, not only for themselves, their children and servants, but for the soldiers in camp and at the front of battle.

As said in another chapter, it was often a woman's hand that led out the dark battalions, and her brain that made the plans for feeding and clothing the helpless little ones and the equally helpless servants. In docility and obedience for the most part, these faithful creatures performed their daily labors. Regularly and sincerely they inquired about "Marster," "Marse Tom," "Marse Henry," and many were deeply distressed at the sad news that too often came from the battlefield. Of very serious insult offered these defenseless women by the negroes, there is no record; a few cases such as we often read of now would have disbanded the armies of the Confederacy, and privates and officers would have vied with each other in leaving the army in order to protect their homes from insult worse than that which produced secession.

VI

"Gallant Black Tom" and Treacherous Isaac

The friendly relations between the races were for the most part undisturbed. Where the Federal army passed, however, some change was noticed. Some few servants became insolent, and a good many were unwilling to work as usual. Large numbers on the other hand, clung to their "white folks" with noble fidelity. "I'll eat dirt and sleep in de leaves, 'fore I'll leave my ole Mistis and my young Missy," said gallant "black Tom" one morning, when told by the Federals that he was free. Of treachery worthy of an Indian, however, we had some cases, notably that of Gilmore Simms's body-servant Isaac. Though South Carolina was doomed beforehand to havoc and destruction, orders were given by the promoters of the brave "March through Georgia" to spare Simms's house, on the ground that he did not belong to the South alone, but to the whole country. This order was obeyed. The house and library were spared by the enemy. A few months later, however, before Mr. Simms could bring his family home, it was burned by Isaac, to whom the great *littérateur* had ever been a kind and a humane master.

One of the marvels of history is the fidelity of the Southern negro to his master during that awful era. This fidelity is appreciated in the South, and makes the relations between many old colored people and their white neighbors very tender. The old colored women, not being politicians, seem to feel closer to the whites. To meet "old Mammy" is a great treat to many of this writer's generation; and the good creature's eye glistens as she tells her friends, "This is one of my white chillun." Unfortunately these old mammies are dying off, and their places are being left vacant.

VII

War Poets of the South

As Greece had her Tyrtaeus and Germany her Arndt, Körner, and others to stir their soldiers with patriotic odes, so the South had her Timrod, her Hayne, her Thompson, her McCabes, her Randall, her Simms, her Cooke, her Ryan, and other poets. Women also touched the lyre, and thrilled the Southern heart. Catherine Warfield, Margaret Preston, Fanny Downing, Mary B. Clarke, and other gifted women wrote songs that were worth many regiments to the Confederate armies. Many of their poems stir our pulses even in these piping days of peace, and they are invaluable to the student of that fearful revolution. They should be read and memorized by our children and our children's children. As every English child knows the *Battle of the Baltic,* the *Revenge,* and many other such ballads; as German children know the *Sword Song, What Is the German's Fatherland?,* and other heroic songs; so our Southern children should know *Maryland, My Maryland*, the *Sword of Lee*, Catherine Warfield's *Manassas*, the *Song of the Snow, Somebody's Darling*, and other poems that compress into a few lines whole libraries of history and whole centuries of woe.

VIII

"Starvation Parties"

All shadow and no sunshine would make a nation of idiots and madmen. Relief there must be or the o'ercharged heart will break, and reason forsake her seat. In self-defense, therefore, the younger women of the South, wherever possible, and when no fresh sorrow prevented, used to come together to sing, play games, talk and dance with one another, or with the beardless boys of fifteen or sixteen, slurred as "trundle-bed trash" after the return of peace made them no longer needed. If one or two of the soldier boys happened to be at home on a furlough or on sick leave, what a charm would be added to the entertainment! What a hero in the parlor! How the fair maids would hang upon his lips as he graphically described his last battle, told how he captured a "whole company of Yankees," and, like Goldsmith's old soldier, "shouldered his crutch, to show how fields were won." If he had a voice, how beautifully his baritone or his tenor would blend with Lucy's soprano, Julia's alto, and Alice's contralto. While the dancing was going on, the old folks did not come into the parlor;

for many hearts were too anxious and too sad to care for dancing. But—

> "Music hath charms to soothe a savage breast,
> To soften rocks or bend a knotted oak,"

as the poet says; and soon the old gentleman, the old lady, the maiden aunt, the sick cousin from the country, a good many neighbors, not forgetting the Rev. Dr. Hipkins, kissing pastor of half the pretty girls in the neighborhood— all came pouring in to hear the music. *When This Cruel War is Over, Maryland, My Maryland,* the *Bonnie Blue Flag, Dixie, Her Bright Smile Haunts Me Still, Lorena, Stonewall Jackson's Way,* and other favorite melodies, kept the whole neighborhood awake until an unearthly hour between night and morning.

Rarely was that music stopped by a call to supper. Those singers neither wet their whistles nor filled up the vacuum below the diaphragm. Those were "water parties," or "starvation parties." It was always Lent; self-denial, fasting, was the order of the day. Happy were those people that had had two decent meals, "let alone" expecting anything after supper.

Sometimes, however, there would be a sort of subscription party, each family interested contributing one or two dishes, puddings, and so forth. "Sorghum puddings?" do you ask? Goodness gracious! Or one of those delicious puddings that a South Carolina lady who refugeed in Charlotte, North Carolina, during the war called a "master-

JOSEPH E. JOHNSTON

piece of the culinary art"—a dish so tempting that we reserve it for a later paragraph.

IX

"A Ministering Angel Thou"

Self-denial, we said, was the order of the day. Yes, self-denial in a thousand forms; some of it unavoidable, but much of it voluntary. Women delicately reared tore the carpets from their floors and made blankets (so-called) for the soldiers. Planters stopped raising cotton as a selling crop, and raised grain to feed the armies. Ladies sold their jewelry, and would have cut the hair off their heads, if the plan suggested by a niece of President Madison, to sell the hair in order to raise money for the Confederacy, had been thought practicable.

All this time, the women of the South kept up a brave heart and had no idea of failure. Their hopeful letters to friends and loved ones at the front inspired the soldiers, nerved them for greater effort, and gave them fortitude under sufferings and reverses. So well was this known that all through Georgia and South Carolina Sherman's "triumphal" heroes told Southern ladies, "You women could have stopped this war long ago if you had chosen to do so."

The queen of the home, she was in the hospital an angel of mercy. Eternity alone can gauge the work done by the Southern woman in relieving pain, in comforting the weary, and in robbing death of some of its terrors. Friend and foe alike received her tender ministrations. The wounded, she cheered and entertained with an ease and a grace that Southern women have always been known for; before the dying eyes, she held up the cross of Him who "went about doing good;" and the dead she saw decently buried and, if no minister could be found, would herself read a part of the funeral service over his remains rather than let him go without Christian burial.

She wrote letters home for the sick and the wounded, and added a cheering word of her own. To bereaved ones far away, she wrote tenderly and sympathetically, in words that only a Christian and a lady could command, telling them of the dead boy's last hours, of his last messages to dear ones at home, of his trust in a Saviour's love, and of the last words that indicated a triumphant death.

X

Cupid and "General Lee's Socks"

Even hospital life had its sunshine, its brighter aspects. Romance sometimes entered those halls of pain and of suffering; for, after the darts of the enemy had been pulled out and the soldier was being nursed back to health and vigor, the blind god Cupid would enter the hospital and hurl a dart at him, and give him a wound from which he never recovered. To make myself clearer to the young and hitherto unwounded reader: the soldiers often fell in love with the ladies that nursed them—pity being akin to love, and gratitude greatly promoting the tender passion—the two were drawn into the snares of Cupid, and as a result there were many marriages "before that cruel war was over." Difference in age did not balk Cupid, a good many young fellows being so grateful as to marry ladies as old as their mothers, or certainly as old as their "old maid sisters."

In one of the largest hospitals of Virginia, much fun was afforded by "General Lee's socks." They acted, also, as a fine recruiting officer. Of these articles of apparel, Miss Emily Mason, a survivor of the old "effete aristocracy," and one of the "angels of mercy," gives an interesting account in the Charleston *News and Courier*. Mrs. Lee, it seems, once sent Miss Mason some of the General's socks, too much darned to be comfortable. These were kept by the nurses to lend to any soldier well enough to return to duty but not especially eager to do so. They hurt his feet so much that he could hardly walk; and the other soldiers soon saw that he was wearing the famous socks, and they enjoyed the joke immensely. A word to the wise being sufficient, the well soldier soon returned to the post of duty; and, after a while, the mere offer of these socks was considered as an official discharge from the hospital and as an invitation from the ladies to go back to his regiment.

XI

A Starving Nation

As the war went on, starvation literally stared the whole South in the face. Not only the soldiers, but the women and children, also, often suffered the pangs of hunger. Long marches were made by troops on little or no nourishment;

for a soldier's knapsack often contained nothing to eat except a few handfuls of parched corn, and many men died from slow starvation.

At home, the families of these men had a life-and-death struggle to keep the wolf from the door. After the second year of the war, the suffering in many homes was terrible. Flour and sugar oftentimes were unknown quantities. Corn meal was gladly eaten by the most fragile women; for sugar and syrup, the usual substitute was sorghum, made from home-grown sugar cane. A chest of light brown sugar gotten through the blockade, a man of means regarded as a great bonanza. Peas were used considerably instead of flour and meal and had to be given to convalescents. The ill very often suffered for food to tempt the palate. Corn meal was cooked in every way imaginable, "rebel bread" and "Beauregard cakes" being very popular. "Excellent poundcake," too, was made of corn meal.

"A masterpiece of the culinary art" was a "fine pudding" (*sic*) made of corn meal and dried apples boiled together, and eaten with a sauce of butter and sorghum.

Coffee passed out of memory. Even the Rio, generally so distasteful to the higher classes, would have been greatly relished. The usual substitute for coffee were meal, sweet potatoes, wheat, rye, peanuts, chestnuts, and okra seed—all parched.

In numberless homes, tea, also, faded almost out of memory. For black tea, blackberry leaves were used; for green, holly leaves. A good many used sassafras. "Fodder tea" was used in some families.

To get two meals a day of such stuff, with an occasional slice of fat bacon, many were truly thankful. As a result of eating salt meat so constantly, many refined women suffered with scurvy and kindred diseases.

All these and other privations, the women of the South bore unmurmuringly. They thanked God that they could exist, and let the men stay at the front, to fight for home, loved ones, and freedom. A mother and several daughters who belonged to a family known to every schoolboy in America,* and who had sent five sons and brothers into the army, used to sing their "grace" in Richmond over "pea-soup and corn bread for breakfast, corn bread and pea-soup for dinner."

Medicines, also, became very scarce and very expensive. The United States made quinine "contraband of war," that is, would not let it come through the lines to relieve the soldiers. Of course, soldiers, non-combatants, women and children all suffered immeasurably. A substitute for quinine was dogwood and poplar, boiled strong, and made into a paste. Home-made mustard, opium, and castor oil were tried in some places; with what highly beneficial results, one may imagine.

At such sufferings, the demons in Hades must have shivered with horror; but

"Man's inhumanity to man
Makes countless thousands mourn."

---

*But almost ignored by the *Encyclopedia Britannica*. (See pages 101, 102.)

XII

The "Triumphal March" Through Georgia

On May 4, 1864, simultaneously by the watch, General Grant moved upon Lee and Richmond; Gen. W. T. Sherman, upon Joseph E. Johnston and Atlanta. In spite of overwhelming odds, Joe Johnston, that "great master of logistics",* skillfully eluded Sherman, and struck him severely without bringing on a general engagement. Hood, superseding Johnston, surrendered Atlanta; and Sherman, having seized the granary of the Southern Confederacy, determined to march north, via Savannah, Charleston, and Columbia, unite with Grant and "get Lee beeween his thumb and his forefinger."† Sherman's march through Georgia, in which he consumed twenty million dollars' worth of property and destroyed four times as much, is vividly portrayed in some histories and encyclopedias as a "triumphal march;" and Northern poets surprised Sherman by singing him into immortality.‡

All this is written in letters of blood and agony upon the hearts of Southern women. Their sufferings, their fears, their unutterable dread, no pen can describe, and imagination itself turns pale with despair when asked to depict these horrors. As to whether Halleck and Sherman intended that their plan of campaign should be so interpreted

---

*This compliment is quoted from Gen. Richard Taylor, the eminent soldier.

† See Appleton's *Cyclopedia Amer. Biog.*, V, p. 505, for a very striking picture of Sherman showing President Lincoln and others how easily this could be done.

‡Little Laura Galt's refusing quite recently to sing this song in school made her a heroine in the South, and the veterans conferred great honors upon her.

and executed, an omniscient God has already rendered his verdict; but no one can either deny or palliate the pilferings and the plunderings, the bullyings and the brutalities, the oaths and the execrations, committed, uttered, and gloried in by Sherman's "bummers" and Wilson's and Kilpatrick's "raiders," in their "triumphal" march through Georgia into South Carolina.

"But for these women, the rebels would have surrendered long ago," was a favorite ejaculation of the doughty warriors. "Get up, old woman; praying will do you no good now," said an officer to an old lady that was saying her morning prayers as the crowd burst in upon her. A few chivalrous Federal soldiers tried to stop these fearful brutalities; and some, secretly bringing food to those who had seen the last crust snatched from the hands of crying children, apologized for the brutalities.

Graves were opened in the hope of finding treasure, and the bodies of the dead—white and black—literally left to dogs and to vultures.

In Virginia, also, similar atrocities were committed. In Williamsburg, the old College of William and Mary was burned, its tombs rifled, and its books saved only by brave and patriotic women. The noble women of the place were cursed and shot at, but generally by stragglers or other brutes not under McClellan's control. The Military Institute at Lexington was burned, and the Valley of Virginia so desolated that "a crow in passing over it had to carry his rations."*

---

*This classic phrase will make the name of Sheridan's army immortal, long after T. B. Read's poem, *Sheridan's Ride*, has passed into oblivion. When the South produces

One of the most touching pictures of Southern life during the war is the scene around Atlanta after the fall of that city. The Confederate authorities opened a provision store where provisions were exchanged for minie balls. Many of the needy—and nearly all were needy—women of the country around Atlanta turned out with baskets to gather up the balls lying on the battlefields. A perfect godsend was an old exploded magazine, around which great "lead-mines" were discovered by the poor suffering women. Great was their joy when their heavy baskets were exchanged for food to keep the family from actual starvation.

When the army passed by on its "triumphal" march to meet the forces of Joseph E. Johnston, a very prominent commander is reported to have said that he left behind him a very able lieutenant to complete his work, namely, "General Starvation."

XIII

The Women Decline to Surrender

Some grim humor lights up even the lurid horror of this march of the vandals. It was reported that all the boys would be killed to keep them from becoming rebels in the future. In some places, accordingly, mothers dressed up their boys in girls' clothes. One of these boy-girls was sliding down the banisters, and the anxious mother called out, "Bessie, my son, come down from there." "Ah," said

---

another Poe, he will write *The Crow* and give the Southern view of the triumphal ride.

a heroic "bummer," who was paying his respects to the silver and other valuables, "I thought it was strange that all the children in this state were girls."

Caligula said that he wished all the Romans had one neck, so that he might use his famous axe with great effect and with little exertion. A famous hero of the "triumphal march" is reported to have said that he would bring all the women of Georgia and of South Carolina to the washtub. Not all the perfumes of Arabia can sweeten the names of the men that carried torch, famine, and insult to the women and children of the South, or of him who, in his "Order Number 28," offered an egregious and nameless insult to the noble women of New Orleans.

The kindest friends that the famishing women and children found in the "triumphal" army were the horses. They must have had Hebrew owners, for they carried out faithfully the old Mosaic command to leave some gleanings for the poor and the stranger. These kind creatures left corn on the ground, corn in the troughs and mangers, corn in the old mahogany bureau drawers used as troughs by the vandal army. What a godsend to the conquered women and children! After the invading hosts moved on, the wretched, shivering, terror-stricken women scratched up this corn, separated it from the dirt and stuff into which much of it had fallen, and postponed a few days what seemed inevitable starvation.

As a result of these privations, many feeble women, children, and old men actually perished. One of General Longstreet's brigadiers said quite recently that two of his children died from lack of proper nourishment

Salt became very scarce all over the South, and the Southern housekeeper was often at her wits' ends to supply the deficiency. Old meat house floors were carefully scraped and the salt boiled out of the mixed earth and drippings.

Still the "liars" and "rebels," as the "boys" and "bummers" called our dear women, would not surrender; would not write the letters that might have disbanded the armies of Lee, Hood, and Johnston. The Grecian women, during the Trojan war, wrote to their husbands that, if they did not come home, other men would soon usurp their places; the women of the South wrote to their husbands, sons, and lovers not to come home until they had driven the invader back across the Potomac. Again, the South had no faithless Helens to coquette with the Northern soldiery. While the Greeks were besieging Troy to punish Paris, son of Priam, for enticing away the wife of the king of Sparta, that heartless wanton was placidly living in Troy, in the constant society of the man who had thus betrayed his hospitality. The Helens of the South regarded the foe with unutterable loathing, and only abject dread kept them from showing their disgust more than they did. The few marriages that took place between Southern girls and Northern soldiers after the war were generally bread-and-butter affairs, Cupid being absent altogether.

XIV

Heroines in Homespun

In nothing was woman's self-denial more marked than in the clothes with which she gladly disfigured herself for the sake of her country. It may be said without fear of contradiction that no women in the world have ever dressed more tastefully than the ladies of the South. A Southern girl in a cheap muslin is often "queen of hearts" in the ball room or the parlor. During the war, however, the Southern woman willingly parted with fashion plates, mantua-makers, and milliners. Dragging her grandmother's long disused loom out of the dusty attic, she wove herself "homespun" for dresses, used old buttons long out of fashion, and, when these wore out, bored holes in persimmon seeds and covered them with the same fabric that her dress was made of. Her grandmother's old dresses were taken out of chests and drawers long given up to moths and to dust, and the lovely girls of the South walked unflinchingly up the church aisle, flaunting the old gourd and the palm-leaf patterns of bygone generations. Dyeing was much in vogue, and many dresses were, with the aid of sundry plants and herbs, often changed in color to suit the seasons. Curtain chintzes were often used for dress material. Late in the war, the mere wearing of clothes was all that was expected, fit, shape, "set" and material being little noticed. By tacit consent, no lady ever laughed at the costume of another. The one supreme object was to exist, keep soul and body together, while the men were fighting for fireside, home, and country.

At first, old hats were "fixed up" and "made over" until the parts refused to hang together. Then corn shucks and palmetto were called into requisition. After ribbon was out of the question, hats were trimmed with dress goods, such as shepherd's plaid homespun, and with almost any wretched stuff they could find in the attic, or on the shelves of country merchants.

Stockings were knit from cotton spun and twisted on the plantation. Shoes were made of oilcloth by the plantation cobbler, and fit accordingly. Sherman's "triumphal" heroes had no little sport ridiculing Southern ladies into whose presence they could not have come except in companies of thousands supported by pistols and bayonets.

XV

Her Monuments and Histories

The surrender at Appomattox surprised, amazed, stupefied the women of the South. They could not, would not, believe that such a thing was possible. Like General Taylor, they never surrendered. For four long years, they had shut their eyes to the possibility of failure; when it came, it completely dazed them. Erelong, however, their spirits began to rally. They saw that the men needed comfort, help, and inspiration; and where else could they find it save in the smiles of her who had cheered them in the long conflict? The power of recuperation, of rallying after a great blow, for which the Southern people are now noted, came to their assistance, and the women of the South had no little share in that kindly gift of a merciful Providence. In a short while, they began to take heart and to hope for the future. Accordingly, when the soldier limped back to his dismantled home, his fences gone, his slaves either gone away, or waiting sulkily to see what part of Marster's place "Mars Linkum" would give each one of them—penniless, dejected, hopeless—the queen of that once cheerful and happy home met him at the door with a loving embrace and a kiss as fresh as that of the day of betrothal, told him how proud she was that he had done his duty, thanked God that he was spared to her and the little ones, and pointed him hopefully to the future.

As soon as she had had time to give an air of cleanliness and of refinement—not of real comfort—to the dismantled house, and make the place, however humble, look a little homelike, she went out to gather spring flowers to deck the graves of the fallen heroes. Out of their first earnings, she spared a few shillings to help with a monument to the "unreturning." From then till now, her zeal has never abated, and, on court-greens, in cemeteries, in hamlets, towns, and cities all over the South, she is rearing shafts, statues, columns, and pyramids of granite, of bronze and of marble, to hand down to unborn generations the name and the fame of the Confederate soldier.

Like the great mass of the old soldiers, she offers no apologies. She is not sorry for the fight they made, and is sorry they were not successful. If she was the "truest patriot," she was also the "biggest rebel." She has never been reconstructed. She refuses to sympathize with any one-armed Union soldier that she is thrown with, and, if she can say it without being too abrupt and rude, tells him that he would have two arms if he had staid at home and "minded his own business." Her opinion of "the new scalawag" and of certain recent politicians, speakers, and writers of the North can best be expressed in sign language, the English with its 300,000 words being utterly inadequate. Her contempt for renegade Southerners is absolutely beyond the imagination of an unabridged dictionary.

She is now organizing societies to save her father's name from being branded with treason and rebellion. She hurls back in scorn the charge that her father was a traitor and a "rebel." Whether the people that persist in making this charge be penny-a-liners in some newspaper office, or editors of influential journals; whether they be ignorant and uncultured "schoolmarms" in some obscure village, or learned professors in rich universities, she indignantly denounces them as slanderers, and confidently appeals to history to vindicate the name and the honor of her father, either lying in a far-distant soldier's grave, or bearing his "good gray head" proudly aloft in advancing years among a people that delight to honor him.

The women of Carthage are famous for turning their hair into bowstrings, and hurling great stones on the Romans. The women of Jerusalem fought like hyenas when the Holy City was besieged by the armies of Cæsar. The women of Londonderry earned immortal fame during the siege of their city by the French and the Irish. All glory to these, we say, and we envy them not their melancholy honors. But, when Clio, the muse of history, puts her trumpet to her æonian lips and looks down on the nations for a woman to herald to fame, she will turn the star-like glory of her immortal eyes to her who, hungry and thirsty as her soul fainted in her, clad in garments that provoked the ridicule of a brutal soldiery, saw the bread dragged from the mouth of her crying infant and the fire devouring the home of her fathers, saw the graves of her dead rifled and the bones of her children exposed to the dogs and the vultures, and yet hurled defiance at the brutal invader, while crying, "Would God that I had other sons to send to the front of battle!"

CHAPTER VI

LEE AND HIS PALADINS

I

Lee Goes with His State

THIS is a book of sketches. Its object is to pass very rapidly over great wars, especially those treated fully in all the histories. In regard, then, to the campaigns of Lee, Jackson, Joseph E. Johnston, Albert Sidney Johnston, Forrest, and other heroes of the South, we shall speak very briefly, going into details in those matters only which are either overlooked or treated too lightly in many text-books.

The first four men named above were "West Pointers." They were sent to West Point by their states, and their education was paid for out of the taxes paid by the states that sent them. They were not objects of charity. When they left the Academy, they had as much right to resign from the "old army" as any other officers. Some writers of history speak of them as stealing their education from the United States, and treacherously turning their swords against the generous friend that had given them an education.

We have already seen that Lee and other Southern cadets were taught at West Point that a state had the right to se-

R. E. LEE

cede from the Union.* General Lee deplored secession. He simply "went with his state." Most of the Southern men in the "old army" "went with their states." As soon as Albert Sidney Johnston heard that Texas had seceded, he resigned an honorable position in the United States army, rode into the wilderness between his post and his state, and offered her his services. Jackson was a states-rights Democrat, and, after Virginia seceded, accepted a position in her forces, taking the cadets of the Virginia Military Institute with him as drillmasters.

All the Southern leaders believed in states rights. They believed that their supreme allegiance was due the state, and that at her call they should leave the Federal service and help to drive back any army that crossed the Potomac. In 1861, few men in the South believed otherwise.

II

The Hall of Fame

In 1861, Colonel R. E. Lee was prominent in the United States army. He was offered the command of the forces levied to invade Virginia. When Virginia elected him one of her major-generals, he accepted, saying that only in her defense would he ever draw his sword.

In the spring of 1862, General Lee became famous. In defending Richmond against McClellan, he took his place among the greatest commanders of history.

Every student has read often about the Seven Days' bat-

---
*See pages 188, 189.

tles. In these, Mechanicsville, Gaines's Mill, Frazier's Farm, Savage's Station, White Oak Swamp, and Malvern Hill, it will be recalled, Lee with 60,000 troops drove McClellan's 115,000 men away from Richmond to their gunboats in James river. Richmond was saved. The world had a new hero.

John B. Magruder has received slight mention in our histories. This great engineer-soldier ought to be immortal. When McClellan landed at the end of the Peninsula and set out for Richmond, which was totally unprotected, Magruder with 11,000 men blocked his way for a month and held the 115,000 men at bay until General Joseph E. Johnston could come down with 63,000 troops to defend the Confederate capital. General Johnston being seriously wounded, General Lee was put in command, with the results already stated.

These battles cost the South dearly. At Seven Pines fell the noble General Robert Hatton, of Tennessee; General J. J. Pettigrew, the great Carolinian, was wounded and captured; and Wade Hampton, the Rupert of Carolina, was seriously wounded. McClellan's "On to Richmond" made Lee famous. It also immortalized Jeb Stuart. As long as history is read, as long as men love chivalry, Stuart's ride around McClellan will charm readers and hearers. To have been one of Stuart's 1,200 troopers, riding around McClellan's army, being chased by overwhelming numbers, improvising a bridge from an old barn, and getting back safely to tell General Lee all he wished to know about the enemy —this will be enough glory for any old Confederate grandsire. In this ride fell the gallant Captain William Latané (Latany), whose burial at the hands of several Southern women is famed in art, poetry, and tradition. Others besides Stuart won fame by the great ride. The "flower of Cavaliers" was ably supported by Col. W. H. F. Lee, Col. Fitzhugh Lee, Col. W. T. Martin, of Mississippi, and by Breathed's (Breth-ed) artillery.

McClellan made war like a gentleman. His letter of July 7, 1862, to President Lincoln, advising that the war should be conducted so as to command the respect of mankind and the smile of Providence, is one of the noblest chapters in the sad volume of civil conflict.

The North mustered another army. This, under the command of Major-General John Pope, was ordered to crush Lee and capture Richmond. Pope and McClellan must not unite their forces. In order to prevent this, Lee determined to feign an attack upon the Federal capital. On August 29th, 30th, and 31st, 1862, the Confederates under Jackson, Longstreet, Lee, and others crushed Pope on the field of Second Manassas. Here "queer lovable" Dick Ewell lost a leg. Here, also, General W. N. Pendleton, the fighting parson, made a reputation as artillerist, and Colonel Stephen D. Lee, another artillerist, "turned the tide of battle, and consummated the victory."* When their ammunition gave out, the Southern troops fought with rocks most gallantly.

In this battle, Lee had 49,000; the Federals, about 74,000.

---
*Jefferson Davis.

III

"Maryland, My Maryland"

"Johnny Reb" now crosses into Maryland. If he can get to Baltimore, he will meet with a warm reception from thousands of aunts, uncles, and cousins in that center of rebeldom. Had not Randall stirred the Southern heart? Certainly Maryland will rise up and greet her sister Virginia when she comes to drive "the despot's heel" off "her shore," and to hurl his "torch" from her "temple door."

> "The best-laid plans of mice and men
> Gang aft a-gley,"

says the poet. So proved it with the plans of General Lee. The farmers of western Maryland were cooler than icebergs when the "rebel horde," as Whittier calls them, rode into Frederick town; they could not understand that the barefooted, ragged soldiers of Lee and Jackson had come from homes of comfort, cleanliness, and elegance, and that they had marched their shoes off their feet and their clothes off their backs in defense of mighty principles.

McClellan was sent against Lee. At Sharpsburg, or Antietam, on the 17th of September, 1862, McClellan with 87,000 men and Lee with 35,000 fought one of the bloodiest battles in all history. Lee was supported by able lieutenants. He himself commended the Washington Artillery and John R. Cooke's North Carolina regiment for what they did in the battle, and Longstreet, in his war history, speaks admiringly of Hood and D. H. Hill.

After the battle of Sharpsburg, Lee made a leisurely retreat into Virginia. McClellan, for not crushing him, was again superseded.

Maryland, then, did not "breathe" and "burn." She was as cool as an icicle. Thousands of her sons, however, entered the Southern army and navy, and the South will ever honor the names of Semmes, Buchanan, Archer, Winder, and other noble Marylanders.

IV

Marye's Heights and Chancellorsville

Burnside superseded McClellan. With 100,000 men, he moved against Lee, who was entrenched at Fredericksburg, Virginia, with 78,000 troops. Both sides fought with intrepid bravery. At Marye's Heights, just outside of the old colonial town of Fredericksburg, the home of Mary Washington, the two armies engaged in deadly grapple. The Federals charged Marye's Heights, held by 7,000 Georgians and Carolinians, supported by the famous Washington Artillery. The troops of Cobb, Kershaw, and Ransom bore themselves heroically. Cobb and Maxcy Gregg fell dead, and the brave Cooke, of North Carolina, was severely wounded. Lee used only 20,000 of his men; the position secured beforehand served him instead of thousands. This battle added to the fame of Lee. Here, also, appeared "the gallant Pelham," of Stuart's horse artillery, whose Napoleon gun became famous in history, song, and legend.

This was in December. The campaign was over, except that the Confederate cavalry under Hampton, Stuart, W. H. F. Lee, and Fitzhugh Lee raided in the Federal rear and caused great uneasiness in Washington.

Jeb Stuart was fond of a joke. He telegraphed to the Federal quartermaster-general in Washington that the mules he had furnished Burnside were so mean that they could not pull the Federal cannon to the rebel camp. Stuart baffled the small critics. They did not understand how a man could combine mirth and merriment with high seriousness and supreme ability. He is well called "the Rupert of the Confederacy." If he had lived in France in the early part of the nineteenth century, he would have been one of Napoleon's most famous marshals.

Burnside disappears from history. In the spring of 1863, General Joseph Hooker, at the head of "the finest army on the planet," crossed the Rappahannock river above Fredericksburg and grappled with Lee in the now famous Spottsylvania Wilderness. Lee had 57,000 men; Hooker, 113,000. Jackson and Lee planned an attack upon Hooker's right flank, which was brilliantly executed by the dread Stonewall. Alas! the price was terrible. It was during this movement that Jackson fell at the hands of some of his own men and left a vacancy that was never filled. General A. P. Hill was wounded, and Lee was thus doubly crippled. The morning after Jackson fell, Stuart was put in command of Jackson's corps, and charged the enemy, crying, "Charge and remember Jackson."

Lee's fame now reached its meridian. No greater victory

was ever won than that at Chancellorsville, in the Virginia wilderness.

V.

"All the World Wondered"

The South had been suffering serious reverses. Sidney Johnston's place had never been filled in the West, and Sherman, Grant, and Thomas had been gaining advantages in that department. Something must be done to cheer the Southern people.

Lee again crosses the Potomac and "carries the war into Africa." In three corps, under Ewell, A. P. Hill, and Longstreet, the Army of Northern Virginia marches into Pennsylvania. They stumble upon the Federal army, now led by General George G. Meade. The rest is familiar to every schoolboy. Every reader knows that the South received her death blow at Gettysburg.

Some call this "the high water mark of the Rebellion;" we call it the turning-point in the War between the States. Let us take up a few points which are practically ignored in all school histories.

First: Why was Lee ignorant of Meade's whereabouts? For this, some blame Stuart, whose cavalry was "the eyes and ears" of Lee's army. Stuart's men say that he was busy destroying Federal supplies and baggage wagons, while others say that Jeb was playing pranks and was neglecting his business.

Another disputed point is: Where was Longstreet? He was expected to come up very early on the 2nd of July, but did not come till the afternoon. Again: Why did Longstreet not reinforce Pickett in his famous charge? This is a hot question. With five thousand more men, Pickett might have taken the Federal heights and won the battle. What then?

Third: Why did General Lee's lieutenants not carry out his orders instead of arguing with him, or following their own ideas? By their delays, the Federals had time to bring up fresh forces and seize the best positions.

At the end of the second day, the advantage was with the South. Lee's plan for the third day (July 3) was to pierce the Federal center, then attack Meade's right and left, and hurl his army back in confusion. For this great effort 14,000 or 15,000 of Lee's best men were selected, and put under the leadership of Pickett, Pettigrew, and Trimble.

This is usually known as Pickett's charge. "All the world wondered." We may also rhyme, "Some one had blundered." After Pettigrew's division was flanked, Pickett was left unsupported and had to fall back with fearful mortality.

The gallant Armistead, of Maryland, fell at the cannon's mouth, on the heights of Gettysburg. Garnett, Barksdale, Semmes, and Pender were either killed or mortally wounded. Hampton, Pettigrew, Trimble, Hood, Kemper, and G. T. Anderson were more or less seriously wounded.

Some blamed this man; some, that. General Lee blamed no one, but took all the blame upon himself. To Wilcox, who came weeping to him, he said, "Never mind, General; all this has been my fault." To the survivors of the charge, he said, "All this will come right in the end. . . . . All good men must rally."

Lee had 62,000 men; Meade, over 100,000. The Federals had both numbers and position. If the South had followed up her victory of the first day, she would have had the choice of position. If Lee's subordinates had carried out his plans the second day, Meade's fresh thousands would not have seized the commanding points of the battlefield. If Pickett, Pettigrew, and Trimble had been properly supported on the third day, Lee would have marched into Washington and Philadelphia. *If*—"if is a big word," we often say. A Southern poet who served in the Confederate army has written:

> "God lives! He forged the iron will
> That clutched and held that trembling hill."

That poem is popular in the North, but not south of the Potomac. "God lives!" Yes, the South believes that firmly. She believes in a God of Battles, and that God rules the destinies of nations. And yet the great mass of the Southern people believe as firmly that the South would have won the battle of Gettysburg and with that her independence, if General Lee's wishes had been obeyed as Jackson would have obeyed them.

General Lee is reported to have said that, if Jackson had lived, the South would have won the battle of Gettysburg. The Southern people believe so firmly.

Some strong Calvinists in the South believe that Jackson's death was a part of the divine plan to maintain the Union. A few other men believe that God used this four years' war to abolish slavery. But the great majority of our people believe that the failure to carry out General Lee's plans and orders led to the downfall of the Confederacy.

VI

Grapple of the Giants

Many lost heart after Gettysburg; more gave up hope after Vicksburg fell. Still the ragged veterans of Lee would follow him blindly, unquestioningly.

A new star had risen in the Northern heavens. In the spring of 1864, the hero of Fort Donelson and of Vicksburg, General Ulysses S. Grant, was made commander-in-chief of the Union forces. He advanced to the Rapidan river, to the Wilderness already so famous. It was sixty miles to Richmond. In his way lay Lee's army of 64,000; Grant had 141,000. It will take him eleven months to get to Richmond. To crush Lee, he adopts the "hammer policy;" will "fight it out on this line if it takes all summer." He will refuse to exchange prisoners on the ground that it will shorten the war and be more just to the Northern men confined in Southern prisons.

Grant started for Richmond early in May. In his path stood his wily antagonist. Whenever Grant moved southward, Lee threw himself in his way, and dealt a terrific blow. Day after day, in that bloody month, men fought like beasts in the jungles of the Wilderness. The scene shifted rapidly from the Rapidan to the North Anna, the Pamunkey, the Chickahominy, the James. At Cold Harbor came the climax of the duel. In about half an hour, Grant lost

12,737 men.* In the whole campaign from the Rapidan to the James, Grant lost 60,000 men, as many as Lee had in his whole army.

During this campaign, Longstreet was disabled, and General Micah Jenkins killed. Stuart, also, fell in these sad hours. While heading off an attack upon Richmond by General Philip H. Sheridan, Stuart was killed at Yellow Tavern. His grave in Hollywood cemetery, Richmond, should be kept green forever, a Southern Mecca.

Grant crossed the James and laid siege to Petersburg, the key to Richmond. Lee would have let Richmond go. He would have given up Richmond, united his army with that of Joseph E. Johnston in the south, crushed Sherman, and then confronted Grant in Virginia. The Confederate government, however, would not give up Richmond: its mania was to hold cities rather than to crush armies.

General Lee saw that the end was coming. He had only 40,000 men; Grant 111,000. Lee's men were starved and ragged. His wounded were suffering for food and medicine. His one idea now was to keep the enemy from breaking through the long thin gray line that stood sentinel at the back door of Richmond.

April 9, 1865, came the surrender at Appomattox. Only 8,000 men were armed; the rest were either unable to bear arms or had no equipment. "All was lost save honor."

A. P. Hill breathed out his noble spirit on the ragged edge of conflict. John B. Gordon, "the Chevalier Bayard of the

---
*Lee's *Lee*, page 343.

Confederacy," led the last charge, and "fought his corps to a frazzle." The young flag went down in defeat;

> "Yet 'tis wreathed around with glory,
> And 'twill live in song and story,
> Though its folds are in the dust."

CHAPTER VII

JACKSON AND HIS "FOOT-CAVALRY"

I

"Poor White Trash"

A PHRASE to conjure with is "Lee and Jackson." It always elicits applause in the South; frequently, in other sections. Both men "went with their states." Each represented a civilization—one the Cavalier and the other the Puritan.

Mrs. Jackson's life of her husband is one of the notable books of the last century, and should be read by every schoolboy. One part of it has been grossly misunderstood. She tells us that General Jackson's first two American progenitors came over as "indented servants," and married some time after their arrival. This plain statement has been distorted by some writers. It has been construed to mean that Jackson's people were "poor white trash," and that he was a social miracle. The whole thing is nonsensical. Many fine men and women, unable to pay their passage, permitted planters or others to advance the money for their passage—a large sum in those days—and let them "work it out" after their arrival. The Jacksons were a sturdy, substantial stock, which has produced fine, able, and progressive men for several generations. Thomas J. Jackson, as boy and youth, was very ordinary. No one at West Point dreamed that he would ever be distinguished. Few people in Lexington thought that he was anything more than a "cranky professor." In those days, he showed no special capacity for anything except for doing his duty at all times and in all places.

Only when powder was burning did his eye gleam with a mighty lustre. He was like the steed that snuffeth the battle from afar. His genius is for war. It will begin to show itself on the fields of Mexico, when he is rapidly promoted for gallantry at Vera Cruz, Contreras, Churubusco, and Chapultepec; will oft and anon give some inklings of its presence, when at the cannon's roar on the drill ground at the Virginia Military Institute, Major Jackson "would grow more erect, the grasp upon his sabre would tighten, the quiet eyes would flash, the large nostrils would dilate, and the calm, grave face would glow with the proud spirit of the warrior." It will disclose itself more fully at Manassas when he says to General Bee, "Sir, we will give them the bayonet;" but will reach its meridian glory when he drives four Federal armies out of his beloved Valley, falls like lightning upon McClellan's flank at Gaines's Mill and afterwards upon Hooker's at Chancellorsville, hurling battalion after battalion of the enemy back upon one another in wild confusion.

II

Jackson's Political Views

What led Major Jackson to enter the Southern army?

Was it ambition? No; for, though he might have been swayed by that motive in his earlier days, he was now too conscientious—morbidly conscientious—to fight for any cause that he did not believe in heartily. Was he, as some would say, driven by public opinion? As well try to browbeat the falls of Niagara or intimidate the rock of Gibraltar. We have Mrs. Jackson's statement: he "was strongly for the Union, but believed firmly in states rights. If Virginia secedes, he will go with his state." He would have preferred to fight in the Union rather than secede. This was the feeling of a large number of Southern people.

Lincoln's call for troops decided Virginia. Up to the day of that call, Lexington was almost solid against secession. After that, Lexington and the whole state east of the Alleghanies were in favor of secession.

Major Jackson believed, also, in slavery. Moreover, he owned a few "servants." He believed that slavery was sanctioned by the Bible, and that it was God's mode of christianizing the African. He conducted a Sunday school for negroes; had his servants regularly at his family prayers; treated them kindly and tenderly.

III

"Stone Wall"

Major Jackson offered his sword to Virginia. He was commissioned colonel, then brigadier-general. At Manassas, July 21, 1861, his great career began. There he was dubbed "Stonewall." All day long, that hot July day, the men of the North and of the South dashed against each other, bravely, madly, frantically. The pent-up hatred of decades and of generations vented itself in the whistling bullet, the clashing bayonet, and the screaming mortar. The very demons of hell must have danced for joy as they saw two great Christian civilizations surging and foaming towards each other in bloody billows on the red fields of Manassas. Who, in God's name, shall give account thereof in the day of judgment?

Who is there? Carolina and her sisters, led by Hampton, Bee, Bartow, and others; Louisiana with her Tigers and the Washington Artillery, and the "peerless Beauregard;" Virginia, led by Joe Johnston, and following Stuart's plume. "General, they are beating us back," cries Bee to Jackson. "Sir, we will give them the bayonet," answers the Spartan of Lexington. "Look! there stands Jackson like a stone wall. Rally behind the Virginian," cried Bee, as he yielded up his noble spirit.

So Jackson became "Stonewall." All other theories are utterly without foundation.

Who saved the day at Manassas? Who was the hero of that battle? "I," said the sparrow, "with my bow and arrow; I killed Cock Robin." There is glory enough for all. Jackson checked the onset at the Henry house; Kirby Smith and Elzey, later in the day, brought reinforcements that turned the tide of battle.

Jackson was at first anxious to take Washington. After hearing the statements of President Davis, General Johnston, and others as to the condition of the troops and the

T. J. JACKSON

scarcity of cavalry, he, however, changed his mind. For not taking Washington or allowing Jackson to do so, President Davis used to be soundly berated in some quarters. At the time, Jackson was eager. He wished to introduce then and there his policy of "ceaseless invasion."

IV

The True Stonewall Jackson

We have *The True George Washington* and *The True Abraham Lincoln*: we need a volume entitled *The True Stonewall Jackson*.

Of no other great man has so much nonsense been written. Even Southern tradition has given us a somewhat distorted picture of this great hero. A few plain facts may be given.

Jackson is often spoken of as a cold, fanatical, cranky man that would throw a damper over any social gathering. This is a very unfair picture. We admit that he was not generally what is called sociable or genial. He was a taciturn, self-contained man, a good listener, not given to much talking. General Dick Taylor says, "If silence is golden, Jackson was a bonanza." Nor was he addicted to jesting or jocularity. He, however, enjoyed a clean joke, but in his own way, laughing quietly, and soon turning to some moral or religious question.

His home life was simple and beautiful. The accounts that we have of the last winter he spent in the bosom of his family are extremely touching. His devotion as a husband was tender beyond expression.

His religious life is often misunderstood. He was given to neither bigotry nor cant. He was emphatically a man of faith and of prayer. He believed implicitly in a God of Battles, and always prayed for divine assistance.

Some have charged him with being proud, and too tenacious of his personal rights. These charges are utterly misleading. He did tender his resignation when the government at Richmond interfered in the internal affairs of his department; but he did it in the interests of the Confederacy. Some thought that he was unjustly harsh towards inferior officers; but he was, we believe, never severe except when his orders had been neglected or disobeyed. We do not say that he was perfect. We do say, however, that, if General Jackson's ideas of discipline had prevailed throughout the Southern army, the South would have had not only the best fighters but the best soldiers in modern history.*

Jackson believed in "war to the hilt." He seems to have been originally in favor of giving and receiving no quarter, so as to make the war "short, sharp, and decisive." This view he waived in deference to General Lee and President Davis. Later on, he seems to have favored adopting the "black flag" in dealing with a few special leaders of the Union forces.

As to General Jackson's plans of warfare: As said already, he was in favor of "ceaseless invasion." He did not believe in trying to hold cities like Richmond and Vicksburg. He proposed to form movable columns of cavalry and horse artillery, to be used in carrying the war into the North,

---

*This distinction, we believe, was drawn by Gen. Joseph E. Johnston.

destroying crops, capturing cities, and rarely risking a battle. If—(but there's the big word 'if' again)—Jackson's plan had been adopted, and such men as Morgan, Forrest, Stuart, Sidney Johnston, and Jackson himself had led these ceaseless columns across the Potomac, the South might have gained her independence.

This is a book of polemics. Its object is to defend the South, her leaders, and her soldiers. We shall eradicate the poison wherever we find it.

A popular ballad is *Barbara Frietchie*. Every boy and girl has read it and declaimed it. Few have ever seen Whittier's explanations or the refutations of Southern writers. Let us look at it closely. Whittier says that "a blush of shame" came over Jackson's face, as he saw the flag of the Union waving. Does any reader believe that? Was the pious, God-fearing hero of 1862 ashamed of what he had done in 1861? Again, Jackson is made to threaten with the death of a dog any man that touches a hair of Dame Barbara's head. What language! What an idea! No man in that army of Scotch Covenanters needed any such warning. Another flaw may be stated. Dame Barbara was bedridden and could not have got to the window to save her life. Another serious flaw is that Jackson's corps did not pass up the street that Dame Barbara lived on. The most serious flaw, however, is that the whole story is a myth, palmed off on the poet by some ill-informed person.

These points have been made in print before. So strong are they that few now believe the story. Recently, however, a prominent writer of history tells us that the Barbara

Frietchie incident really occurred at Fredericksburg, Virginia—which we can say is absolutely without foundation, another myth. Possibly it was Frederick's Hall, Louisa county, Virginia. Try that!

V

The Thunderbolt of War

The Valley Campaign is immortal. It put Jackson among the great soldiers of Christendom. Though treated in some volumes as raids on Banks and others, it is studied in some military schools of Europe as one of the greatest campaigns of history. The outlines are familiar to the young student.

Why is Kernstown immortal? Certainly not on account of the numbers. Nor can we claim it as a Confederate victory. It is immortal because with 3,400 men Jackson stopped the advance of 175,000 men upon the Southern capital. If the Valley forces under Shields and others had been permitted to join McDowell, and all these had marched to unite with McClellan's 105,000 advancing up the Peninsula, Richmond might have fallen; and, at that time in the war, the fall of the capital would probably have meant the collapse of the Confederacy.

Again: The battle of McDowell would seem to be unimportant. Jackson had superior forces and a very ordinary antagonist; but McDowell was part of a campaign in which 16,000 Confederates kept 35,000 Federals from advancing upon Richmond and joining McClellan; and thus again a few thousand men under Jackson neutralized the great armies of the enemy. This was May 8, 1862.

Jackson's victory over Banks at Winchester was worth $300,000 in supplies to the Confederacy, and won Banks the sobriquet of "Jackson's commissary." The boys of the Valley were in high spirits. The grandsons of the men that had followed Andrew Lewis, Daniel Morgan, and William Campbell felt that they had a leader worthy of their metal. At Cross Keys and Port Republic, they drove four Federal generals rapidly to the Potomac. The "crazy professor" was now a world hero.

We have already seen Jackson at Gaines's Mill, June 27. Some claim that he turned the tide of battle against McClellan, and thus saved Richmond.

Another disputed question is, Who planned the Valley Campaign? Some say Lee; some, Jos. E. Johnston; others, Jackson. Could any other man in America have executed it? That is the question before us.

"There were heroes before Agamemnon." There were other great soldiers in the Valley besides Jackson. The South should never forget "queer Dick Ewell"—Ewell the Unique—and Turner Ashby, the cavalier of the Valley.

Cedar Run was a noble victory. With 18,000 men Jackson defeated Banks and Sigel with 32,000. Under these heavy odds, Jackson's genius rose to its great proportions. Drawing his sword—the only time during the war, it is thought—dropping his bridle rein on his horse's neck, he reached over and took a flag from a standard bearer close by, and, waving it over his head, cried "Rally men! Remember Winder! Where's my Stonewall Brigade? Forward, men! Forward!" The battle was soon over.

CHAPTER VIII

SHILOH AND ITS HEROES

I

The Hero of Texas

EVERY Southern boy and girl should know about General Albert Sidney Johnston. His death may have lost the South her independence.

Johnston was born in Kentucky, but lived in Texas. He was a distinguished officer in the "old army," and, in 1861, went out of the Union with Texas. He was a typical Southerner of the old school. After Texas seceded, General Johnston forwarded his resignation to Washington, but kept the whole matter secret so as not to permit his rank as general-commanding the Department of the Pacific to influence the many adventurous Southerners settled in California. He had foreseen the war between the sections. While deploring the sad state of affairs, he sympathized heartily with the Southern people. His dearest friends were Leonidas Polk and Jefferson Davis. As said already, they had been taught the right of secession at the West Point Military Academy. Johnston was of course censured bitterly for "deserting his flag." Polk was censured for laying aside his duties as bishop of Louisiana and giving the

South the benefit of his military education, although the "fighting parsons" of the Revolution, such as Thruston and Muhlenburg, are national heroes.

General Johnston was put in charge of the Western Department. His centre was Bowling Green, Kentucky. With only 21,000 or 22,000 men he had to face 100,000 under such able generals as Grant, Buell, and Thomas. He called in vain for adequate reinforcements.

Grant was not yet distinguished. Polk, supported by Pillow, Cheatham, and other heroes of the Southwest, defeated him at Belmont, in spite of overwhelming numbers. Johnston's thin line was soon broken. The 100,000 Federals swarmed up the Southern rivers and took Forts Henry and Donelson. Johnston was bitterly censured by bombproof brigadiers and editorial ink-pots. President Davis stood by him courageously, and refused to remove this "incompetent" and "cowardly" general. Lack of troops paralyzed Johnston's efforts. Great generals he had in abundance; for besides those already mentioned, he had John Morgan and N. B. Forrest, two of the greatest cavalrymen ever seen on this continent.

II

"Freedom Shrieked When Kosciusko Fell"

So says Campbell of the Polish hero. So say many in regard to the death of Sidney Johnston. He was the brother of Jackson. The latter was Lee's "right arm;" the former, the greatest soldier of the Southwest.

Shiloh was a "decisive battle" of the war. If Johnston had lived to follow up his victory, there would have been no Vicksburg, no siege of Petersburg, no capture of Richmond, no Appomattox; Grant was defeated when Johnston fell. Two hours more would have driven the Federals into the river or forced them to surrender. "To-night," said Johnston, "we will water our horses in the Tennessee river." The Federals were in the way of the horses. "Freedom shrieked when Johnston fell."

Shiloh was a noble battle. The very flower of the Southwest was there under Beauregard, Bragg, Polk, Hardee, and Breckenridge. Other great spirits were on the field. George W. Johnston, Provisional Governor of Kentucky, fell on the second day while serving as a private in a Kentucky regiment. General A. H. Gladden, of Louisiana, fell while leading his brigade with conspicuous gallantry. Some noble spirits survived the battle. Among them were Forrest, "the Wizard of the Saddle;" "Little Joe Wheeler," the hero of three wars; Morgan, famous for his raids; Pat Cleburne, "the Stonewall of the West," who later fell on the bloody field of Franklin.

III

"Common Errors"

There are "common errors" in the use of English; there are equally as many in some histories.

One of these is that General Johnston exposed himself recklessly at Shiloh in order to retrieve his reputation, and

ALBERT SIDNEY JOHNSTON

mayhap show the "bomb-proof brigadiers" and others that his failure to hold the Bowling Green-Cumberland line with 22,000 against 100,000 was not due to cowardice.

The whole thing is preposterous. All the prominent Southern generals exposed themselves too frequently. Joe Johnston and Beauregard did it at Manassas. Jackson did it habitually. Ewell frequently rushed to the very front of battle. Stuart's black plume was always in front, just as Henry of Navarre's white plume beckoned his men ever onward. In the Wilderness, General Lee's horse was seized by the Texans, who said, "If you will go back, General, we will go forward." It was a bad though noble habit of the Southern leaders. In the early days of the war, the sentiment of the troops rather demanded it. A sad experience taught them better. The loss of Sidney Johnston and Stonewall Jackson was the price paid for their experience.

This custom of the Southern generals, even Grant could not understand. He says in his *Personal Memoirs* that the Southern troops at Shiloh could not have felt confident of victory, as they permitted Johnston to ride along the front of battle. What chains could have bound that man after he smelt the powder?

Johnston was first buried in New Orleans. After the war, his remains were removed to Austin, Texas. Among his pall-bearers were Beauregard, Bragg, Buckner, Hood, Longstreet, and "Dick Taylor." All but one of these have "crossed over the river" and are resting "under the shade of the trees" with the dread Stonewall.

CHAPTER IX

THE SOUTH SINCE THE WAR

I

A Prostrate Nation

GENERAL LEE, as already stated, surrendered April 9, 1865. On April 26, followed the surrender of General Joheph E. Johnston in North Carolina; in May, that of General Richard Taylor in Mississippi, and that of General E. Kirby Smith west of the Mississippi river. By the last of June, there was not a Confederate soldier in arms against the United States government. Never did an army lay down its arms in better faith, or with more sincere acceptance of the terms offered by the conqueror. How these terms were kept by some of the conquerors, history will tell in flaming letters, calling to her aid essay, fiction and drama, and the eloquence of tongues yet unborn. General Grant acted honorably and kindly. Mr. Lincoln seems to have nursed no mean grudge against the fallen foe; but, if General Lee could have foreseen the events of the years from 1865 to 1876, he would have hidden his ragged remnant in the Appalachian mountains, and two new generations of Southern youth would have kept up the contest to the present moment. But for the personal influence of General Grant, General Robert E. Lee would have been prosecuted for treason. President Davis, Vice-President Stephens, Governor Brown, of Georgia, Governor Clark, of Mississippi, General Howell Cobb, Senator Hill, of Georgia, and other prominent men were arrested and put in prison. The greatest sufferer was President Davis. His treatment by some government officials at Fortress Monroe reads like a chapter from the Spanish Inquisition or from a history of the Indians. Mrs. Davis's account of that treatment and of the disrespect shown her by one or two prominent officials at Fort Monroe, challenges the credulity of mankind. Mr. Davis was never brought to trial. The United States Government knew that an impartial jury might well fail to find him guilty of treason against the government, and that eminent lawyers were ready to argue his case before the world. The failure to try Mr. Davis was a great constitutional victory for the South, and posterity will so regard it. The North could not have proved that he had committed treason against the government.

The cost of the war is almost beyond calculation. Besides slaves worth about two thousand million dollars, the South lost values of every kind, footing up at least two thousand million more. There was practically no money in circulation, her banks had gone to ruin, her credit was totally gone, all basis of credit was destroyed, her stocks and bonds were utterly worthless, provisions almost exhausted, bankruptcy was universal. The whole land lay in utter paralysis and ruin.

II

The Wolf at the Door

The soldier, returning to his dismantled home, saw starvation standing at his door, shaking his gaunt finger at wife and little ones. Soon a worse sight met his gaze: an idle, shiftless mass of freedmen hung around the courthouse, the post office and other public places, wondering when they could crowd the soldier's family out of their home, and move into it. Some of the slaves were still faithful and respectful; many were sullen, suspicious, grum; some insolent. Many looked on with maudlin curiosity and with ill-suppressed delight as they saw the gentlemen of the South hoeing their gardens, ploughing the fields, driving their own ox carts, or hiring themselves to some neighbor that could manage to give them three meals a day and a few dollars a month to work as laborers. The freedmen crowded to the towns and cities. Freedom they thought meant eternal rest. Wonderful stories came to them of bounteous stores from the boundless treasury in Washington; and visions of forty acres and a mule; or, grander yet, of moving into the "big house" of their bankrupt masters, where they might smoke their pipes in the library of the "effete aristocrats," lie on old Marster's feather beds, and use the master's silver.

Agriculture was totally demoralized, factories generally destroyed, railroads worn out and useless, farming implements gone, neither ox nor mule nor horse left to plough with; fences had been burnt by the armies; many houses were totally dismantled, the whole land lying under the curse of Nineveh.

Having made a heroic fight, the South determined to accept heroically the arbitrament of war. Slavery she willingly surrendered; secession as a remedy for grievances, she embalmed among the mummies of Egypt; the right of a state to judge of infractions of the constitution, she marked "obsolete," and laid on the shelf with Lilly's Latin grammar. She threw herself on the mercy of her conquerors.

The Southern people were willing and anxious to settle down and begin life over again. They were willing to accept any fair government that would protect their persons, and the little property the war had left them; believed that Mr. Lincoln would treat them humanely if not kindly; and were ready to bear anything to which self-respecting men could submit.

Mr. Lincoln had already shown that his plan of restoring the Union was not one of cruelty. On December 8, 1863, he had offered "full pardon" to all persons (except the leaders of the "rebellion") that would lay down their arms, swear allegiance to the constitution, and promise to obey all acts of Congress that had been passed up to the date of his amnesty proclamation (December 8, 1863). He further said that, if one-tenth of the votes of 1860 in any seceded state should establish a government upon the basis outlined above, he would recognize it as "the true government of the state." Representation in Congress, he said, did not rest with him, but with Congress. No mention was made of negro suffrage. Indeed, we have it on record that Mr.

Lincoln did not believe that the negro should be a voter or a juror, or be put upon any political or social equality with the white man.

When the war closed, Mr. Lincoln said, "Let 'em up easy, let 'em up easy." When the question was raised whether to regard the Southern states as never out of the Union but as having temporarily cut themselves off as aliens, Mr. Lincoln brushed it aside as not a practical question, but as rather what is called "academic," that is, technical and not worthy of serious discussion at such a crisis. His idea was to bring the seceded states into practical touch with the other states and restore them as soon as possible to their place in the Union, on condition that they surrender slavery and the right of secession and accept the constitution of the United States as the fundamental law of the land. His method was one of conciliation and of restoration. When violent men wished to treat the states as conquered provinces that had forfeited all the rights of statehood, he said, "We shall sooner have the fowl by hatching the egg than by smashing it."

III

The Hounds of Peace

This policy did not please Congress. A large number in both houses thought that Mr. Lincoln was too lenient, and that he was violating "the rights of humanity" and "the principles of republican government." Chaos reigned supreme. Many were so angry with the South that they could not hear the voice of mercy, which "droppeth as the gentle dew from heaven." Shylock was whetting his knife, not on his sole but on his soul, demanding his pound of flesh from Antonio, whose argosies had gone to the bottom of the ocean. Mr. Lincoln was firm and inflexible, and, on April 11, 1865, said publicly that he still clung to his plan of restoration.

To add fuel to the flame, came the assassination of President Lincoln. None deplored this wild act more than the South and her noble ex-president. It now seems incredible that Andrew Johnson, the successor of Mr. Lincoln, offered a reward of $100,000 for the capture of Mr. Davis as an accomplice of the assassin. Nor was the South in any sense responsible. John Wilkes Booth was not strictly a Southern man, did not represent the South, but killed the president on his own motion, and probably from personal motives.

While deploring the assassination and regretting that Mr. Lincoln did not live to carry out his policy, the South has never professed to love Mr. Lincoln. To do so would be arrant hypocrisy. She cannot put him along with Washington, and rank him with the demigods. She cannot forget his campaign cry of 1858; his leading a ticket avowedly hostile to her institutions; his saying that he had no authority to interfere with slavery, and yet issuing the Emancipation Proclamation; and his straining and rending the constitution that he promised in his oath of office faithfully to maintain. She, however, admires his great ability, his shrewd common sense, his keen sagacity, and believes that he had more of "the milk of human kindness," less small bitterness, less desire to gloat over a fallen foe, than Andrew Johnson, or than the Radical majority in Congress.

The poet tells us of fearful creatures that, "never ceasing, barked with wide Cerberean mouths full loud, and rang a hideous peal." Not to push the comparison to the very farthest, we may say that such a chorus broke upon the ears of the prostrate South after Lincoln's assassination. Many believed that Booth was her appointed agent. Many accused Jefferson Davis of being an accomplice, and, as said already, President Johnson offered $100,000 reward for his arrest; and smaller amounts were offered for other Southern gentlemen equally above such atrocious crimes as assassination. Thank Heaven that such charges found little credence even in those fearful days! We regret that history has to notice them in this better era; but the historian more than the poet must deal with "the unrelenting past," enter its most ghastly precincts, and walk with shuddering horror among its grinning sepulchres.

We have all heard of "the dogs of war"; but the South suffered more from the hounds of peace.

IV

The Reign of Terror

With the accession of Andrew Johnson to the presidency, the South had new visions of horror. Harsh measures were in the air. The imprisonment of Jefferson Davis and of others already mentioned, the summons issued against General Lee by the United States court at Norfolk, and the violent language used by the new president—all these things alarmed those that had figured prominently in the war; and a number of them left the United States, and went, some to Cuba, some to Egypt, some to Mexico, and some to Europe.

The Radical party in Congress thought that providence had come to their assistance. Now should the conquered South lick the dust at the feet of her enemies. Soon their faces fell. The president's tone changed; he became less bitter; it was soon found out that he would not hang, draw and quarter all the Confederate leaders, but that "my policy" would be more human and humane than he first intended. This change is generally attributed to the influence of Mr. Seward, secretary of state, who is said to have urged Mr. Johnson to pursue milder methods.

If Congress was dissatisfied with Mr. Lincoln's leniency, they raved at Mr. Johnson's mildness. Then began the deadlock between the legislative and the executive branches of the government which culminated in the unsuccessful impeachment and trial of the president. There was a roaring chaos of opinions. No two men in Congress agreed as to how the South should be got back into the Union; whether she should be hung, drawn, and quartered first, and then brought back in a million coffins; or brought back first, then tied to a post, whipped till the blood flowed in streams, and then carried off to execution. All the Radical party agreed that the president had nothing to do with it; that he was not in the game even as referee or umpire, certainly not as captain. Meantime the South was lying in "misery and irons, hard by at death's door." Her brave sons had gone to work; but the negroes were totally demoralized, and little labor could be had to work the crops. Untold thousands of freedmen threw down all work, flocked to the towns, cities and camps, expecting to be supported if not made rich from the Federal treasury.

V

The Freedman's Bureau

This state of affairs, Mr. Lincoln had already foreseen and tried to provide against. Among the negroes that had followed the Federal armies, especially Sherman's army in its march through Georgia, there had been great suffering and destitution. To keep these runaways from starving, Congress, on March 3, 1865, established the Freedman's Bureau, but did not make any adequate appropriation; so that at first the act did little towards relieving want, but a great deal towards making the negroes feel and know that they were, in some sense, "the wards of the nation," and believe that the Southern people were their worst enemies.

This act, with amendments and "variations," was in force till 1872, and relieved a great deal of suffering among the blacks, and among whites that had "stuck" to the Union. It also established schools, colleges, and universities for the freedman, and spent a good many million dollars in caring for the negro. So far so good. The abandoned and deserted lands which this Bureau took charge of to give the negroes, was the property of the wretched, impoverished people of the South, and much of it was recovered by the owners only after great delay and after grievous treatment at the hands of some of the officials.

Theoretically, this Bureau sounds very noble. As described by General O. O. Howard, the commissioner appointed by President Johnson, it reads like an extract from the writings of John Howard, Elizabeth Fry, or some other great philanthropist. Practically, however, it did not work so well. To disburse all these millions and see that hundreds of thousands were fed daily required a very large corps of assistants; and many of these were very questionable characters. All this, however, might have gone on without adding to the woes of the South; and we must refer briefly to the reasons why the name Freedman's Bureau is unsavory in the nostrils of the Southern people.

One of its clauses made its agents "guardians of freedmen, with power to settle their disputes with employers;" and thereby hangs a tale ghastlier than any that ghost or goblin damned ever hissed into the ear of Hamlet. Under this clause, our fathers suffered untold annoyance, indignity, and insult. Any shiftless negro girl could threaten her employer with arrest by the provost-marshal, and all through the South cases of this kind were of daily occurrence. Our people in these years drank the cup of humiliation to its very dregs, the "wine of astonishment" to its very bottom.

VI

The Schoolmarm in Tradition

At this time, and as part of the machinery of this Bureau, appeared "the Yankee schoolmarm," famous in Southern tradition. Under the ægis of the provost-marshal and his assistants, who protected her from the imaginary bullets of the imaginary assassin and from the real contempt of our mothers and grandmothers,

> In her noisy mansion, skilled to rule,
> The village schoolmarm taught her little school.

Ladies of refinement there may have been among these teachers; but many of them came for what they could make by it. We shall describe "the schoolmarm" as the older people generally remember her. She came as a philanthropist, but had her eyes on the loaves and fishes. She told the little "darlings" what sacrifices she had made to come South to raise them to a level with the "proud aristocrats over yonder;" and, at the end of the session, took up a collection in which forks, spoons, and family heirlooms figured instead of silver dollars. She brought a stigma upon the sacred name of teacher, and left behind her the flavor of asafœtida.

The last interview of one of these "marms" with old Aunt Susan is interesting:

"Good-bye, Mrs. Brown; remember now what I say: You are as good as any of these white people, and have a perfect right to eat with them and sit in the parlor with them. Do you understand?"

"Yes'm," replied Aunt Susan, *alias* Mrs. Brown.

"Now, Mrs. Brown," continued the retiring head of Cross Roads College, "I want you dear people to know what brought me down here. I used to make dresses and bonnets up in my own state, but came South to help elevate your precious children to equality with the proud aristocracy of the South. Understand?"

"Yes'm," said Aunt Susan; "lemme see. Does you say I is good as my ole mistis?"

"Oh, yes, certainly," answered the philanthropist.

"An' you sez yo' biz'ness at home wuz to make dresses and bonnits?"

"Yes," answered the schoolmarm.

"Well, my white folks never 'sochiates wid dressmakers and millners, an' I ain't gwine do it; good mornin', marm." (Exit Mrs. Brown, usually known as Aunt Susan.)

This illustration is taken from an article published by a Southern lady in 1885, after the heat of passion had subsided. It represents exactly the schoolmarm in tradition.

VII

Reconstruction Through Destruction

President Johnson soon showed that he thought the president was "in the saddle." He proposed to carry on the policy of "restoration"—what is called in our history presidential reconstruction; but Congress violently opposed his policy. Most of the seceded states accepted the new president's suggestions, called conventions, adopted constitutions, repealed their ordinances of secession, accepted the thirteenth amendment abolishing slavery forever, and elected representatives and senators to seats in Congress. Here came the rub. When these representatives and senators got to Washington, they met with a cold reception from the Northern members, and found that their names were not on the roll of Congress. The clause of the constitution making each branch of Congress the judge of the eligibility of its members was used as a pretext to reject these Southern representatives and senators.

Then began the contest between Congress and the president. February 26, 1866, Congress appointed a committee of fifteen, twelve Republicans and three Democrats, to look into Southern affairs. On June 18, this committee reported against the president's policy, treated the South as still in a state of rebellion, and, under the leadership of violent South-haters, entered upon a new era of persecution.

Meantime, the prostrate South was fast in the grip of the Freedman's Bureau, the shiftless freedman himself, and the schoolmarm, and could not be reinstated in the Union. Her great offenses—what led Congress to denounce her as still in rebellion—were first, that she had passed laws against vagrancy; but this had been done to protect property from millions of idlers, mostly of the freedman class; and, second, that she was unwilling to receive the slaves as political equals, competent to vote and to hold public office. These bitter pills she could not swallow in a moment. After a while, however, she submitted to the inevitable, and, in order to get some kind of government and go to work to rebuild her shattered fortunes, accepted the fourteenth and fifteenth amendments to the constitution. These two amendments, with the thirteenth abolishing slavery, are the constitutional results of the War between the States, *alias* the "Rebellion."

The thirteenth amendment confirmed the Emancipation Proclamation. No one wishes to see it repealed.

The fourteenth amendment brought a new being into existence, that is, a citizen of the United States. Before its adoption, men were citizens of their respective states, and incidentally residents of the United States. Its object of course was to make citizens of the negroes emancipated by the war.

The fifteenth amendment went farther, and gave votes to all negro males over 21 years of age. For thirty years or more, these votes were cast almost solidly in the interests of one political party, and the Southern people saw that there was no probability that the negro vote would ever be divided between the parties. This led to the restriction of the suffrage in several Southern states. The results are excellent. As said elsewhere, a good many whites are disfranchised by the new constitutions of the Southern states. The best class of colored men retain their votes, and the mass of idle and vicious ones are disfranchised. In these results, the North has practically acquiesced, and the Supreme Court of the United States has shown no inclination to upset the new constitutions. All this is a happy omen. It is one of the most significant signs that "the war is at last over."

March 2, 1867, is the "Black Friday" of the South. On that day, Congress passed, over the president's veto, a bill dividing the territory of secession, except Tennessee, into five military districts, to be commanded by generals of the United States army. These military governors were ordered to ignore the state governments and the state officers as illegal and as insufficient to protect the freedman in his rights under the constitution. Under this act, the mass of intelligent white men in the South were disfranchised, and all negro males over twenty-one were given the ballot. The results may be imagined.

VIII

The Carpetbagger and the Scalawag

In the midst of this hurlyburly of wrack and ruin, and as a part of the diabolical machinery, appears that monstrosity, that vulture of society, the "carpetbagger." He is the product of putrefaction, the child of carrion and decay. In our day, he packs his bag and speeds to the sister isle of Cuba, and his odor is even now borne to us on the southern zephyr. When the Philippines are "pacified," he will take ship to "loot" the treasury of that territory.

The carpetbagger of 1865 was the lowest of his ilk, the basest of his species. Often he was an apostate in religion, a preacher driven out of some community for political corruption, for immorality, or for robbing his church's treasury. He refugeed to the prostrate South to recoup his fortunes by plundering bankrupt commonwealths.

To inflame the negroes against their former masters; to speak contemptuously of the "poor white rebel trash;" to point the negro to the home of "that broken-down aristocrat" and ask him how he would like to have it; to ogle him and embrace him, calling him "Mister" and "Brother," and count upon his vote at the next election,—such was the employment of this bird of prey, this cross between the cormorant and the buzzard.

Forth from this cesspool of corruption, sprang another creature forever infamous as the "scalawag." He is a renegade Southerner, who joined the carpetbagger and the negro in dividing offices, plundering citizens, and robbing the public treasury. Before the war, he was a blatant "day-before-yesterday secessionist." During the war, he probably held a bomb-proof position far from the post of danger. When Congress quarrelled with the president, he saw the opportunity of his life, sneaked slimily out of his hole, and with oily tongue ingratiated himself with the august representatives of the conqueror, while gleams of the gubernatorial mansion and of senatorial honors flashed before his snaky vision.

The carpetbagger is no new character in history. He has lived in all periods and among all nations. He crossed the Mediterranean, and checked his carpetbag for Utica and Magnesia. He was with the infamous Verres, whom Cicero denounced for plundering Sicily. He crossed the Channel with William the Norman, and battened on the decaying carcass of Anglo-Saxon civilization. History repeats itself.

Scalawags, also, were produced in earlier ages; but ours seem fouler. Sicily, Africa, and Asia Minor had them in abundance; but those were pagan days, and men were sunk in superstition and brutality. England under the Conqueror had them in plenty; but that was before the days of nice honor and chivalric ideals. The scalawag of 1865, we repeat, was "the basest of his species."

IX

The Third Triumvirate

When Cæsar, Crassus, and Pompey divided the Roman world among them, they were indulging "that vaulting ambition which o'erleaps itself," but were themselves the worst sufferers. When Octavius, Antony, and Lepidus drew up their deadly proscription, they were but following the precedents of a pagan age; but their deeds, though bloody and heinous, did not undermine the civilization of the Roman world. Not so with the third triumvirate, composed of the carpetbagger, the scalawag, and the negro. They rode roughshod over private rights, piled up huge debts for posterity, plundered the public treasury, and made heinous plots against the hearth and home of the Southern family.

We must say, however, that the poor ignorant freedman was but a pliant tool in the hands of unprincipled men of the other two classes. Rascality and robbery ran riot. Enormous debts were piled up against the states; the bonds were sold cheap to adventurers from every section; and colossal fortunes were made by depraved and corrupt men like Legree, famous in *ante-bellum* fiction. The debt of Alabama increased from about six million to about thirty-eight million; that of Florida from two hundred and twenty-one thousand to nearly sixteen million; that of South Carolina from five million to thirty-nine million; and the debts of other states in about the same proportion. The debts of the eleven seceding states were increased from eighty-seven million to three hundred and eighty million.* A former congressman from Maine says that the military government of South Carolina in 1867 was "a carnival of crime and corruption," "a morass of rottenness," "a huge system of brigandage." Justice L. Q. C. Lamar says that the reconstruction policy of Congress was intended to reverse every natural, social, and political relation on which the civilization not only of the South, but of the whole Union rested.

The black man was stirred up against the white man by incendiary speeches in public and by the basest suggestions in private. To get the "proud aristocrat's" house and home was held up as immediately possible; to get his daughter in marriage was to follow. Compared with the last suggestion, all others sank into insignificance. To stand by disfranchised and see great masses of ignorant and insolent men of an inferior race casting their votes against one's property, and laying up boundless debts and burdens for posterity—this was bad, yet for a time endurable; but the attack upon the home, upon the racial integrity of the Anglo-Saxon—this would make every Southern father draw the sword of Virginius, and smile with joy that he yet lived to thrust it into the vitals of his daughter.

Behind all this reign of atrocity, stood the Radical majority in Congress. In this era of better feeling, it is almost incredible that men of Anglo-Saxon blood could have given countenance to plans of reconstruction that could lead to such results. In their fury, they impeached President Johnson because his plan seemed too lenient; possibly they

---
*Dr. J. L. M. Curry's figures.

would have impeached even Abraham Lincoln, had he lived to urge his temperate and humane policy.

A quotation from the records of that period will interest the student. Let us see what Mr. D. H. Chamberlain, of Massachusetts, attorney-general of South Carolina from 1868 to 1872, writes of the situation. First, as to the "unwise and unfortunate" conduct of the white men of that noble old commonwealth, sprung from the best blood of the French Huguenot and of the Anglo-Saxon. Says Mr. Chamberlain: "One race (that is, the whites) stood aloft and haughtily refused to seek the confidence of the race which was just entering on its new powers." Shades of Alfred and of Washington! Men of the great Anglo-Saxon race expected to "seek the confidence," to acknowledge the leadership, of a race known to history only as "hewers of wood and drawers of water" through all the ages!

So much for Mr. Chamberlain's knowledge of history. Now for his opinion of the carpetbagger and the scalawag. "Three years have passed," says he, "and the result is—what? Incompetency, dishonesty, corruption in all its forms, have 'advanced their miscreated fronts,' have put to flight the small remnant that opposed them, and now rules the party that rules the State." Mr. Chamberlain's candor and truthfulness compel our admiration, in spite of his monstrous twaddle about the Anglo-Saxons of Carolina.

X

The Ku Klux Klan

This state of affairs could not last; moderate wickedness might have lasted longer. Respectable Northern men living in the South revolted against it, and began to think about their Anglo-Saxon civilization. As a result, there sprang up the Ku Klux Klan,* a secret order instituted by the whites in self-preservation, but later on used for unworthy purposes. Great throngs of men clothed in white sheets rode single file on horseback through negro sections of the country; their horses drank water by the barrel, and the riders, by the bucketful; skulls and crossbones were drawn on the doors and walls, and on all the voting places: the appeal to superstition won the victory; the great reign of terror was over.

It was anarchy; but self-preservation is the first law of nature. Let him that is without sin among us throw the first stone, we say reverently. The nation that holds the continent bought from the Indian with beads and bracelets, or taken from him at the point of the bayonet, the nation that gave Spain twenty million dollars for a principality, can ill afford—whether North or South—to blame the Anglo-Saxon for using ghosts and goblins to save his property and maintain his civilization.

This fearful period may be said to have lasted from 1865 to 1876. During these years, many of the young men went to new states to seek their fortunes; capital shrank from the South as men shrink from a leper; two-thirds of

---
*In Thomas Dixon's play, *The Clansman*, Gen. N. B. Forrest is represented as being the grand commander of the Ku Klux Klan.

the wealth of the South had been swept away; money, if any one would lend it, was held at the fabulous rate of 75 per cent or 80 per cent; colossal ruin reigned supreme.

Even President Grant, so kindly in some ways, had kept soldiers in the South to terrorize elections. Hayes relieved the South of this incubus. From his accession to the presidency, the new era of reconstruction set in—reconstruction by the Southern people, the only kind that could be sound or permanent.

Of the "black-and-tan" conventions that drafted the new constitutions, we have already briefly spoken. Virginia's great (!) convention was probably more decent, or less barbarous, than some others; that worthy body drafted the constitution under which Virginia lived till July 10, 1902. A handful of Virginia gentlemen of brains and character were powerless against the enormous black-and-tan majority in the "famous" Underwood convention. An anecdote of two of the statesmen will lighten up our ghastly narrative. The question of issuing certain stock and bonds was being discussed by the carpetbaggers and the scalawags, when one ebony statesman turned to another and said, "What is dis yere storck de is talkin' about so much? Whar's de gwine ter put all dat storck?" "Oh, shur! Jim, ain't you done listen to de 'schusion? De storck is gwine ter be kep in de barns." Both solons were ready to vote; carpetbagger and scalawag were ready to divide the office and the plunder.

XI

Reconstruction by the Southern People

The real restoration of the South may be said to have begun about 1880. In that year, she had about $17\frac{1}{2}$ per cent of the assessed property of the whole country, against 44 per cent in 1860. By 1890, she had added $3,800,000,000 to her assessed values, a gain of more than 50 per cent in ten years. In farm products, she gained 16 per cent in the same period. In 1896, she made one-third of the corn crop of the country; she now makes more than half the total wheat crop. In the period 1880-1895, she increased her cotton crop from five million to almost ten million bales. In 1894, she manufactured 718,515 bales; in 1903, 2,000,729 bales. In 1903, her cotton crop was nearly eleven million bales; in 1904, more than ten million; in 1905, nearly fourteen million; and in 1906, it was more than eleven million bales.

In the *ante-bellum* period, the South grew rich on grains, sugar, rice, indigo, and tobacco. Now she has all these sources of wealth, and many others. Since 1863, the wheat shipments of New Orleans have increased from 2,744,581 bushels to 15,643,745 bushels a year, and the corn shipments from less than 1,000,000 bushels to 12,832,139 bushels. The shipments from Galveston have increased in the same proportion. In 1902, the shipments from these two ports together almost equalled those from New York. Cotton mills are springing up in all directions. New England mills, also, are moving south, so as to save freights, and thus be able to compete better with Southern mills. In 1902, for the first time, the number of bales and pounds used by Southern mills exceeded those of the North and East.

Before the war, the seed of the cotton was fed to the hogs. To-day, it is used for fertilizing after a valuable oil has been extracted. The income from this new source of wealth increased almost ten-fold in fifteen years.

The South is developing vast mines of coal and of iron. In fifteen years, the output of coal from her mines increased fivefold. She is "sending iron to Pennsylvania and coal to Newcastle," says a distinguished educator.* By putting iron ore, coke, coal, and limestone close together, nature enables the South to undersell the world in manufactured iron.

The railroads of the South are developing rapidly. Since 1894, the Southern Railway has increased in mileage from 4,159 to 7,550; the Louisville and Nashville, from 2,673 to 4,279; the Norfolk and Western, from 1,327 to 1,861. In the same period, the united earnings of these three systems have more than doubled.

Cotton will yet be "king." By building mills near the cotton fields, the South can soon dictate the price of cotton to the world. The proposed canal across Central America, by bringing the Southern states much closer to China, will greatly promote the cotton interests of the South, and in various ways add to the wealth of the whole nation.

In farm produce, in garden products, in foreign commerce, in banking, and in many other sources of wealth, the South is making substantial progress in building up her

---

*Chancellor J. H. Kirkland, of Vanderbilt University.

N. B. FORREST

waste places and restoring her shattered fortunes. She is no longer dependent upon negro labor, though she prefers the negro for her rice, her sugar, and her cotton fields. Her farmers are rapidly learning to diversify their crops so as to be less injured by the decline in this or that market. The brains and the energy formerly devoted to politics will soon make the South wealthy, and make her educational institutions equal to those of any other section in training intelligent citizens.

In educational matters, also, the South has made most substantial progress. A Northern expert says that the South is spending as much on public education as Great Britain, though the population is little more than half. The magnanimity of the Southern people in giving negro children the same advantages as their own, in spite of the fact that the whites pay over 90 per cent of the taxes, is one of the greatest proofs of the true nobility of our people. The South has forgiven the poor hoodwinked freedman, but despises the white men that used him as a cat's-paw.

The colleges and the state universities of the South are doing a great work in training the youth of both sexes, proving that our people believe in an intelligent citizenship. It is said that no Southern college was extinguished by the war, but that the people, by private and by state funds, have revived all that were closed or seriously crippled by war and its results. In the twenty years from 1875 to 1895, school attendance increased 130 per cent, while population increased only 54 per cent; the value of school property more than trebled; the attendance upon the colleges and universities increased in fifteen years 150 per cent.

To the buoyancy and the hopefulness of our people, we have referred in foregoing pages. The power of recuperation, with peoples as with individuals, is one of the sweetest gifts of Heaven; and this gift in large measure has been bestowed upon our people. The French people, also, have wonderful recuperative power, but the South has eclipsed that nation. After the Franco-Prussian War (1870-1871), France lay apparently prostrate and helpless at the feet of the new German Confederation. It seemed as if all were lost including honor; and a superficial observer might have thought that France might never resume her place among the "great powers of Europe." Such gloomy fears were soon dissipated. In a short time, France paid a war indemnity of over a billion dollars, and, in spite of the loss of valuable territory ceded to the conqueror, soon resumed her place among the great nations of Europe. Even greater power of recuperation has been shown by our noble people. Though one-third of her able-bodied men had died from the effects of war; though she had lost two-thirds of her assessed property by the forcible confiscation of her slaves, by plunder, and by the legitimate results of failure; though the era of reconstruction had paralyzed her energies and made life a mere existence—yet, since her people regained control of their local governments, the South has rallied beyond expression, and now her pulses throb with the fullness of the spring and with the buoyancy of a new vitality.

The war was worth all it cost. It has made labor more universal. Before the war, a good many young men lived on their fathers and helped languidly to manage the plantation. Now every young man is expected to adopt a trade, a business, or a profession, and the first question asked of a young man of twenty-five is, "What is your business or profession?" Gentlemen of easy leisure are little respected. Labor is more honored than ever before.

Being cut off from political honors and preferment, the brains of the South have been devoted to other matters. Politics used to be the bane of her civilization; to every statesman, she had a thousand small politicians. Now our people are as a rule too busy to go into politics, and it is very hard to induce good business men, or men of standing in the professions, to take public office. Consequently, we are producing great leaders of industry, great financiers, fine lawyers, noble educators, and excellent scholars. Statesmen we can hardly hope to produce while occupying our isolated position, politically, in the Union. A Clay or a Calhoun from the South could not muster a majority in the Senate.

XII

The Race Problem

The "negro question" is one of the great problems now awaiting solution. Not whether the negro shall sit at the white man's table, smoke in his library, and marry his daughter—that question is never discussed south of the Potomac; but whether he shall take part in the government of the Southern people, and hold public office and other positions of honor and responsibility. This race question is one that vitally concerns the individual states, and must be left to them for solution. If many negroes are disfranchised by the new constitutions of North Carolina, Virginia, Louisiana, Alabama, and other Southern states, it is because they cannot meet the requirements as to intelligence and as to amount of property laid down by those constitutions. That no man can be deprived of his vote on account of race, color, or previous condition of servitude is known to everyone who has ever heard of the war amendments to the constitution of the United States, or who ever reads a newspaper. A good many whites lose their votes under the new constitutions of the South, but vastly more negroes are disfranchised. It is needless to say that the South believes that this is a white man's country; and it would seem that the North is rapidly coming to the same opinion.

This race question has been a bone of contention ever since the formation of our government. In 1787, it came near defeating the plan for a "more perfect union;" and the so-called "Federal ratio," whereby five slaves were counted as three citizens in fixing the number of representatives in Congress, was resorted to as a compromise. Then came the long wrangle as to "free states" and "slave states;" the Missouri compromise of 1820; the angry debates in Congress; the rise of the Abolition party; the publication of *Uncle Tom's Cabin;* John Brown's raid, and, to cap the climax, the great war outlined in foregoing chapters. Worse than all that, came the era of reconstruction, when a merciless Radical majority in Congress attempted to put the freedman in control of millions of what an English historian has called the flower of the Anglo-Saxon race. This problem long refused to admit of solution. White men in the South used this negro vote to elevate themselves into public office, until the South was driven to the conclusion that the negro must get out of politics and let the white man govern both races unassisted. This is the true solution. Since retiring largely from the field of statesmanship, the negro is less objectionable to his Anglo-Saxon neighbor; and, if the United States government and its courts will let the South alone and not interfere in her suffrage questions, we shall have peace, happiness, and fraternal union.

As said before, the negro question has long been the apple of discord between the sections of our country. How preposterous it seems for brethren of the great Anglo-Saxon race to quarrel over a race so manifestly inferior, and so clearly intended by providence to occupy a position of inferiority! It simply proves the perversity and the stupidity of human nature.

As said in an earlier chapter, many of the ablest men of the *ante-bellum* period were in favor of colonizing the negroes in Africa. Some of the thoughtful men of our day are in favor of deportation. At present, however, the cotton states are opposed to the separation of the races. They believe that the labor of the negro is indispensable on the rice and cotton plantations; but the time may come soon when this idea will vanish before statistics.

Rudimentary education the Southern people intend to give the negro if he stays out of politics; but, if his so-called friends in other sections should upset the suffrage laws now prevailing in the South, the next step would probably be to let the colored children have no schools except those that could be maintained by the taxes of the colored people alone. This would give them one school where they now have ten. At present, comparatively few Southern whites favor a division of the school tax on the basis of color; if, however, the United States courts should interfere with suffrage laws in the South, there would be a tidal wave of indignation that would submerge the colored schools sustained by the whites, and produce other results too painful to predict.

Bad advice and pernicious leadership have injured the colored man beyond expression. Alienated from his white neighbors, first by scalawags and carpetbaggers, more recently by artful politicians, he has left the white man's church, protested against white teachers, and lost the training that contact with a higher civilization used to give him. The difference between the old colored people and the younger is very noticeable, and to this deterioration is due the present state of feeling between the races. The only solution of the problem, if the colored man is to remain in the South, is for him to get out of the white man's way, politically and otherwise: competition will inevitably destroy him. His only place in the South is that of a servant without servitude.

At school and at church, also, he is often wofully misled, even totally ruined. Many of his teachers set him against his white neighbors. Instead of reminding him that the schoolhouse was built with the white man's money and the teacher's salary paid out of the white man's treasury, the teacher too often plants the seeds of race bitterness in the black child's bosom. At home, too, a great many parents are doing the same thing, thus sowing the wind to reap the whirlwind in the future. We are glad to say, however, that there are some wiser teachers and some wiser colored parents. A most respectable colored teacher in Virginia, on being asked quite recently why his pupils were so offensive to white citizens on the streets, replied, "I try to teach them right at school, but they are taught wrong at home."

At church, also, they get some pernicious instruction, though we rejoice to say that there are a number of faithful colored ministers trying to lift their people to a higher moral level. To illustrate our statement as to pernicious instruction, we cite an incident related to us by a Virginia gentleman of high Christian character. His family had but one servant, a colored woman, whom they trusted as a member of the family and for whom they all felt a deep affection. Handkerchiefs, pieces of jewelry, and other things disappeared mysteriously; but at first no one suspected the servant. Finally, the losses became so heavy that they were compelled to suspect her, as she was the only person that had access to the trunks and bureaus. One day they searched her trunk, and in it found the missing articles. They called her up, told her how they had felt towards her and how they had trusted her, and asked her why she had betrayed their confidence. She replied: "Well, my preacher tells us that the Lord told the Jews, when they went out of Egypt to plunder the Egyptians, to get even with them for keeping them in bondage; and he says that we have a right to get all we can out of the white people for having kept us in slavery."

Shakespeare makes one of his characters say that the devil can cite scripture for his purpose. So with this negro preacher. He might be pardoned for not understanding the command given by Moses to the Jews in verse 22 of the 3rd chapter of Exodus; but the application of it to the colored race is a clear perversion of scripture. How shall the blind lead the blind?

A strong feeling for employing white teachers for negro children is developing in parts of the South. There are many ladies in the Southern states who would take charge of schools for colored children, and thus guarantee them several hours a day of good moral teaching and moral influence.

What the negro needs is kind but firm restraint such as he had in slavery. He is the child-race of the world. Instead of letting him live in idleness, or work only one day in six, as numbers of them do, many are in favor of putting him under tutelage, and compelling him to earn honest wages. If his hands and his brain were employed, his evil propensities would be to a large degree curbed, and thus the most potent cause of bad feeling between the races would be removed, partially if not entirely.

He needs, also, good leaders of his own race. Most of his representative men, when they meet, pass resolutions against lynching, but rarely condemn the monstrous crimes that drive the white man to such frenzy.

XIII

Morals and Religion

In morals and religion, the Southern people are still quite sound at bottom. Divorce, though more common than before the war, still puts one on the defensive, if not under a social stigma.

Immorality is condemned; drunkards are despised; the temperance movement is sweeping large parts of the country, the elimination of the vicious vote giving the temperance cause a wonderful impetus, even in such conservative states as Virginia. The negro vote always went in the main on the side of liquor; and in temperance elections the colored preacher could not control his members.

To decline a drink used to cause duels. Now, duelling is put among the antiquities, and liquor is rarely offered in private houses.

In religious matters, the Southern people are still very conservative. New fads and *isms* find little favor among them. To go to church at least once on Sunday is expected of every good citizen, and a public violation of the Sabbath injures a man's standing in most communities. The two races no longer worship together. The colored race demand their own churches, and preachers of their own color. Many of the preachers were used by the white politicians, and lost caste with their white neighbors; but some of them have been very useful in maintaining law and order.

The people of the so-called "New South" still honor religion, respect the Sabbath, and despise cant and hypocrisy.

Social swearing, if we may coin the phrase, is no longer "good form" in the South. An oath uttered audibly in the Westmoreland Club of Richmond would cause amazement; swearing is relegated to the barroom and other haunts of the sons of Belial. Gentlemen of standing rarely swear in public; but most youths have a touch of the habit just after measles and roseola.

Lynching is just now bringing censure upon some Southern communities; but it is an erroneous idea that it is confined to the South or that negroes are the only victims. It is true, however, that about three-fourths of the lynchings occur in the South, and that over half of the victims are negroes. It is equally true that the principal cause of lynching is the freedman's crime; and it may be added that, as long as this cause continues, lynching will be resorted to. Southern men will not allow certain facts to be dragged through the courts, while police-court lawyers delight police-court rabbles with their indecent questions. We regret to say, moreover, that the colored people as a rule do not condemn the crimes leading to lynching half as vigorously as they do the lynching. The colored man does not seem to have the least conception of the awful sanctity of the white man's home: the chasm at this point is as wide as eternity.

As some of the brutal element of the negro race move north and west, these sections are resorting to lynch law almost daily. The people there are beginning to sympathize with the South considerably. Foreigners, however, do not understand the awful situation. Says an Englishman living in Mississippi: "It is perfectly useless to try to explain to a foreigner the true inwardness of lynch law. . . . . . . I do not uphold them in wrong-doing, and yet I tell my English kinsmen and friends that, if they were surrounded by the same conditions, they would undoubtedly act just as the Southerners do. Human nature, especially Anglo-Saxon nature, is the same in all lands."

In the matter of honor, we still have much to be proud of. We cannot claim, however, that we are as strictly scrupulous as the generations before us. Civil wars always affect the honor and the morals of a people, and we cannot claim total exemption from this law of nature. While our election officers have, in many cases, used very questionable methods to maintain the political supremacy of the white race, our people as a mass regret that such methods were considered necessary, and are recasting their constitutions so as to eliminate the vicious and purchasable vote by fair and honorable means. Upon the youth of our day devolves the responsibility of carrying out hereafter the election laws created under these new state constitutions. The temptation to corrupt methods will exist no longer. Cheating in elections will train our people to cheat in other matters. The habit of dishonesty and prevarication grows into a second nature.

Though making the concessions in the last paragraph, we can still say that we have not been "sinners above all the Galileans."

The young men of the South are still sound in the essentials of honor. The college honor spoken of in our second chapter is still maintained to a degree that augurs well for the future. While cheating on examinations is more frequent than "before the war," it is generally condemned by the public sentiment of the students, and the student body will often secure the necessary evidence and present the culprit before the faculty for trial. Northern colleges and universities have been trying recently to introduce the honor system: prominent students sometimes write south to inquire as to its details, and its methods of operation.

Municipal corruption figures a good deal in our daily papers. Councilmen are bought up; some are convicted of bribery, and others go unpunished. In this matter, also, we are not "sinners above all the Galileans." Some of the pious and self-righteous cities of the other sections are worse than those of the old "slave-driver" and "lashing planter." Two wrongs, however, do not make a right. We must make our town councils and our legislatures, like Cæsar's wife, above reproach. It devolves upon us to elect men of character to these positions. If such men say that they are too busy to accept office, our boys must determine, first to be men of character, and then to make some personal sacrifice in order to serve the city and the commonwealth. We still have much to be thankful for. In these cases of municipal corruption, the men under suspicion rarely represent the real civilization of our communities. They are generally men of little previous standing, itching for public office, and using it, when gained, for their own personal ends and objects.

Our educated men are generally men of honor. The teachers and the scholars of the South are as a rule highly respected as representing the best type of the citizen and of the gentleman. Few of them can be bought at any figure. A few Southern states have been accused of rottenness and corruption in the matter of "book adoptions;" but the men suspected of selling their votes are generally not educators and scholars, but men of the type described in the foregoing paragraph pushing their way into school boards and state boards of education. We must mark these men, and by our votes bury them in the obscurity from which they sprang.

XIV

Zaccheus* is Coming Down

Love for the Union is increasing in the South. Though she is practically ignored in the national government, and though many objectionable men represent the Federal government in Southern communities, the South is proud of the Union, would fight for it against any foreign nation, and welcomes overtures from friendly Northerners like Mr. Charles Francis Adams and others that are leading the way to full reconciliation. The young men love the Union more than the older; but state loyalty is still very strong among all classes. If compelled to choose between the State and the Union, the men of the South would undoubtedly "go with the state;" but the possibility of a rupture is never discussed with any seriousness. The right of secession,

*See page 122.

"though not by gunpowder determinable," is not regarded as a live question, but rather as what editors call "dead matter." It would take a number of wild-cat presidents and pestiferous politicians to resurrect the doctrine of secession as a burning question.

A Southern youth, if asked which he loves most, the state or the Union, would probably say, "I love not Cæsar less but Rome more," Cæsar being the Union, and Rome his native state. Possibly we should say he loves the Union well, and his state better.

President Cleveland's official recognition of Southern men did no little to cement the sections. In his cabinet, sat several Southern men of high standing; and, during the great naval review in 1893, when the fleets of the world met our navy in Hampton Roads, a Confederate veteran, who was secretary of war, was welcomed to the harbor by the screaming of hundreds of whistles, American and foreign.

President McKinley was respected, if not loved, by the Southern people. His tragic death was greatly deplored by our people, and public sentiment in the South demanded the execution of the assassin.

In the war with Spain in 1898, the South showed great loyalty to the Union. The greatest diplomat of that era was Fitzhugh Lee, consul-general to Havana. This noble son of Virginia was selected for this position when the relations between Spain and the United States were becoming "strained" on account of our sympathy with Cuba. General Lee was a brilliant success, and helped to distinguish Mr.

McKinley's administration. The president, it is thought, permitted small politicians to "sidetrack" this eminent Southerner and Democrat in the slashes of Florida, instead of sending him as the liberator of Cuba.

In the war with Spain, Worth Bagley, of North Carolina, was the first man killed in battle. The heroic deed of Hobson, of Alabama, in attempting to block up the harbor of Santiago; the bravery of "Little Joe Wheeler" in the same campaign; the gallantry of Schley, the noble son of Maryland—all helped to unite the different sections of our country.

If we may judge by the signs of the times, the day of true union and full reconciliation is fast approaching. Mr. Charles Francis Adams's Charleston address, in which he said that both sides were right in 1861; Mr. Cleveland's Madison Square Garden speech, in which he praised the magnanimity of the South towards the negro, and urged the North to leave the solution of the negro problem to the Southern people; the endorsement of that speech by the Philadelphia *Press,* long the exponent of the warmest anti-Southern sentiment; the addresses made in Richmond, Va., in April, 1903, by Mr. St. Clair McKelway, editor of the Brooklyn *Eagle,* and by Dr. Lyman Abbott, in which they spoke tenderly of Southern heroes and sympathetically on Southern questions—these and other significant events have made the heart of the South beat faster, and prepared the way for a union not "pinned together by bayonets," but "resting upon the consent of the governed."

Mutual forgiveness and reparation! This, as already

said, is the open sesame to fraternal union and to the full measure of our national greatness. If such Northern men as those named above could write our histories, compile our encyclopedias, and edit all our great journals, this book might not be needed, or certainly many of its paragraphs might be dispensed with. Alas! however, ink-pots of Liliput and pygmy politicians have so shaped public sentiment, so filled our bookshelves with pestilential libels, that, unless Southern men write the truth, the South will be handed down to infamy. Books are still pouring from the press, encyclopedias still being printed, that demand refutation from Southern writers.

We are not waving the "bloody shirt," but telling the truth, "naught extenuating and naught setting down in malice." Truth is the great healer. Truth crushed to earth will rise again. To tell the truth to the people of the South, and to all elsewhere that care to know it,—such is the object of this volume, and we invoke upon it the blessing of high Heaven, that it may increase the self-respect of our beloved South, disabuse some fair minds in other sections of false ideas as to her history, her customs, her institutions, and her motives, past and present, and hasten the day when "Ephraim shall not envy Judah and Judah shall not vex Ephraim."

CHAPTER X

CONCLUSION

I

Recapitulation

WE have finished our talks. Before parting, let us take time for a few words of review, of recapitulation, and a few words by way of warning to the young reader of these pages.

We have tried to show the Southern youth how much he has to love and to be proud of, and how much there is to inspire him. In our earlier talks, we dwelt upon some of the poetic features of our country, and tried to appeal to the sentiment for the venerable, the lofty, in our history. We stood together at Roanoke Island, Saint Augustine, and Jamestown, and gave ourselves up to the thoughts too deep for utterance that surge in upon our souls as we stand at such sacred places. Then we took up the heroic phases of the colonial era. We saw how our Southern fathers rose up against the tyranny of Harvey and of Berkeley, and left us as a legacy eternal hatred of tyranny and of tyrants.

Coming to the last half of the 18th century, we saw the men of the South coöperating with those of Massachusetts in opposing the tyranny of George III and his ministers. Along with Otis of Massachusetts, we named Henry, the

Virginian, whom both tradition and history have made preëminent. In the war that the colonies waged for independence, the South, we saw, played a noble part. We passed rapidly in review the career of some of her greatest soldiers, spoke briefly of some of the critical battles of the Revolution, and saw clearly that the South played a noble and heroic part in achieving American independence.

Then came the era of constitutions. The South's part in drafting the Federal constitution of 1787, we found to be very great; and we saw later on that the violation of this great compact or agreement by many Northern and Western states led eleven Southern states to secede from the Union in 1861.

Between the formation of the Union (1789) and its dissolution (1861), came, it will be remembered, the War of 1812 and the Mexican War (1846). That our states did nobly in these wars, we showed very clearly. We then reviewed the cause of ill-feeling between the sections. We showed that the South bore patiently for many years the attacks made by fanatics upon her people and her institutions, bore slurs and abuse from many quarters, bore the nullification on the part of many Northern and Western states of clauses of the constitution and of acts of Congress in which she was deeply interested. We saw that, when, in 1860, a great party avowedly hostile to her and her interests got possession of the government, seven Southern states seceded, and that four others, because they did not believe in coercion, joined the secession movement.

That the doctrine of secession was not confined to the

South but was also a New England doctrine, we proved conclusively; and that nullification, also, was a New England doctrine, we showed very clearly.

We then gave a rapid sketch of the great war for Southern independence. We discussed the rearing, the motives, the courage, and the self-sacrificing heroism of the soldiers and the sailors of the Confederacy; gave a rapid outline of the campaigns of Lee, Jackson, and Albert Sidney Johnston, and of the sufferings of the noble women of the South, the wives and the mothers of heroes.

We wrote as a Southern man for Southern youth. While glorifying the South, we did not heap maledictions and denunciations upon every one in the North, but upon those alone that came under the head of fanatics, vilifiers, marauders, plunderers, and heroes of "triumphal" marches over women, children, and graves. Any one that takes offense must either belong to one of these classes or condone the crimes referred to. "If any, speak, for him have I offended." Hatred towards any section, we have not encouraged. Love for the South, admiration for her heroes, belief in her sincerity, and in the eternal justice of her cause —all this we have taught to the best of our ability and with all the earnestness of conviction. "If this be treason, make the most of it."

II

Patriotism

What we all, old and young, need, is real patriotism. We need a larger vision of our relation to our country.

Local patriotism killed ancient Greece, and, if encouraged, may kill modern America.

In ancient Greece, men used to say, " I am an Athenian," "I am a Spartan," "I am a Theban;" and the system of city-states indicated by these phrases led Greece to disintegration, decay, and ruin.

General Henry Lee in 1798 needed a larger vision when he cried in the Virginia legislature, "Virginia is my country." John Randolph, of Roanoke, needed it. We in the twentieth century need it also. Let us lift up our eyes unto the hills and catch the inspiration.

Patriotism means love of country, love of one's native land. Some men spell *country* without *r*; but even Westmoreland county is no man's country. If we love only Texas, Georgia, or Virginia, we cannot say that we are patriotic. We must love our country as a whole. We must love the flag that has braved a hundred years the battle and the breeze. If we have not this love, we are orphans in the universe, we are cut off from one of the deepest sources of joy. A man without patriotism is a man without a country, and a man without a country is more to be pitied than the man without a shadow—the famous but wretched being of German literature.

A great German author depicts in vivid language the sufferings of the man without a shadow; how he was pursued by the sidelong glances of every passer-by and by the curious stare of vulgar mobs, and so driven to desperation. Worse than this is the suffering of the man without a country. Better migrate to the bleak hills of Labrador and, sitting on the shivering edges of a glacier, cry, "My country 'tis of thee I sing," than live in a land of perpetual sunshine and of golden harvests, with lips that cannot sing that thrilling anthem.

Already I hear your comments, "gentle" reader. The Northern sympathizer is saying, "Good; he's advising the youth of the South to forget the war and love the Union." The overzealous Southerner is saying, "Bah! he's gone over to the enemy, and is catering to the majority."

Both are wrong, especially the Southerner. His sneer is as false as Lucifer's when he told the Almighty that Job knew which side his bread was buttered on, and that he served God for the loaves and fishes. Wrong, too, was the Northerner, when he thought that this writer was urging the Southern youth to "forget the war." When I forget the war, let my tongue cleave to the roof of my mouth, and let my right hand forget its cunning.

What, then? Both are wrong, I repeat. I am just where I started: we need a larger vision of patriotism.

Virginia is not your country. Carolina is not your country. Alabama, Florida, Tennessee, though all call up sweet and solemn memories, are not your country. You need what the Romans call *patria* and the Germans *fatherland*—and would that we had the word, and the same lofty sentiment that thrills the bosom of the German as he sings, *What is the German's Fatherland?*

A man may say that the old Abolition party destroyed his love for this country. That party is out of date, but the fatherland still lives. Another may say that he does not love the flag because so many South-haters have sung of that flag in verse or have glorified it in their orations. Rise to a larger vision. Do you hate the Bible because many blatant and pernicious sects have quoted it as authority for their perverted teachings?

We can denounce the abolitionists, but love our country. We can denounce the slurs of pestiferous poets, pulpiteers, and orators, but still love the flag which our fathers helped to make respected and feared on land and ocean. It is our country, our flag. Shall we let these men and their modern imitators scratch our names out of the old family Bible and drive us out of the halls of our fathers, and leave us shivering in the cold without a home where we may meet around the old hearth and the old Yule log?

For forty years, this has been our blunder; let us up and rectify it. Let us go up and keep the feast. If some of the family give us cold looks and treat us as the prodigal son who has wasted his substance with riotous living, let us not be driven from the ancestral halls and the graves of our fathers; but, led by Virginia, the oldest of all the sisters, and "Carolina bright and fair," let us take our place at the old fireside and sing together the songs of "Auld Lang Syne."

INDEX

Abolition Party: rise of, .. 171
Abolition Societies 173
Abbott, Lyman: 303
Adams, Charles Francis: ..
    77, 84, 187, 301, 303
Adams, John Quincy: ......
    150, 151, 184, 185, 187
Alabama: secedes; 193
    debt of, ... 282
Alamance: battle of, ... 40
Alien and Sedition Acts, ... 191
Andros, Governor: 30
Antietam: battle of, ... 244
Anti-Federalists and Federalists: 156, 158
Appomattox: surrender at, 251
Arkansas: secedes, ... 193
Articles of Confederation:
    80, 83
Ashe, John: 59
Atlanta: privations in, ... 232
Aunt Phillis' Cabin: 101

Bacon's Rebellion: 28, 29
Bagley, Worth: 303
Bee, Barnard E.: 254
Berkeley, Sir William: ..27, 30
Biglow Papers: 47
"Black Friday": 279
"Book Adoptions": 301
Boone, Daniel: 71
Booth, John Wilkes: ...271, 272

Boston Massacre: 37, 38
Boyd, Belle: 218, 219
Brown, John: 178, 179
Buchanan, James: 193
Buell, D. C.: 200, 201
Burgesses, House of: ..163, 164
Burnside, A. E.: 245, 246

Calhoun, John C.: 156, 190, 191
Campbell, William: 57, 58
Carolina and Virginia: ...36-44
Carpetbagger: 280, 284
Carrington, Edward: 41
Caswell, Richard: 61
Cavalier and Puritan: .....
    119, 123, 147, 149
Cedar Run, Battle of: 261
Chamberlain, D. H.: 284
Chancellorsville and Marye's
    Heights: 245, 247
Christ in the Camp: ..207, 208
Civilization, the Planter: 116-119
Civil War (See *War between the States.*)
Clark, George Rogers: 58
Clarke, Elijah: 68
Clay, Henry: 86, 175
Cleveland, Benjamin: 60
Cleveland, Grover: 302, 303
Code Duello: 127
Cold Harbor; battle of 250
Commercial, Cincinnati: ... 186

[311]

Committees of Correspondence 40
Committee of Safety: 43
Common Sense: 47
Confederate Candle: 219
Confederate States: government organized, ... 193
Confederate Veteran: 195
Confederacy, Women of the 213, 240
Congress: the first American 24
  of 1765, ...35, 36
  continental, ...
    36, 49, 80
  stamp act, ...35, 36
  representation fixed 81, 82
  secession discussed in, ... 183
  and Lincoln, 270, 271
  and Andrew Johnson, ..273, 277, 278
Constitution: remarks on, 20
  and the south 78-86
  views of the 150-158
  and "higher law," 172
  amendments to, ...278, 279
Constitutional Convention of 1787: 79-82
Conway, Cabal: 59
Cooke, John Esten: 25
Cooke, John R.: 244, 245
Cotton Gin: effect of the, 171, 172
Croghan, George: 88

Cross Keys: battle of, ... 261
Curry, J. L. M.: 101, 109

Davidson, William: 61
Davie, William R.: 60
Davis, Jefferson: 94, 153, 156, 175, 189, 193, 194, 258, 266, 271, 272.
Declaration of Independence: passed, ... 49
Declaration of Rights: 49
Dixon, Thomas: 285
Dred Scott Case: 177
Dunmore, Lord: 30, 46, 53
Dwight, Dr. Timothy: 182, 184
Eagle, Brooklyn: 303
Education in the South: ..
  107, 108, 289
Emancipation: in Virginia, 163, 170
  the beginning of, .. 166
  growth of, 169-172
  proclamation, ... 271
Embargo Act: 189, 190
Encyclopedia Britannica: 101-103, 192, 229
Estrangement: early cause of, ...146-158
  later causes of, ...158-162
  greatest cause of, 162-181
Ewell, Richard S.: 243

Faneuil Hall: 38

INDEX

Federalists: and anti-Federalists, ...156-158
Federal Ratio: 168
Female College: the first in America, ... 25
Fifteenth Amendment: ... 279
Fiske, John: 24, 42, 71, 72, 84, 148, 184, 185, 190
Five Resolutions: 34, 35
Florida: secedes, ... 193
    debt of, ...282
Fort Donelson: 263
Fort Henry: 263
Forrest, N. B.: ...240, 263, 285
Fourteenth Amendment: .. 278
Fredericksburg: battle of, .. 245
Freedman's Bureau: 274
Fremont, John C.:......... 177
Frietchie, Barbara: 213, 259, 260
Fugitive Slave Laws: ..173, 191

Gadsden, Christopher: ..35, 46
Gambling: 129
Geiger, Emily: 67, 68
Gentlemen of the Old School: 144
George III and his Friends: 30-36
Georgia: first female college in, ...25, 116
    and independence, ... 47
    heroes of, ...68-71
    in the Revolution, ... 76
    in convention of 1787, ... 79
    in Mexican War, 95
    cedes claims to territory, ... 167

Georgia: and emancipation, ... 170
    secedes, ... 193
    "triumphal march" through 230-232
Gettysburg: battle of, ..247-249
Gist, Mordecai: 52
Gordon, John B.: 251
Grady, Henry W.: 116
Grant, U. S.: 123, 230, 250, 251, 266, 267
Great Bridge: battle of, ... 53
Greeley, Horace: 186
Greg, Percy: on Mexican War, ... 96
    on slavery, 133, 134

Habersham, Colonel: 43
Hatton, Robert: 242
Hamilton, Alexander: 20
Hampton, Wade: 130, 242, 248
Harnett, Cornelius: 62
Harrison, William Henry:.. 87
Hartford Convention: 184, 185, 188, 190
Hart, Nancy: 70, 71
Harvey, Sir John: 27, 30
Henry, Patrick: ....
    33, 34, 41, 58, 81
Herald, New York: on secession, ... 186
Heroes: and Heroines, ...51-72
    of the frontier, ..71-72
    homes that made, 98-146
Heroines in Homespun: 234-236
"Higher Law, The": ...173-174

Hill, A. P.: 246, 251
Hoar, George F.: 77
"Honor System": 107, 108, 129
Hooker, Joseph: 246
House of Burgesses: 36, 38
Houston, Sam: 88
Howard, John Eager: ..51, 55
Hundred Years Wrangle, The: 146-196
Hunter, William: 61, 62

Independence: 44-51
Intolerable Acts: 39

Jackson, Andrew: 87, 88
Jackson, James: 69
Jackson, T. J.:............
   94, 178, 240, 253, 261
Jackson, Mrs. T. J.: 255
Jamestown: 22, 23
Jamestown Exposition: 129
Jasper, William: 69, 70
Jefferson, Thomas: ....
   84, 85, 156, 158
Johnson, Andrew:
   271-274, 277, 278
Johnson, Richard M.: ...87, 88
Johnston, Albert Sidney:
   189, 240, 241, 247, 262, 265
Johnston, Joseph E.:
   94, 189, 230, 232, 240, 266

Kansas: and slavery question, ... 176
Kentucky: and Dan'l Boone, 71
   in Mexican War, 193
   stays in Union, 193
Kernstown: battle of, ... 260
Ku Klux Klan: 285, 286

Latané, William: 243
Lee, Fitzhugh: 18, 243, 302, 303
Lee, Guy Carleton: 165
Lee, Henry: 55, 56
Lee, Robert E.: 56, 59, 94, 123, 130, 178, 189, 194, 240-252, 266, 267, 272
Lee, Stephen D.: 243
Lewis, Andrew: 53
Lincoln, Abraham: 150, 156, 175, 178, 180, 181, 192, 193, 196, 257, 266, 267, 270, 271
Lodge, Henry Cabot: 122
London Company: 25
Longstreet, James: 244, 257
Louisiana: effect of purchase
   of, ... 172
   secedes, ... 193
Lowell, James Russell: ... 77

McClellan, George B.: ..241-245
McDowell: battle of, ... 260
McDowell, Grace Greenlee: 63
McDowell, Joseph: 60
McIntosh, Lachlan: 68, 69
McKelway, St. Clair; 303
McKinley, William: 302
Madison, James: 20, 84
Manassas: battle of, ... 243
Marion, Francis: 64, 66
Marshall, John: 53, 157, 158
Marye's Heights: and Chancellorsville, ...245-247
Maryland: and independence, ... 47
   heroes of, ..51, 52
   in the convention of 1787, 79
   and slavery, .. 164

INDEX

Maryland: cedes claim to territory, ... 167
   stays in Union, 193
   Lee in, ...244, 245
"Maryland, My Maryland": 244, 245
Mason, George: 49
Massachusetts: assembly dissolved, ... 38
   and independence, 45
   and Virginia, ...75, 77
   and states rights, 150, 152
   establishes slavery, 162
   abolition movement in, ... 166
   and secession, ..182-185
   and nullification, .. 191
Maury, Dabney H.: 130
Meade, George G.: 247
Mecklenburg Declaration: 41, 42, 44
Mercer, C. F.: 163
Mercer, Hugh: 57
Mexican War: 90, 96
Mississippi: in Mexican War, 94
   secedes, ... 193
Missouri: and slavery question, ... 172
   stays in Union, 193
Mobile Cadets: 202
Monroe Doctrine: 90
Monroe, James: 90, 97
Monuments and Histories: 236-239
Moore's Creek: battle of, .. 61
Morgan, Daniel: 53-55
Morgan, John H.: ..64, 263, 264
Mosby, John S.: 64

Motte, Rebecca: 68
Moultrie, William: 63, 64
Municipal Corruption: 300

Nash, Francis: 60
Navigation Laws: 31
Negro Questions: and the constitution, ... 82
   in the South, ..291-296
New England: and War of 1812, ...88-90
   in Mexican War, .. 95
   settlers in, ...119, 120
   and states rights, 151
   slavery in, ... 162
   threatens secession, 172
   pioneers of secession, ...181-185
   nullification, ...189-192
New Orleans: 233
News and Courier: 227
New York: and independence, ... 48
North Carolina: and Tryon, 30
   aids Boston, ... 39
   first blood spilt in, 40
   and Mecklenburg Declaration, ..41, 42
   Provincial Congress of, ... 42
   and independence, 45, 47
   heroes of, ...59, 63
   University of, ... 60
   in convention of 1787, ... 79
   adopts constitution, 83
   in Mexican War, .. 94
   and slavery, ... 164

North Carolina: and emancipation, ... 170
    secedes, ... 193
Norfolk: burned, ... 46
North, The: in the revolution, ...73, 74
    in the War of 1812, 88-90
    pronunciation in, .. 106
    and slavery, ... 127
    differences between the South and, 147-149
    and states rights, 150-158
    slavery in, ...162-164
    sells slaves, ...165-167
    imports slaves, 166, 168
    nullifies, ...189-192
Northwest Territory: ...58, 167
Nullification: defined, ... 156
    advocated by Jefferson, ...157, 158
    threatened in South Carolina, ... 159
    by the North, 161, 162, 173, 189, 192

"Ole Marster": 111-114
"Ole Mistis": 114-116
Omnibus Bill: 191
"Order Number 28": 233
Otis, James: 32

Page, Thomas Nelson: 144
Parsons Cause: 33, 34
Pendleton, W. N.: 243
Pennsylvania: and independence, ... 48
Personal Liberty Bills: 173, 191

Pettigrew, J. J.: 242, 248
Pickens, Andrew: 66, 67
Pickett, George E.: 248
Pinckney, Charles Cotesworth: 157
"Pirates": 208-212
Planter Civilization: ...116-119
Planter, The "lazy": ...138-141
Planters: 134-138
Pocahontas: 24
Point Pleasant: battle of, .. 52
Polk, Thomas: 42
Pope, John: 243
Port Republic: battle of, .. 261
Press, Philadelphia: 303
Prisons: in the North, ... 127
    in the South, ... 128
Private Soldier, The: and the Sailor, ...197-212
Puritan and Cavalier: 119-123; 147-149

Quakers: petition of, ... 167
Quartering Act: 37
Quincy, Josiah: ..155, 183, 184

Race Problem: 291-296
Randolph, Edmund: 79
Randolph, John: 152
Randolph, Peyton: 35
Rawle, William: 189
Rawlings, Moses: 52
Rebellion, Bacon's: 28, 29
Rebellion: Records of the, 194, 211
Reconstruction: 287-291
Recruiting Officer: 216, 217
Redemptioners: 165
Religious Liberty: 61, 85

Revolutionary War: troops and battles, ... 72, 74
Rhode Island: and religious freedom, ... 50
Richmond Blues: 202
Roanoke Island: 23
Roanoke Island, St. Augustine, and Jamestown: ..21-26
Robertson, James: 45, 71
Rockbridge Artillery: 206
Roosevelt, Theodore: 45, 71, 72, 83, 95, 122, 159, 201, 202
Rutherford, Griffith: 61

Sailors: in the War of 1812, 89, 90
Sailor, The: and the private Soldier, ... 197-212
St. Augustine: 22
St. John's Church: 41
Sansom, Emma: 218
Scalawag: 280-284
Schoolmarm in Tradition: 275-277
Secession: in 1787, ... 83
  and Texas, ... 91
  first speech in congress on, ... 155
  early believers in, 156
  threatened by New England, ... 172
  by the South, ..179, 180
  the right of, ...181-192
  Northern advocates of, ... 182-189
  threatened by Massachusetts, ... 185
  taught at West Point, ...188, 189

Secession: name of the war of, ... 195
  doctrine abandoned, 269
Semmes, Raphael: 209
Seven Days' Battles; ...241-242
Seymour, Horatio: 184, 185
Sharpsburg, battle of; 244
"Sheridan's Ride": 231
Sherman, W. T.: 230
Shiloh and its Heroes: 262-265
Shiloh: battle of, ... 264
"Sic Semper Tyrannis": ..27-36
Simms, William Gilmore: .. 221
Slavery: and Texas, 92, 93, 160
  in the North, ... 127
  in the South, 131-134
  and religion, 143, 168, 169
  cause of war, ... 161
  abolished in the North, ... 161
  established by Massachusetts,.. 162
  in the North and the South,.. 162-164
  and Virginia, 163, 164, 166
  and Federal ratio, 168
  abolition of, ... 169
  moral side of, ..171
  and Missouri Compromise, ... 172
  and California, 175, 176
  extinguished by war, ... 196
  surrendered by South, ... 269
Slaves: treatment of, ...134-138

Slaves: number of, ... 164
    insurrections of, 165, 166
    runaway, ... 168
Slave Trade: 164, 166, 167
Smith, Goldwin: on secession, ... 188
Smith, John: 24
Smith, Kirby E.: 266
Smallwood, William: 51
South Carolina: and the congress of 1765, ..35, 36
    aids Boston, ... 39
    provincial Congress of, ...44, 45
    and independence, 46-48
    heroes of, ...63-68
    in the Revolution, 73, 76
    in convention of 1787, ... 79
    in Mexican War, .. 94
    divorce in, ... 120
    and states rights, .. 152
    and nullification, .. 159

    and slavery, ..163, 164
    threatens nullification, ...190, 192
    secedes, ... 193
    Sherman's March through, ... 231
    during reconstruction, ...283, 284
South, The: in olden days, 15-97
    no solid, ...17-19
    and the constitution of 1787, ... 20

South, The: and continental congress, ... 36
    in the Revolution, 51-78
    and the constitution, 78-86
    and the Union, ...86-97
    and Texas, ..92, 93, 96
    literature unjust to, 98-104
    English of, ...105, 106
    the *ante-bellum*, ... 111
    in 1860, ...116, 117
    yeomanry of, ..123, 126
    education in, ..125, 126
    slavery in, ...131-134
    ill-feeling towards the North, ...147-150
    and states rights, 150-158
    outvoted in Congress, 160
    and slaves, ...162-164
    secedes, ... 179
    war poets of, ..222, 223
    since the war, ...266-304
Southern Literary Messenger: 101
Stamp Act: 34, 36, 37
Stamp Act Congress: ...35, 36
"Starvation Parties": ..223-225
States Rights: 150-158
Stephens, Alex. H.: 193, 199
"Stonewall": (See *Jackson, T. J.*)
Stowe, Mrs. H. B. 77, 176
Stuart, J. E. B.: 178, 242, 246, 247, 251
Sumter, Fort: 67
Sumter, Thomas: 66

Taney, Roger B.: 177

INDEX

Tariff: 158, 159
"Taxation without Represen-
   tation": 30-33
Taylor, Richard: 257, 266
Tea Parties: Boston, ...38, 39
        Annapolis, ... 39
        Charleston, ... 39
Tennessee; settled by Rob-
   ertson, ...45, 71
Telfair, Edward: 43
Texas: and Mexico, ...91, 92
      and slavery, ... 92
      secedes, ... 193
      the hero of, ...262, 263
Text-books: misstatements
   in, ...132, 133
Thirteenth Amendment: .. 278
Townshend Acts: 37
Tryon, Gov.: 30
Tyler, John: 92, 163
Tyler, Lyon G.: 163

Uncle Tom's Cabin: 47, 101,
   132, 135, 138, 142-144, 176
"Underground Railroad": .. 173
Underwood Convention: ... 286
Union: created by states, 83-86
   maintained and ex-
   panded by South, ..86-97
   love for the, ...301-304
University of Virginia: 108, 206

Valley Campaign: 260, 261
Virginia: and Five Resolu-
      tions, ...34, 35
      and Carolina, ..36, 44
      and committees of
      correspondence, .. 40
      and independence,
            46, 47, 48

Virginia: and Bill of Rights, 49
   heroes, ...52-59
   in convention of
     1787, ... 79
   and Connecticut, .. 82
   settled by Cavaliers,
           120, 121
   aristocrats in, 124, 125
   and her debt, ... 129
   and states rights,
           152, 154
   slavery in, ...162, 163
   cedes Northwest
     Territory, ... 167
   constitutional con-
     vention of 1829, . 170
   and Massachusetts,
          75, 77
   and nullification,
           191, 192
   secedes, ... 193
   atrocities in, ... 231
   Underwood Consti-
     tution, ... 286
Virginia: and Monitor: 209-212
Virginia and Kentucky Resolutions: 191
Virginia Military Institute:
        231, 241, 254

War between the States: before the, ...15-17
   causes: 146, 150
   slavery question, .. 161
   name adopted, ... 195
   cost of, ... 267
War of 1812: 86-90, 306
War Poets: 222, 223
Washington Artillery:
       202, 244, 245

Washington, George: 39, 59, 85, 157, 257
Washington, William: ..55, 56
Webster, Daniel: denounced by Whittier, ... 174
Westmoreland Club: 298
West Point: secession taught at, ...188, 189
Wheeler, Joseph: 264
Wilderness: battle of the, 250, 251

William and Mary College: 26, 107, 206, 231
Williams, Otho Holland: .. 52
Williams, Roger: 50
Wilmer, Bishop R. H.: 131, 132, 142, 143
Winchester: battle of, ... 261
Women of the Confederacy: 213-240
Woodford, William: 53
Wyatt, Sir Francis: 25

www.ingramcontent.com/pod-product-compliance
Lightning Source LLC
Chambersburg PA
CBHW070228230426
43664CB00014B/2246